THE CREATION OF THE CONSTITUTION

OPPOSING VIEWPOINTS®

Other Books in the American History Series:

The American Frontier
The American Revolution
The Bill of Rights
The Civil War
The Cold War
The Great Depression
Immigration
Isolationism
Puritanism
Reconstruction
Slavery

THE CREATION OF THE CONSTITUTION

OPPOSING VIEWPOINTS®

David L. Bender, *Publisher*
Bruno Leone, *Executive Editor*

William Dudley, *Series Editor*
John C. Chalberg, Ph.D., professor of history,
  Normandale Community College, *Consulting
  Editor*

William Dudley, *Book Editor*

Greenhaven Press, Inc.
San Diego, California

Cover photos, clockwise from upper left: 1) portrait of James Madison (Library of Congress); 2) the Constitution (Library of Congress); 3) oil painting of the signing of the Constitution (Historical Pictures/Stock Montage); 4) engraving of Patrick Henry (Historical Pictures/Stock Montage).

Library of Congress Cataloging-in-Publication Data

The Creation of the constitution : opposing viewpoints / William Dudley, book editor.
    p.   cm. — (American history series)
    Includes bibliographical references and index.
    ISBN 1-56510-221-5 (lib. : alk. paper) — ISBN 1-56510-220-7 (pbk. : acid-free paper)
    1. United States—Constitutional history—Sources.
I. Dudley, William, 1964-   . II. Series: American history series (San Diego, Calif.)

JK113.C74   1995   94-9518
342.73′029—dc20   CIP
[347.30229]

© 1995 by Greenhaven Press, Inc., PO Box 289009, San Diego, CA 92198-9009

Printed in the U.S.A.

Every effort has been made to trace the owners of copyrighted material.

"America was born of revolt, flourished in dissent, became great through experimentation."

Henry Steele Commager, American Historian, 1902-1984

Contents

Foreword

Aboard the *Arbella* as it lurched across the cold, gray Atlantic, John Winthrop was as calm as the waters surrounding him were wild. With the confidence of a leader, Winthrop gathered his Puritan companions around him. It was time to offer a sermon. England lay behind them, and years of strife and persecution for their religious beliefs were over, he said. But the Puritan abandonment of England, he reminded his followers, did not mean that England was beyond redemption. Winthrop wanted his followers to remember England even as they were leaving it behind. Their goal should be to create a new England, one far removed from the authority of the Anglican church and King Charles I. In Winthrop's words, their settlement in the New World ought to be "a city upon a hill," a just society for corrupt England to emulate.

A Chance to Start Over

One June 8, 1630, John Winthrop and his company of refugees had their first glimpse of what they came to call New England. High on the surrounding hills stood a welcoming band of fir trees whose fragrance drifted to the *Arbella* on a morning breeze. To Winthrop, the "smell off the shore [was] like the smell of a garden." This new world would, in fact, often be compared to the Garden of Eden. Here, John Winthrop would have his opportunity to start life over again. So would his family and his shipmates. So would all those who came after them. These victims of conflict in old England hoped to find peace in New England.

Winthrop, for one, had experienced much conflict in his life. As a Puritan, he was opposed to Catholicism and Anglicanism, both of which, he believed, were burdened by distracting rituals and distant hierarchies. A parliamentarian by conviction, he despised Charles I, who had spurned Parliament and created a private army to do his bidding. Winthrop believed in individual responsibility and fought against the loss of religious and political freedom. A gentleman landowner, he feared the rising economic power of a merchant class that seemed to value only money. Once Winthrop stepped aboard the *Arbella*, he hoped, these conflicts would not be a part of his American future.

Yet his Puritan religion told Winthrop that human beings are fallen creatures and that perfection, whether communal or individual, is unachievable on this earth. Therefore, he faced a paradox: On the one hand, his religion demanded that he attempt to live a perfect life in an imperfect world. On the other hand, it told him that he was destined to fail.

Soon after Winthrop disembarked from the *Arbella*, he came face-to-face with this maddening dilemma. He found himself presiding not over a utopia but over a colony caught up in disputes as troubling as any he had confronted in his English past. John Winthrop, it seems, was not the only Puritan with a dream of a heaven on earth. But others in the community saw the dream differently. They wanted greater political and religious freedom than their leader was prepared to grant. Often, Winthrop was able to handle this conflict diplomatically. For example, he expanded, participation in elections and allowed the voters of Massachusetts Bay greater power.

But religious conflict was another matter because it was grounded in competing visions of the Puritan utopia. In Roger Williams and Anne Hutchinson, two of his fellow colonists, John Winthrop faced rivals unprepared to accept his definition of the perfect community. To Williams, perfection demanded that he separate himself from the Puritan institutions in his community and create an even "purer" church. Winthrop, however, disagreed and exiled Williams to Rhode Island. Hutchinson presumed that she could interpret God's will without a minister. Again, Winthrop did not agree. Hutchinson was tried on charges of heresy, convicted, and banished from Massachusetts.

John Winthrop's Massachusetts colony was the first but far from the last American attempt to build a unified, peaceful community that, in the end, only provoked a discord. This glimpse at its history reveals what Winthrop confronted: the unavoidable presence of conflict in American life.

American Assumptions

From America's origins in the early seventeenth century, Americans have often held several interrelated assumptions about their country. First, people believe that to be American is to be free. Second, because Americans did not have to free themselves from feudal lords or an entrenched aristocracy, America has been seen as a perpetual haven from the troubles and disputes that are found in the Old World.

John Winthrop lived his life as though these assumptions were true. But the opposing viewpoints presented in the American History Series should reveal that for many Americans, these assumptions were and are myths. Indeed, for numerous Americans, liberty has not always been guaranteed, and disputes have been an integral, sometimes welcome part of their life.

The American landscape has been torn apart again and again by a great variety of clashes—theological, ideological, political, economic, geographical, and social. But such a landscape is not necessarily a hopelessly divided country. If the editors hope to prove anything during the course of this series, it is not that the United States has been destroyed by conflict but rather that it has been enlivened, enriched, and even strengthened by Americans who have disagreed with one another.

Thomas Jefferson was one of the least confrontational of Americans, but he boldly and irrevocably enriched American life with his individualistic views. Like John Winthrop before him, he had a notion of an American Eden. Like Winthrop, he offered a vision of a harmonious society. And like Winthrop, he not only became enmeshed in conflict but eventually presided over a people beset by it. But unlike Winthrop, Jefferson believed this Eden was not located in a specific community but in each individual American. His Declaration of Independence from Great Britain could also be read as a declaration of independence for each individual in American society.

Jefferson's Ideal

Jefferson's ideal world was composed of "yeoman farmers," each of whom was roughly equal to the others in society's eyes, each of whom was free from the restrictions of both government and fellow citizens. Throughout his life, Jefferson offered a continuing challenge to Americans: Advance individualism and equality or see the death of the American experiment. Jefferson believed that the strength of this experiment depended upon a society of autonomous individuals and a society without great gaps between rich and poor. His challenge to his fellow Americans to create—and sustain—such a society has itself produced both economic and political conflict.

A society whose guiding document is the Declaration of Independence is a society assured of the freedom to dream—and to disagree. We know that Jefferson hated conflict, both personal and political. His tendency was to avoid confrontations of any sort, to squirrel himself away and write rather than to stand up and speak his mind. It is only through his written words that we can grasp Jefferson's utopian dream of a society of independent farmers, all pursuing their private dreams and all leading lives of middling prosperity.

Jefferson, this man of wealth and intellect, lived an essentially happy private life. But his public life was much more troublesome. From the first rumblings of the American Revolution in the 1760s to the North-South skirmishes of the 1820s that ultimately produced the Civil War, Jefferson was at or near the center of American political history. The issues were almost too many—and too crucial—for one lifetime: Jefferson had to choose between sup-

11

porting or rejecting the path of revolution. During and after the ensuing war, he was at the forefront of the battle for religious liberty. After endorsing the Constitution, he opposed the economic plans of Alexander Hamilton. At the end of the century, he fought the infamous Alien and Sedition Acts, which limited civil liberties. As president, he opposed the Federalist court, conspiracies to divide the union, and calls for a new war against England. Throughout his life, Thomas Jefferson, slaveholder, pondered the conflict between American freedom and American slavery. And from retirement at his Monticello retreat, he frowned at the rising spirit of commercialism he feared was dividing Americans and destroying his dream of American harmony.

No matter the issue, however, Thomas Jefferson invariably supported the rights of the individual. Worried as he was about the excesses of commercialism, he accepted them because his main concern was to live in a society where liberty and individualism could flourish. To Jefferson, Americans had to be free to worship as they desired. They also deserved to be free from an over-reaching government. To Jefferson, Americans should also be free to possess slaves.

Harmony, an Elusive Goal

Before reading the articles in this anthology, the editors ask readers to ponder the lives of John Winthrop and Thomas Jefferson. Each held a utopian vision, one based upon the demands of community and the other on the autonomy of the individual. Each dreamed of a country of perpetual new beginnings. Each found himself thrust into a position of leadership and found that conflict could not be avoided. Harmony, whether communal or individual, was a forever elusive goal.

The opposing visions of Winthrop and Jefferson have been at the heart of many differences among Americans from many backgrounds through the whole of American history. Moreover, their visions have provoked important responses that have helped shape American society, the American character, and many an American battle.

The editors of the American History Series have done extensive research to find representative opinions on the issues included in these volumes. They have found numerous outstanding opposing viewpoints from people of all times, classes, and genders in American history. From those, they have selected commentaries that best fit the nature and flavor of the period and topic under consideration. Every attempt was made to include the most important and relevant viewpoints in each chapter. Obviously, not every notable viewpoint could be included. Therefore, a selective, annotated bibliography has been provided at the end of each book to aid readers in seeking additional information.

The editors are confident that as this series reveals past conflicts, it will help revitalize the reader's views of the American present. In that spirit, the American History Series is dedicated to the proposition that American history is more complicated, more fascinating, and more troubling than John Winthrop or Thomas Jefferson ever dared to imagine.

John C. Chalberg
Consulting Editor

Introduction

"The Constitution was a product of division, debate, and disagreement, yet the very process of its writing and ratification helped America redefine itself and create a sense of unity."

Independence from Great Britain meant both opportunity and crisis for the thirteen American colonies along the Atlantic seaboard. No longer were they under the authority of King George III and the British Parliament. No longer were the colonies subject to a constitutional monarchy. On the other hand, no longer did there seem to be *any* sovereign authority in the new United States of America.

Radical revolutionaries such as Tom Paine believed that sovereignty now resided in the individual American citizen. But were Americans prepared to accept this prescription? Could the crisis of sovereignty created by the Declaration of Independence of 1776 be resolved simply by declaring each American sovereign and autonomous? Was the American Revolution a fight for anarchy? No doubt most newly independent Americans would have answered no to all of these questions.

The Declaration of Independence posited that sovereignty was to be found in "governments . . . deriving their just powers from the consent of the governed." But how was this consent to be granted? The answer, many Americans believed, lay in written constitutions specifying the duties, structures, and limitations of government. Unlike the British constitution familiar to educated Americans, which was simply the aggregate of that country's laws and structures of government as they had evolved over centuries, the charters Americans resolved to adopt would be antecedent to government. As historians Oscar and Mary Handlin explain in *The Dimensions of Liberty*:

> In the New World the term, constitution, no longer referred to
> the actual organization of power developed through custom,

prescription, and precedent. Instead it had come to mean a written frame of government setting fixed limits on the use of power. The American view was, of course, closely related to the rejection of the old conception that authority descended from the Crown to its officials. In the newer view—that authority was derived from the consent of the governed—the written constitution became the instrument by which the people entrusted power to their agents.

By the end of 1781, ten of the thirteen former colonies had drafted and ratified state constitutions. (Connecticut and Rhode Island had simply revised their colonial charters by removing all references to royal authority; New Hampshire, on its fourth try, finally ratified a state constitution in 1783.) The new state constitutions and the 1777 Articles of Confederation (America's first national constitution) all reveal a broad consensus on the ideals of government, marked by a suspicion of political power. To the revolutionary generation, power was not to be a commodity available for the taking by ambitious politicians. This generation was wary of authority—and of politicians who desired it. Power was to be husbanded, divided, limited.

Accordingly, governors of many states were given limited veto and appointive powers. Most control was granted to the legislatures, which were presumably more responsive to the people. To ensure this responsiveness to their constituents, legislators and governors were in many state constitutions subject to rotation in office. For instance, in Virginia the governor was elected to a one-year term and could hold office for no more than three consecutive terms. The distrust of authority was particularly evident in the Articles of Confederation, which provided for no executive or judicial authority at all, and which gave its national legislature, the Continental Congress, no direct powers over the states.

The End of Consensus

The debates of 1786-1788 surrounding the creation of the Constitution, which are described in this book, reflect the end of this national consensus on the necessity of establishing sovereign governments coupled with the reluctance to grant them power. The development of opposing views can be understood by examining the actions and reactions of two noted Virginians, James Madison and Patrick Henry, to three critical events—Shays's Rebellion of 1786, the Constitutional Convention of 1787, and the Virginia state ratifying convention of 1788.

Although Madison and Henry were both plantation owners active in politics and both supporters of American independence, they had important dissimilarities, not the least of which was a difference in age. Henry was part of the generation that had attained political power when Great Britain still ruled the colonies; their defining event was the American Revolution. Following the Revolution they were well positioned to assume political leadership of the states, and Henry indeed did dominate public life in Virginia in the 1770s and 1780s, serving as governor several times. Traveling outside of Virginia only once in his life, Henry gave his primary allegiance and concern to his state. Madison was of a younger generation, being only in his mid-twenties when America declared independence in 1776. Madison's college education in New Jersey and his service in the Continental Congress from 1779 to 1783 gave him a different perspective, focused on the problems facing the country as a whole.

These differences in age and perspective help account for Madison and Henry's differing reactions to the series of events known as Shays's Rebellion. This revolt against state authority occurred at a time when economic and political tensions were on the rise in many of the thirteen states. Several years of depressed prices, tight money, and burdensome taxes following the Revolutionary War had spelled ruin for farmers everywhere, but especially for backcountry farmers already near poverty. Petitions for legislative relief, especially for infusions of paper money and mortgage moratoriums, mounted in many states. (The issue of paper money was especially divisive in many states, with farmers and other debtors calling for the printing of state money with which to pay off debts, while creditors were opposed to being paid with depreciated currency.) In Massachusetts in 1786, farmers, after failing to gain any legislative help, used mob action to force suspensions of court-ordered foreclosures and imprisonment for debt. They went so far as to organize themselves into an impromptu militia whose first target was the state arsenal at Springfield. The Massachusetts legislature appealed to the Continental Congress for a troop commitment to put down the rebellion. When Congress balked, eastern Massachusetts merchants and creditors organized and financed what was essentially a private militia, albeit one sanctioned by the state legislature. The farmers-turned-rebels (one of whose leaders was Revolutionary War veteran Daniel Shays) were overwhelmed by the state's mercenary force, and by February 1787 the revolt was crushed.

Differing Views on Rebellion

Shays's Rebellion was a brief episode, but the controversy surrounding it did not soon die. Frightened calls for a more "energetic" (i.e., powerful) government were heard from points as far away as Virginia. George Washington, for one, worried about "combustibles" in other states "which a spark might set fire to." Many anti-Shays pamphlets railed against what one labeled the "prevailing rage of excessive democracy" (e.g., Shays's efforts to take matters into his own hands).

Patrick Henry did not share these concerns. Certainly he was not inclined to engage in public condemnation of Daniel Shays or to publicly express anxious worries about the future of the country. After all, he had lived among the hard-pressed farmers of Virginia. More than most public men in Virginia or elsewhere, Patrick Henry understood the grievances of a Daniel Shays. In fact, for years he had championed the passage of debtor relief laws for Virginians, out of both a desire for justice and the hope that Virginia could avoid the strife of Massachusetts. As economic conditions worsened in the mid-1780s he advocated the printing of paper money to alleviate the problems faced by beleaguered farmers. The problems facing the nation were not caused by the farmers, Henry believed, but rather by the machinations of urban merchants, bankers, and other creditors.

Madison did not go as far as those who saw in Shays's Rebellion the "excess of democracy." To Madison, Shays's Rebellion was a warning signal. His primary fear was that anti-republican, perhaps even monarchist, forces might try to exploit this episode of rural discontent to foment a counterrevolution against the "spirit of 1776," reversing the gains in liberty and in the establishment of republican government made during the American Revolution. He did not agree with Henry, however, in seeking to pass laws to benefit current debtors in hopes of blunting future revolutions, believing such laws to be harmful to the country as a whole.

Madison was prepared to concede that some of the optimistic "spirit of 1776" had been lost. The generation that fought for and won American independence had believed that the American people were united—that a kind of natural concord existed among the citizens. But events such as Shays's Rebellion convinced many that Americans were no longer filled with a sense of public virtue, that America was no longer a place where harmony reigned. Madison was one of the convinced. Patrick Henry was not, and here can be found the makings of the great debate between the two Virginians surrounding the creation and ratification of America's second (and still existing) constitution in 1787 and 1788.

The Constitutional Convention

Due to the efforts of people such as Madison and Washington and others, including Alexander Hamilton, the states and the Continental Congress agreed to authorize a convention to meet in Philadelphia in May 1787 to examine and revise the Articles of Confederation. Madison and Henry were elected by the state of Virginia as delegates to the convention. Madison went and was perhaps its single most important participant. Henry decided to stay on his farm in Virginia.

Henry did accept the need for some alteration of the Articles of Confederation; for instance, he agreed that the disarray created by thirteen separate state imposts (trade tariffs) was intolerable, and that a national impost was necessary. But he was not persuaded to attend the Constitutional Convention of 1787. Henry's refusal to participate was the subject of much speculation among his fellow Virginia politicians. Governor Edmund Randolph suggested in a letter to Madison that recent financial reverses had led to Henry's decision to remain at home. Madison, who declared Henry's nonparticipation potentially "ominous," suspected that his fellow Virginian simply preferred to remain "unfettered."

Whatever the reasons, Henry's absence, and that of other elected delegates with similar convictions, left the Constitutional Convention dominated by those who *did* think that drastic change in the American government was necessary. Over the next few months, they went beyond the mere revision of the Articles and drafted an entirely new document. The creation of the Constitution was a thoroughly collective endeavor—the product of the deliberation and debates of fifty-five delegates, ranging from the precocious Charles Pinckney to the venerable Benjamin Franklin, from the loquacious Gouverneur Morris to the reticent George Washington, from the nationalist Alexander Hamilton to the states' rights defender William Paterson. But of all the delegates the most influential was James Madison. Because of his thorough study and preparation, his tireless politicking, and his many ideas and innovations, the Constitution revealed to the public on September 18, 1787, was largely, if not entirely, based on his ideas.

Madison's work at the Convention was motivated by the belief that this was the time "for all real friends of the revolution to perpetuate the Union and redeem the honor of the Republican name." To Madison that redemption demanded more than mere revision of the Articles of Confederation. Only a completely new constitution, one that would at once strengthen the fragmented union and preserve republican values, could restore the flagging "spirit of 1776." At the same time he did not want to move toward a centralized state that ignored—or, worse yet, crushed—either states' rights or individual freedoms. His answer was a system in which governmental power was expanded but divided—shared between state governments and a more powerful central government, between a national congress and a national executive, and between individual citizens and government at every level.

The Ratification Debate

The creation of the Constitution did not end with the Constitutional Convention. The document required ratification by at least nine of the thirteen states, and for that it had to be explained, defended, and debated nationwide. George Washington started the process by mailing copies of the Constitution to Virginia's former governors, including Patrick Henry. He wrote a cover letter expressing the hope that those about to read the new Constitution "will at once discover the good, and the exceptional parts of it." Washington, who had presided over the Constitutional Convention, went on to endorse the final product as "the best that could be obtained at this time." Without it, he concluded, "anarchy would soon have ensued."

Henry, for one, was put off by such alarmist statements, but he did manage a courteous reply. "I have to lament that I cannot bring my mind to accord with the proposed constitution," he wrote to Washington. "Perhaps mature Reflections may furnish me Reasons to change my present Sentiments into a Conformity with the opinions of those personages for whom I have the highest Reverence."

Beneath Henry's studied good manners ran strong feelings of betrayal. Had not the Convention greatly exceeded its authority? Its charge had been to amend the Articles of Confederation, not abolish them. Instead, the Convention created a new national government with potentially coercive power over every state. Laws passed by the new national Congress would take precedence over any state law. A new national judiciary would assure the "supremacy" of the new Constitution. In addition, individual states would be formally prohibited from legislating on a number of critical issues, including the printing of paper money, or on any matter that could be construed to impair the obligation of contracts (such as debtor relief laws).

In sum, Patrick Henry objected to the principle of "consolidated" (i.e., centrally controlled) government that he saw at work in this document. To him, such a principle violated the spirit of the Revolution. It was his contention that each state had formed its own independent government during the Revolution. True, those states had allied with one another for a common defense against Great Britain, and later had agreed to remain in "perpetual union" to achieve mutual peacetime objectives. But, Henry believed, to adopt this new Constitution was to shatter the existing confederation of states and replace it with a national government whose legislature and executive bore a striking—and worrisome—resemblance to Great Britain's. Rather than securing Americans from a misplaced fear of anarchy, Henry believed, the Constitution of 1787 invited a new era of oppression.

Patrick Henry was but one of many people who shared these ideas and who disputed and criticized the Constitution in newspapers, pamphlets, and the state ratification debates. They unwillingly became known as anti-federalists. (Preferring "federalists," they argued it was they who supported the sharing of power between state and federal governments, as opposed to the "consolidators" who wished to centralize government; but the proponents of the Constitution succeeded in appropriating the term "federalist" for themselves.)

What was Henry's strategy for preventing ratification? "The friends of Liberty will expect support from the back people," he declared, referring to the poorer farmers of western Virginia. Just as many western farmers in Virginia and other states had taken the lead in the fight against Great Britain and were in sympathy with the grievances of Daniel Shays, so would many follow the lead of Patrick Henry in opposing the Constitution and "consolidated" government. Such government, Henry argued, inevitably worked to the advantage of those few who controlled the eastern commercial and mercantile interests.

Henry was correct in that much of the support for the Constitution came from these wealthier parts of American society. These federalists argued that the opposition to the Constitution from Henry and others stemmed from political and economic self-interest. For example, a Richmond merchant wrote that the opposition to the Constitution could be reduced to "two classes," both of which Henry represented: "those who have power [under the Articles] and are unwilling to part with an atom of it" and the "people who are very unwilling to pay their debts and are afraid this constitution will make them Honest Men."

The Virginia Convention

Although Madison and Henry were both leading figures in the ratification debate, they did not directly confront each other until the Virginia state ratifying convention began on June 2, 1788. By that time, eight of the required nine states had already ratified the Constitution—a fact federalists were hoping would increase the pressure on Virginia and other states to support it. Henry, however, had repeatedly declared that he alone would keep Virginia independent until the Constitution was to his liking. "Other states cannot do without us," he argued. "Therefore, we can dictate to them what terms we please."

Henry's terms—and grievances—were spelled out in dramatic fashion in a series of impassioned speeches beginning on June 4. The famous orator extolled the value of liberty, which he had in the past said was the "greatest of all earthly blessings." But liberty and "energetic" government, Henry warned, were inevitably at odds. Calling himself an "old-fashioned fellow," Henry hearkened back to the days of the American Revolution, when republican virtue animated the entire population and the state constitu-

20

tions and Articles of Confederation created governments accountable to the people. But, he asserted, the liberty gained by the Revolution was now threatened by this new Constitution the federalists were foisting on an unsuspecting populace.

What alternatives did Henry propose? Restore the principle of annual elections and rotation in office, both of which had been common features in many state constitutions. How could a nation call itself a republic, he asked, and yet permit a president not only to hold power for a long term of four years but also to stand for reelection again and again? How could a truly republican government tolerate a judiciary whose members were appointed for life and a Senate whose members served for six years before having to stand for reelection? "Where annual elections end, slavery begins," Henry warned ominously.

The Constitution, he argued, would require large armies, navies, and a host of tax gatherers and government officials to serve the interests of the "ambitious few" and would "oppress and ruin the people"; only a government small in scale could be held accountable. "There is no true responsibility" under the proposed Constitution, Henry claimed, and "this, sir, is my great objection to it."

Madison did not respond to Henry immediately, and when he finally spoke at the convention he did so without Henry's oratorical flair. Pale and speaking in a low voice, Madison argued that the Constitution actually *preserved* republicanism against the dangers posed by both agrarian rebellions and aristocratic repression. "Commotions" such as Shays's Rebellion, he argued, more often than not "produced despotism." The trick was to find the proper balance between the federal government and state governments, between majoritarianism and republicanism, between rich and poor, between east and west. Madison was convinced that the new Constitution struck that balance.

Madison conceded that the new government would be one of greater "energy," but argued that any government needs sufficient energy to function. The Constitution did centralize more power in the national government, but "thirteen individual sovereignties" could only be a "solecism in theory and a mere nullity in practice." The desired alternative was not a consolidated government, he stated, but rather a government of "mixed nature" that could ensure stability and freedom, both necessary ingredients for human happiness. The Constitution, he concluded, provided such an alternative.

The Constitution Is Ratified

The two sides debated vigorously until the vote to ratify was taken on June 25. On the eve of the decision neither side was certain of victory. Madison confided to his brother that there was no reason for "either party [to] despair absolutely." Henry told his colleagues that if the Constitution were ratified he would remain a "peaceable citizen," but one filled with "painful sensations which arise from a conviction of being overpowered in a good cause." The vote was narrow but decisive. Virginia, by an 89-79 tally, ratified the Constitution.

In a sense, both Madison and Henry can be considered victors. Madison, of course, was eminently successful in incorporating his ideas into the Constitution and seeing it ratified. But Henry's opposition was not entirely in vain. Because of the efforts of the anti-federalists, the Bill of Rights was added to the Constitution three years later—creating a bulwark protecting individual liberties from the new federal government. In addition, Henry's pledge to accept ratification as a "peaceable citizen" helped to ensure that the divisions surrounding the creation of the Constitution—divisions dramatically revealed by the following selection of documents—would not permanently fragment the new nation. The Constitution was a product of division, debate, and disagreement, yet the very process of its writing and ratification helped America redefine itself and create a sense of unity. America demonstrated that it could establish new foundations, with at least a measure of harmony and tranquility, under a Constitution that has lasted for more than two hundred years.

John C. Chalberg
Consulting Editor

CHAPTER 1

Does America Need a Constitution?

Chapter Preface

For most of the 1780s the United States of America was governed under the Articles of Confederation, America's first written constitution. It was written by the Continental Congress, America's first national governing body. First meeting in 1774 as an advisory council to the British colonies, the Congress evolved into an ad hoc legislature, which—after declaring independence from Great Britain—organized the war effort against that nation. Ratified by all thirteen states by 1781, the Articles established the Continental Congress as America's national legislature. Delegates were elected annually by the states, each state having one vote in the body. There was no chief executive or national judiciary. Rather than a centralized government, the Articles were meant to establish a "firm league of friendship" between states, each of which "retains its sovereignty."

The structure of government created by the Articles of Confederation reflected the feelings against a strong national government shared by many people at that time. Americans were fighting a war of independence against a central government (Great Britain) whose powers and taxes were deemed oppressive. They were loath to create a new one. Historian Paul Goodman writes in *The American Constitution:*

> Ratification of the Articles . . . left the states virtually sovereign and gave them the power to surrender only as much power to the national government as seemed absolutely necessary. Americans were deeply suspicious of power. Government, they thought, was a necessary evil because without it citizens could not enjoy order, security, or liberty. But government had a tendency to aggrandize power and become oppressive. The best defense against tyranny was to keep power close enough to the people where they could more effectively scrutinize public officials and zealously guard their freedom. This was the theory underlying the Articles of Confederation.

Among the official responsibilities of the government under the Articles of Confederation were assignments to manage foreign affairs, make treaties, raise and maintain an army and navy, and to coin and borrow money. However, its effectiveness was severely hampered in that it had no enforceable power to collect taxes from the states. While the former colonies cooperated sufficiently during the Revolutionary War to defeat the British, following peace in 1783 the new states found themselves increasingly divided even as they faced severe economic and political difficulties. States refused requests of the national government for funds. They took matters into their own hands on the regulation of commerce, leading to trade wars and disputes between states. Some passed laws creating paper money and other measures favorable to debtors and harmful to creditors. The lack of a strong central government hampered relations with foreign nations, including Spain and Great Britain, which still controlled territories in North America on the western and northern borders of the United States.

Throughout the 1780s advocates of a stronger national government, such as Alexander Hamilton, called for changes in the Articles of Confederation. By 1787 most Americans involved in public affairs agreed that changes in the Articles of Confederation were necessary. However, they disagreed on the scope and content of such changes. Some argued for relatively minor modifications in the Articles, such as giving the national government greater powers over trade. Greater changes ran the risk of creating "baleful aristocracies" and would "prepare the way to a ruinous system of government" as Massachusetts Continental Congress delegates Elbridge Berry and Rufus King wrote in 1785 while arguing against a general convention for revising the Articles. But others argued that merely revising the Articles would not be sufficient to deal with the problems facing the United States, and that, as George Washington wrote in a letter to James Madison in March 1787, "a thorough reform of the present system is indispensable." The differing opinions over the Articles of Confederation carried over into the federalist/anti-federalist split between those who favored the Constitution proposed in 1787 and those who argued that it represented too radical a change from the Articles.

VIEWPOINT 1

"Most of the present difficulties of this country arise from the weakness and other defects of our governments."

America Under the Articles of Confederation Is in Crisis

Benjamin Rush (1745-1813)

Benjamin Rush was a noted physician who was a pioneer in the humane treatment of the mentally ill. He was also deeply involved in public affairs and social reforms. A signer of the Declaration of Independence in 1776, Rush served as the physician general for George Washington's Continental Army during the Revolutionary War. After the war he wrote prolifically on various medical, educational, and social issues, and became a critic of the Articles of Confederation. The following was originally printed February 1, 1787, in the premier issue of the *American Museum*, a Philadelphia magazine published monthly from 1787 to 1792. Rush makes reference to the Constitutional Convention, which had been authorized by the Continental Congress and the states to meet in Philadelphia in May. He criticizes the existing national government under the Articles of Confederation and urges the creation of a strong national government. His arguments foreshadow many ideas that are found in the U.S. Constitution.

There is nothing more common than to confound the terms of American Revolution with those of the late American war. The American war is over, but this is far from being the case with

From Benjamin Rush, "Address to the People of the United States," Philadelphia, May 1787. In *Pamphlets and Acts of the Revolution in America*, Hezekiah Niles, ed. Baltimore, 1822.

American Revolution. On the contrary, nothing but the first act of the great drama is closed. It remains yet to establish and perfect our new forms of government; and to prepare the principles, morals, and manners of our citizens for these forms of government after they are established and brought to perfection.

The confederation, together with most of our state constitutions, were formed under very unfavorable circumstances. We had just emerged from a corrupted monarchy. Although we understood perfectly the principles of liberty, yet most of us were ignorant of the forms and combinations of power in republics. Add to this, the British army was in the heart of our country spreading desolation wherever it went; our resentments, of course, were awakened. We detested the British name, and unfortunately refused to copy some things in the administration of justice and power in the British government which have made it the admiration and envy of the world. In our opposition to monarchy, we forgot that the temple of tyranny has two doors. We bolted one of them by proper restraints; but we left the other open, by neglecting to guard against the effects of our own ignorance and licentiousness.

Our Present Difficulties

Most of the present difficulties of this country arise from the weakness and other defects of our governments.

My business at present shall be only to suggest the defects of the confederation. These consist first, in the deficiency of coercive power; second, in a defect of exclusive power to issue paper money and regulate commerce; third, in vesting the sovereign power of the United States in a single legislature; and fourth, in the too frequent rotation of its members.

A convention is to sit soon for the purpose of devising means of obviating part of the two first defects that have been mentioned. But I wish they may add to their recommendations to each state to surrender up to Congress their power of emitting money. In this way a uniform currency will be produced that will facilitate trade and help to bind the states together. Nor will the states be deprived of large sums of money by this means, when sudden emergencies require it; for they may always borrow them, as they did during the war, out of the treasury of Congress. Even a loan office may be better instituted in this way, in each state, than in any other.

The two last defects that have been mentioned are not of less magnitude than the first. Indeed, the single legislature of Congress will become more dangerous, from an increase of power, than ever. To remedy this, let the supreme federal power be divided, like the legislatures of most of our states, into two distinct, independent branches. Let one of them be styled the council of the states and the other the assembly of the states. Let the first consist of a single delegate and the second, of two, three, or four delegates, chosen annually by each state. Let the President be chosen annually by the joint ballot of both houses; and let him possess certain powers, in conjunction with a privy council, especially the power of appointing most of the officers of the United States. The officers will not only be better, when appointed this way, but one of the principal causes of faction will be thereby removed from Congress. I apprehend this division of the power of Congress will become more necessary, as soon as they are invested with more ample powers of levying and expending public money.

The custom of turning men out of power or office as soon as they are qualified for it has been found to be absurd in practice. Is it virtuous to dismiss a general, a physician, or even a domestic as soon as they have acquired knowledge sufficient to be useful to us for the sake of increasing the number of able generals, skillful physicians, and faithful servants? We do not. Government is a

Problems with the Confederation

John Jay was the chief foreign secretary of the United States under the Articles of Confederation. He was a strong supporter of the Constitution and one of the co-authors of The Federalist, *a series of pro-Constitution newspaper essays now viewed as classics of American political theory. This passage, taken from* An Address to the People of the State of New-York, *a pamphlet published on September 17, 1787, argues that the loosely organized government under the Articles accomplished little and weakened America in dealing with other nations.*

By the Confederation as it now stands, the direction of general and national affairs is committed to a single body of men, viz. the Congress. They may make war, but are not empowered to raise men or money to carry it on. They may make peace, but without power to see the terms of it observed—They may form alliances, but without ability to comply with the stipulations on their part—They may enter into treaties of commerce, but without power to enforce them at home or abroad—They may borrow money, but without having the means of repayment—They may partly regulate commerce, but without authority to execute their ordinances—They may appoint ministers and other officers of trust, but without power to try or punish them for misdemeanors—They may resolve, but cannot execute either with dispatch or with secrecy—In short, they may consult, and deliberate, and recommend, and make requisitions, and they who please, may regard them.

From this new and wonderful system of Government, it has come to pass, that almost every national object of every kind, is at this day unprovided for; and other nations taking the advantage of its imbecility, are daily multiplying commercial restraints upon us.

science, and can never be perfect in America until we encourage men to devote not only three years but their whole lives to it. I believe the principal reason why so many men of abilities object to serving in Congress is owing to their not thinking it worth while to spend three years in acquiring a profession which their country immediately afterwards forbids them to follow.

Two Dangerous Errors

There are two errors or prejudices on the subject of government in America which lead to the most dangerous consequences.

It is often said "that the sovereign and all other power is seated in the people." This idea is unhappily expressed. It should be, "all power is derived from the people"; they possess it only on the days of their elections. After this, it is the property of their rulers; nor can they exercise or resume it unless it be abused. It is of importance to circulate this idea, as it leads to order and good government.

The people of America have mistaken the meaning of the word sovereignty; hence each state pretends to be sovereign. In Europe, it is applied only to those states which possess the power of making war and peace, of forming treaties and the like. As this power belongs only to Congress, they are the only sovereign power in the United States.

We commit a similar mistake in our ideas of the word independent. No individual state, as such, has any claim to independence. She is independent only in a union with her sister states in congress.

To conform the principles, morals, and manners of our citizens to our republican forms of government, it is absolutely necessary that knowledge of every kind should be disseminated through every part of the United States.

For this purpose, let Congress, instead of laying out $500,000 in building a federal town, appropriate only a fourth of that sum in founding a federal university. In this university let everything connected with government, such as history, the law of nature and nations, the civil law, the municipal laws of our country, and the principles of commerce, be taught by competent professors. Let masters be employed, likewise, to teach gunnery, fortification, and everything connected with defensive and offensive war. . . .

For the purpose of diffusing knowledge, as well as extending the living principle of government to every part of the United States, every state, city, county, village, and township in the Union should be tied together by means of the post office. This is the true nonelectric wire of government. It is the only means of conveying heat and light to every individual in the federal commonwealth. "Sweden lost her liberties," says the Abbé Raynal, "because her citizens were so scattered that they had no means of acting in concert with each other." It should be a constant injunction to the postmasters to convey newspapers free of all charge for postage. They are not only the vehicles of knowledge and intelligence but the sentinels of the liberties of our country.

Becoming Good Republicans

The conduct of some of those strangers who have visited our country since the peace and who fill the British papers with accounts of our distresses shows as great a want of good sense as it does of good nature. They see nothing but the foundations and walls of the temple of liberty; and yet they undertake to judge of the whole fabric.

Our own citizens act a still more absurd part when they cry out, after the experience of three or four years, that we are not proper materials for republican government. Remember, we assumed these forms of government in a hurry, before we were prepared for them. Let every man exert himself in promoting virtue and knowledge in our country, and we shall soon become good republicans. Look at the steps by which governments have been changed or rendered stable in Europe. Read the history of Great Britain. Her boasted government has risen out of wars and rebellions that lasted above 600 years. The United States are traveling peaceably into order and good government. They know no strife but what arises from the collision of opinions; and in three years they have advanced further in the road to stability and happiness than most of the nations in Europe have done in as many centuries.

There is but one path that can lead the United States to destruction, and that is their extent of territory. It was probably to effect this that Great Britain ceded to us so much wasteland. But even this path may be avoided. Let but one new state be exposed to sale at a time; and let the land office be shut up till every part of this new state be settled.

The Revolution Is Not Over

I am extremely sorry to find a passion for retirement so universal among the patriots and heroes of the war. They resemble skillful mariners who, after exerting themselves to preserve a ship from sinking in a storm in the middle of the ocean, drop asleep as soon as the waves subside, and leave the care of their lives and property during the remainder of the voyage to sailors without knowledge or experience. Every man in a republic is public property. His time and talents, his youth, his manhood, his old age—nay, more, his life, his all—belong to his country.

Patriots of 1774, 1775, 1776—heroes of 1778, 1779, 1780! Come forward! Your country demands your services! Philosophers and friends to mankind, come forward! Your country demands your studies and speculations! Lovers of peace and order who declined taking part in the late war, come forward! Your country forgives your timidity and demands your influence and advice! Hear her proclaiming, in sighs and groans, in her governments, in her finances, in her trade, in her manufactures, in her morals, and in her manners, "The Revolution is not over!"

VIEWPOINT 2

"We are at peace with all the world. . . . The state governments answer the purposes of preserving the peace, and providing for present exigencies."

America Under the Articles of Confederation Is Not in Crisis

Melancton Smith (1744-1798)

Melancton Smith was a landowner and merchant from Pough-keepsie in Dutchess County, New York. He served at various times in the first Provincial Congress of New York, as a captain of a minuteman militia company, and as sheriff of Dutchess County. A member of the Continental Congress from 1785 to 1788, Smith was one of the leading opponents of the new Constitution, which he viewed as giving too much power to the national government.

The following is taken from a pamphlet written in 1788 by Smith. In it he questions whether the Articles of Confederation are as bad as claimed by the Constitution's supporters. Smith charges that critics of the Articles have exaggerated the difficulties facing the United States in order to press for the hurried creation of a new central government. He contends that America is relatively well off, and that economic difficulties can be attributed to the recent war rather than to weaknesses in the Articles. Smith's views were shared by many who argued that the Articles of Confederation should be amended or changed gradually, rather than be replaced by a whole new scheme of government.

From Melancton Smith, "An Address to the People of the State of New-York: Showing the Necessity of Making Amendments to the Constitution, Proposed for the United States, Previous to Its Adoption," New York, 1788. In *Pamphlets on the Constitution of the United States*, Brooklyn, 1888.

It is insisted, that the present situation of our country is such, as not to admit of a delay in forming a new government, or of time sufficient to deliberate and agree upon the amendments which are proper, without involving ourselves in a state of anarchy and confusion.

On this head, all the powers of rhetoric, and arts of description, are employed to paint the condition of this country, in the most hideous and frightful colors. We are told, that agriculture is without encouragement; trade is languishing; private faith and credit are disregarded, and public credit is prostrate; that the laws and magistrates are contemned and set at naught; that a spirit of licentiousness is rampant, and ready to break over every bound set to it by the government; that private embarrassments and distresses invade the house of every man of middling property, and insecurity threatens every man in affluent circumstances: in short, that we are in a state of the most grievous calamity at home, and that we are contemptible abroad, the scorn of foreign nations, and the ridicule of the world. From this high-wrought picture, one would suppose that we were in a condition the most deplorable of any people upon earth. But suffer me, my countrymen, to call your attention to a serious and sober estimate of the situation in which you are placed, while I trace the embarrassments under which you labor, to their true sources. What is your condition? Does not every man sit under his own vine and under his own fig-tree, having none to make him afraid? Does not every one follow his calling without impediments and receive the reward of his well-earned industry? The farmer cultivates his land, and reaps the fruit which the bounty of heaven bestows on his honest toil. The mechanic is exercised in his art, and receives the reward of his labour. The merchant drives his commerce, and none can deprive him of the gain he honestly acquires; all classes and callings of men amongst us are protected in their various pursuits, and secured by the laws in the possession and enjoyment of the property obtained in those pursuits. The laws are as well executed as they ever were, in this or any other country. Neither the hand of private violence, nor the more to be dreaded hand of legal oppression, are reached out to distress us.

The War's Effects

It is true, many individuals labour under embarrassments, but these are to be imputed to the unavoidable circumstances of things, rather than to any defect in our governments. We have just emerged from a long and expensive war. During its existence few people were in a situation to increase their fortunes, but many to diminish them. Debts contracted before the war were left unpaid while it existed, and these were left a burden too heavy to be borne at the commencement of peace. Add to these, that when the war was over, too many of us, instead of reassuming our old habits of frugality, and industry, by which alone every country must be placed in a prosperous condition, took up the profuse use of foreign commodities. The country was deluged with articles imported from abroad, and the cash of the country has been sent to pay for them, and still left us labouring under the weight of a huge debt to persons abroad. These are the true sources to which we are to trace all the private difficulties of individuals: But will a new government relieve you from these? The advo-

Economic Difficulties the Result of War

Richard Henry Lee was a Virginian political leader who opposed the Constitution during the ratifying debates. He is widely credited with writing Letters from the Federal Farmer to the Republican, *a series of anti-federalist essays that were widely printed and distributed. In the following passage from the first of the* Letters, *originally published October 8, 1787, he argues that America is in no crisis under the Articles of Confederation. He asserts that the economic difficulties the country faces can be attributed to the fact that the nation has just been through the Revolutionary War.*

If we remain cool and temperate, we are in no immediate danger of any commotions; we are in a state of perfect peace, and in no danger of invasions; the state governments are in the full exercise of their powers; and our governments answer all present exigencies, except the regulation of trade, securing credit, in some cases, and providing for the interest, in some instances, of the public debts; and whether we adopt a change three or nine months hence, can make but little odds with the private circumstances of individuals; their happiness and prosperity, after all, depend principally upon their own exertions. We are hardly recovered from a long and distressing war: The farmers, fishermen, &c. have not fully repaired the waste made by it. Industry and frugality are again assuming their proper station. Private debts are lessened, and public debts incurred by the war have been, by various ways, diminished; and the public lands have now become a productive source for diminishing them much more. I know uneasy men, who with very much to precipitate, do not admit all these facts; but they are facts well known to all men who are thoroughly informed in the affairs of this country. It must, however, be admitted, that our federal system is defective, and that some of the state governments are not well administered; but, then, we impute to the defects in our governments many evils and embarrassments which are most clearly the result of the late war.

cates for it have not yet told you how it will do it—And I will venture to pronounce, that there is but one way in which it can be effected, and that is by industry and economy; limit your expences within your earnings; sell more than you buy, and everything will be well on this score. Your present condition is such as is common to take place after the conclusion of a war. Those who can remember our situation after the termination of the war preceding the last, will recollect that our condition was similar to the present, but time and industry soon recovered us from it. Money was scarce, the produce of the country much lower than it has been since the peace, and many individuals were extremely embarrassed with debts; and this happened although we did not experience the ravages, desolations, and loss of property, that were suffered during the late war.

With regard to our public and national concerns, what is there in our condition that threatens us with any immediate danger? We are at peace with all the world; no nation menaces us with war; nor are we called upon by any cause of sufficient importance to attack any nation. The state governments answer the purposes of preserving the peace, and providing for present exigencies. Our condition as a nation is in no respect worse than it has been for several years past. Our public debt has been lessened in various ways, and the western territory, which has been relied upon as a productive fund to discharge the national debt has at length been brought to market, and a considerable part actually applied to its reduction. I mention these things to shew, that there is nothing special, in our present situation, as it respects our national affairs, that should induce us to accept the proffered system, without taking sufficient time to consider and amend it. I do not mean by this, to insinuate, that our government does not stand in need of a reform. It is admitted by all parties, that alterations are necessary in our federal constitution, but the circumstances of our case do by no means oblige us to precipitate this business, or require that we should adopt a system materially defective. We may safely take time to deliberate and amend, without in the meantime hazarding a condition, in any considerable degree, worse than the present.

VIEWPOINT 3

"It is no longer doubted that a unanimous and punctual obedience of 13 independent bodies to the acts of the federal Government ought not to be calculated on."

The National Government Should Be Granted Direct Powers over the States

James Madison (1751-1836)

James Madison, a Virginia planter who eventually was elected president of the United States, was one of the main instigators and most influential participants in the 1787 Constitutional Convention in Philadelphia. His education at Princeton University in New Jersey and subsequent reading and study (he requested numerous books from his friend Thomas Jefferson in Paris) gave him a broad background in the history of government. That, combined with his experience as a member of the Continental Congress from 1780 to 1783, convinced him of the need for a stronger central government than that created by the Articles of Confederation. Prior to attending the Constitutional Convention, Madison wrote down his views on the "Vices of the Political System of the U. States" in one of his many notebooks. The views expressed in this list provide a glimpse into Madison's motives for creating a new Constitution that gave the national government greater power over the states. Madison's arguments articulate the view that the Articles of Confederation were fundamentally flawed in placing ultimate sovereign power in thirteen separate states rather than in one nation.

From James Madison, "Vices of the Political System of the United States." In *Letters and Other Writings of James Madison.* Philadelphia: Lippincott, 1867.

Failure of the States to Comply with the Constitutional Requisitions. This evil has been so fully experienced both during the war and since the peace, results so naturally from the number and independent authority of the States, and has been so uniformly exemplified in every similar Confederacy, that it may be considered as not less radically and permanently inherent in, than it is fatal to the object of, the present system.

Encroachments by the States on the Federal Authority. Examples of this are numerous, and repetitions may be foreseen in almost every case where any favorite object of a State shall present a temptation. Among these examples are the wars and treaties of Georgia with the Indians, the unlicensed compacts between Virginia and Maryland and between Pennsylvania and New Jersey, the troops raised and to be kept up by Massachusetts.

Violations of the Law of Nations and of Treaties. From the number of Legislatures, the sphere of life from which most of their members are taken, and the circumstances under which their legislative business is carried on, irregularities of this kind must frequently happen. Accordingly, not a year has passed without instances of them in some one or other of the States. The Treaty of Peace, the treaty with France, the treaty with Holland, have each been violated. [See the complaints to Congress on these subjects.] The causes of these irregularities must necessarily produce frequent violations of the law of nations in other respects.

As yet, foreign powers have not been rigorous in animadverting on us. This moderation, however, cannot be mistaken for a permanent partiality to our faults, or a permanent security against those disputes with other nations, which, being among the greatest of public calamities, it ought to be least in the power of any part of the community to bring on the whole.

Alarming Symptoms

Trespasses of the States on the Right of Each Other. These are alarming symptoms, and may be daily apprehended, as we are admonished by daily experience. See the law of Virginia restricting foreign vessels to certain ports; of Maryland in favor of vessels belonging to her *own citizens*; of N. York in favor of the same.

Paper money, instalments of debts, occlusion of courts, making property a legal tender, may likewise be deemed aggressions on the rights of other States. As the citizens of every State, aggregately taken, stand more or less in the relation of creditors or debtors to the citizens of every other State, acts of the debtor State in favor of debtors affect the creditor State in the same manner as they do its own citizens, who are, relatively creditors towards other citizens. This remark may be extended to foreign nations. If the exclusive regulation of the value and alloy of coin was properly delegated to the federal authority, the policy of it equally requires a controul on the States in the cases above mentioned. It must have been meant—1. To preserve uniformity in the circulating medium throughout the nation. 2. To prevent those frauds on the citizens of other States, and the subjects of foreign powers, which might disturb the tranquillity at home, or involve the union in foreign contests.

Part of the manuscript for Madison's "Vices of the Political System of the U. States," written in April 1787.

The practice of many States in restricting the commercial intercourse with other States, and putting their productions and manufactures on the same footing with those of foreign nations, though not contrary to the federal articles, is certainly adverse to the spirit of the Union, and tends to beget retaliating regulations, not less expensive and vexatious in themselves than they are destructive of the general harmony.

Want of Concert in Matters Where Common Interest Requires it. This defect is strongly illustrated in the state of our commercial affairs. How much has the national dignity, interest, and revenue, suffered from this cause? Instances of inferior moment are the want of uniformity in the laws concerning naturalization and literary property; of provision for national seminaries; for grants of incorporation for national purposes, for canals, and other works of general utility; which may at present be defeated by the perverseness of particular States whose concurrence is necessary. . . .

No Sanctions for Lawbreakers

Want of Sanction to the Laws, and of Coercion in the Government of the Confederacy. A sanction is essential to the idea of law, as coercion is to that of Government. The federal system being destitute of both, wants the great vital principles of a Political Constitution. Under the form of such a Constitution, it is in fact nothing more than a treaty of amity, of commerce, and of alliance, between independent and Sovereign States. From what cause could so fatal an omission have happened in the articles of Confederation? From a mistaken confidence that the justice, the good faith, the honor, the sound policy of the several legislative assemblies would render superfluous any appeal to the ordinary motives by which the laws secure the obedience of individuals; a confidence which does honor to the enthusiastic virtue of the compilers, as much as the inexperience of the crisis apologizes for their errors. The time which has since elapsed has had the double effect of increasing the light and tempering the warmth with which the arduous work may be revised. It is no longer doubted that a unanimous and punctual obedience of 13 independent bodies to the acts of the federal Government ought not to be calculated on. Even during the war, when external danger supplied in some degree the defect of legal and coercive sanctions, how imperfectly did the States fulfil their obligations to the Union? In time of peace we see already what is to be expected. How, indeed, could it be otherwise? In the first place, every general act of the Union must necessarily bear unequally hard on some particular member or members of it; secondly, the partiality of the members to their own interests and rights, a partiality which will be fostered by the courtiers of popularity, will naturally exaggerate the inequality where it exists, and even suspect it where it has no existence; thirdly, a distrust of the voluntary compliance of each other may prevent the compliance of any, although it should be the latent disposition of all. Here are causes and pretexts which will never fail to render federal measures abortive. If the laws of the States were merely recommendatory to their citizens, or if they were to be rejudged by county authorities, what security, what probability would exist that they would be carried into execution? Is the security or probability greater in favor of the acts of Congress, which, depending for their execution on the will of the State legislatures, are, tho' nominally authoritative, in fact recommendatory only?

Want of Ratification by the People of the Articles of Confederation. In some of the States the Confederation is recognized by and forms a part of the Constitution. In others, however, it has received no other sanction than that of the legislative authority. From this defect two evils result: 1. Whenever a law of a State happens to be repugnant to an act of Congress, particularly when the latter is of posterior date to the former, it will be at least questionable whether the latter must not prevail; and as the question must be decided by the Tribunals of the State, they will be most likely to lean on the side of the State.

2. As far as the union of the States is to be regarded as a league of sovereign powers, and not as a political Constitution, by virtue of which they are become one sovereign power, so far it seems to follow, from the doctrine of compacts, that a breach of any of the articles of the Confederation by any of the parties to it absolves the other parties from their respective obligations, and gives them a right, if they choose to exert it, of dissolving the Union altogether.

Viewpoint 4

"Some have weakly imagined that it is necessary to annihilate the several States, and vest Congress with the absolute ... government of the continent. ... This, however, would be impracticable and mischievous."

State Governments Should Not Be Supplanted by the National Government

"Z"

"Z" is the pseudonym for the author of several essays originally published in the *Freeman's Journal,* a Philadelphia newspaper. In the essay originally published on May 16, 1787, nine days before the Constitutional Convention officially began, the author questions the necessity of usurping state government powers with a new centralized government. While he concedes that changes strengthening the Articles of Confederation are necessary, he argues that these changes should be limited to matters of foreign trade and commerce, leaving the basic structure of the Confederation intact.

Historian John K. Alexander notes in his book *The Selling of the Convention* that American newspapers and pamphlets were dominated by pro-Constitution writers. "Z" was one of the few authors, Alexander points out, who challenged the prevailing editorial opinion that America should accept whatever the convention delegates decided:

> "Z" deviated from the standard booster line when he advocated a plan that hardly fit with the theme of deferring to the delegates.

While emphatically asserting that Congress needed augmented

"Z," *Freeman's Journal,* May 16, 1787, Philadelphia.

powers, "Z" declared that granting Congress the exclusive right to regulate shipping and foreign trade would be sufficient. He clearly advocated limited change and opposed merely accepting whatever the convention might recommend.

It seems to be generally felt and acknowledged, that the affairs of this country are in a ruinous situation. With vast resources in our hands, we are impoverished by the continual drain of money from us in foreign trade; our navigation is destroyed; our people are in debt and unable to pay; industry is at a stand; our public treaties are violated, and national faith, solemnly plighted to foreigners and to our own citizens, is no longer kept. We are discontented at home, and abroad we are insulted and despised.

In this exigency people naturally look up to the continental Convention, in hopes that their wisdom will provide some effectual remedy for this complication of disorders. It is perhaps the last opportunity which may be presented to us of establishing a permanent system of Continental Government; and, if this opportunity be lost, it is much to be feared that we shall fall into irretrievable confusion.

Complicated Schemes

How the great object of their meeting is to be attained is a question which deserves to be seriously considered. Some men, there is reason to believe, have indulged the idea of reforming the United States by means of some refined and complicated schemes of organizing a future Congress in a different form. These schemes, like many others with which we have been amused in times past, will be found to be merely visionary, and produce no lasting benefit. The error is not in the form of Congress, the mode of election, or the duration of the appointment of the members. The source of all our misfortunes is evidently in the want of power in Congress. To be convinced of this, we need only recollect the vigor, the energy, the unanimity of this country a few years past, even in the midst of a bloody war, *when Congress governed the continent*. We have gradually declined into feebleness, anarchy and wretchedness, from that period in which the several States began to exercise the sovereign and absolute right of treating the recommendations of Congress with contempt. From that time to the present, we have seen the great Federal Head of our union clothed with the authority of making treaties without the power of performing them; of contracting debts without being able to discharge them, or to bind others to discharge them; of regulating our trade, and providing for the general welfare of the people, in their concerns with foreign nations, without the power of restraining a single individual from the infraction of their orders, or restricting any trade, however injurious to the public welfare.

A Warning Against Change

In 1785 the Massachusetts state legislature instructed its delegation in the Continental Congress to introduce a resolution calling for a constitutional convention. The delegation, which included Elbridge Gerry and Rufus King, refused. In a September 3, 1785, letter to the legislature, they expressed their fears of granting too much power to the Continental Congress.

If an alteration, either temporary or perpetual, of the commercial powers of Congress is to be considered by a convention, shall the latter be authorized to revise the Confederation *generally*, or only for express purposes? The great object of the Revolution was the establishment of good government, and each of the states, in forming their own as well as the federal constitution, have adopted republican principles. Notwithstanding this, plans have been artfully laid and vigorously pursued which, had they been successful, we think, would inevitably have changed our republican governments into baleful aristocracies. Those plans are frustrated, but the same spirit remains in their abettors. . . .

We are for increasing the power of Congress as far as it will promote the happiness of the people, but at the same time are clearly of opinion that every measure should be avoided which would strengthen the hands of the enemies to a free government; and that an administration of the present Confederation, with all its inconveniences, is preferable to the risk of general dissensions and animosities, which may approach to anarchy and prepare the way to a ruinous system of government.

To remedy these evils, some have weakly imagined that it is necessary to annihilate the several States, and vest Congress with the absolute direction and government of the continent, as one single republic. This, however, would be impracticable and mischievous. In so extensive a country many local and internal regulations would be required, which Congress could not possibly attend to, and to which the States individually are fully competent; but those things which alike concern all the States, such as our foreign trade and foreign transactions, Congress should be fully authorized to regulate, and should be invested with the power of enforcing their regulations.

The ocean, which joins us to other nations, would seem to be the scene upon which Congress might exert its authority with the greatest benefit to the United States, as no one State can possibly claim any exclusive right in it. It has been long seen that the States individually cannot, with any success, pretend to regulate trade. The duties and restrictions which one State imposes, the neighboring States enable the merchants to elude; and besides, if they could be enforced, it would be highly unjust, that the duties collected in the port of one State should be applied to the sole use of that State in which they are collected, whilst the neighboring States, who have no ports for foreign commerce, consume a part of the goods imported, and thus in effect pay a part of the duties. Even if the recommendation of Congress had been attended to, which proposed the levying for the use of Congress five per centum on goods imported, to be collected by officers to be appointed by the individual States, it is more than probable that the laws would have been feebly executed. Men are not apt to be sufficiently attentive to the business of those who do not appoint, and cannot remove or control them; officers would naturally look up to the State which appointed them, and it is past a doubt that some of the States would esteem it no unpardonable sin to promote their own particular interest, or even that of particular men, to the injury of the United States.

Limit Reforms to Trade Regulations

Would it not then be right to vest Congress with the sole and exclusive power of regulating trade, of imposing port duties, of appointing officers to collect these duties, of erecting ports and deciding all questions by their own authority, which concern foreign trade and navigation upon the high seas? Some of those persons, who have conceived a narrow jealousy of Congress, and therefore have unhappily obstructed their exertions for the public welfare, may perhaps be startled at the idea, and make objections. To such I would answer, that our situation appears to be sufficiently desperate to justify the hazarding an experiment of anything which promises immediate relief. Let us try this for a few years; and if we find it attended with mischief, we can refuse to renew the power. But it appears to me to be necessary and useful; and I cannot think that it would in the least degree endanger our liberties. The representatives of the States in Congress are easily changed as often as we please, and they must necessarily be changed often. They would have little inclination and less ability to enterprise against the liberties of their constituents. This, no doubt, would induce the necessity of employing a small number of armed vessels to enforce the regulations of Congress, and would be the beginning of a Continental Navy; but a navy was never esteemed, like a standing army, dangerous to the liberty of the people.

To those who should object that this is too small a power to grant to Congress; that many more are necessary to be added to those which they already possess, I can only say, that perhaps they have not sufficiently reflected upon the great importance of the power proposed. That it would be of immense service to the country I have no doubt, as it is the only means by which our trade can be put on a footing with other nations; that it would in the event greatly strengthen the hands of Congress, I think is highly probable.

VIEWPOINT 5

"What stronger evidence can be given of the want of energy in our governments than these disorders?"

Shays's Rebellion Indicates the Need for a New Constitution

George Washington (1732-1799)

One of the key events that was much on the minds of the participants of the Constitutional Convention was a series of uprisings by Massachusetts farmers in 1786 and 1787 that became known as Shays's Rebellion. Faced with a combination of bad harvests, a shortage of hard currency, and heavy taxes levied to pay the war debts of Massachusetts, farmers were threatened with the loss of their farms and imprisonment for failure to pay debts and taxes. In response many farmers, following practices used against the British during the American Revolution, held conventions to send petitions to the Massachusetts legislature. The petitions asked for debt relief measures similar to those enacted in other states, including issuing paper money, passing tax reforms, and enacting "stay" laws that postponed court actions against debtors. The Massachusetts legislature, heavily influenced by wealthy creditors and merchants, refused to enact such measures. The farmers then resorted to mob action to shut down local courts, where the cases against them were being heard. Daniel Shays, a former Revolutionary War army officer, began training a group of farmers in military drills and became the symbolic leader of the insurrection. The Massachusetts government raised a strong militia force that crushed the rebellion in battles in January and February of 1787.

News of Shays's Rebellion spread throughout the states and was used by many as evidence that a stronger national government was needed. One important figure to draw this conclusion

From *The Writings of George Washington from Original Manuscript Sources.* Washington, DC: GPO, 1931-1944.

was George Washington. Having resigned as general of the Continental army in 1783 and returned to his Mount Vernon plantation, Washington was officially retired from public life. But he was disturbed by events in Massachusetts and elsewhere that suggested that the new nation he had helped to create would founder without a stronger government. Washington expressed these views in several letters to friends and associates, including a November 5, 1786, letter to Virginian James Madison. In his letter to Madison, reprinted below, Washington refers to a letter from Henry Knox, secretary of war of the Confederation and one of Washington's generals during the Revolution, which described the situation in Massachusetts as a serious one. Washington argues that the United States needs a new and stronger national government in order to preserve internal order and to gain respect from countries in Europe.

Washington's views give some reasons for his eventual agreement to attend the Constitutional Convention in Philadelphia in 1787. His implicit endorsement by attendance at the Convention, and the unspoken understanding among the delegates that Washington would be the first national executive under whatever new government was created, are regarded by many historians as being crucial for the Convention's ultimate success.

M y dear Sir:

I thank you for the communications in your letter of the first instt. The decision of the House on the question respecting a paper emission [issuing of paper money], is portentous I hope, of an auspicious Session. It may certainly be classed among the important questions of the present day; and merited the serious consideration of the Assembly. Fain would I hope, that the great, and most important of all objects, the foederal governmt., may be considered with that calm and deliberate attention which the magnitude of it so loudly calls for at this critical moment. Let prejudices, unreasonable jealousies, and local interest yield to reason and liberality. Let us look to our National character, and to things beyond the present period. No morn ever dawned more favourably than ours did; and no day was ever more clouded than the present! Wisdom, and good examples are necessary at this time to rescue the political machine from the impending storm. Virginia has now an opportunity to set the latter, and has enough of the former, I hope, to take the lead in promoting this great and arduous work. Without some alteration in our political creed, the superstructure we have been seven years raising at the expence of so much blood and treasure, must fall. We are fast verging to anarchy and confusion!

A Crisis of Authority

Reacting to Shays's Rebellion, the American Recorder, *a Charlestown, Massachusetts, newspaper, published an editorial on March 16, 1787, arguing that events demonstrated the need for a stronger national government.*

This is a crisis in our affairs, which requires all the wisdom and energy of government; for every man of sense must be convinced, that our disturbances have arisen, more from a want of power, than the abuse of it—from the relaxation, and almost annihilation of our federal government—from the feeble, unsystematic, temporising, inconstant character of our own state—from the derangement of our finances—the oppressive absurdity of our mode of taxation—and from the astonishing enthusiasm and perversion of principles among the people. It is not extraordinary that commotions have been excited. It is strange, that under the circumstances which we have been discussing, that they did not appear sooner, and terminate more fatally. For let it be remarked, that a feeble government produces more factions than an oppressive one. The want of power first makes individuals pretended legislators, and then, active rebels. Where parents want authority, children are wanting in duty. It is not possible to advance further in the same path. Here the ways divide, the one will conduct us to anarchy, and next to foreign or domestic tyranny: the other, by the wise and vigorous exertion of lawful authority, will lead to permanent power, and general prosperity. I am no advocate for despotism; but I believe the probability to be much less of its being introduced by the corruption of our rulers, than by the delusion of the people. . . .

While the bands of union are so loose, we are no more entitled to the character of a nation than the hordes of vagabond traitors. Reason has ever condemned our paltry prejudices upon this important subject. Now that experience has come in aid of reason, let us renounce them. For what is there now to prevent our subjugation by a foreign power, but their contempt of the acquisition? It is time to render the federal head supreme in the United States.

A letter which I have just received from Genl Knox, who had just returned from Massachusetts (whither he had been sent by Congress consequent of the commotion in that State) is replete with melancholy information of the temper, and designs of a considerable part of that people. Among other things he says,

> there creed is, that the property of the United States, has been protected from confiscation of Britain by the joint exertions of

all, and therefore ought to be the *common property* of all. And he that attempts opposition to this creed is an enemy to equity and justice, and ought to be swept from off the face of the Earth.

Again:

> They are determined to anihillate all debts public and private, and have Agrarian Laws, which are easily effected by the means of unfunded paper money which shall be a tender in all cases whatever.

He adds:

> The numbers of these people amount in Massachusetts to about one fifth part of several populous Counties, and to them may be collected, people of similar sentiments from the States of Rhode Island, Connecticut, and New Hampshire, so as to constitute a body of twelve or fifteen thousand desperate, and unprincipled men. They are chiefly of the young and active part of the Community.

How melancholy is the reflection, that in so short a space, we should have made such large strides towards fulfilling the prediction of our transatlantic foe! "Leave them to themselves, and their government will soon dissolve." Will not the wise and good strive hard to avert this evil? Or will their supineness suffer ignorance, and the arts of self-interested designing disaffected and desperate characters, to involve this rising empire in wretchedness and contempt? What stronger evidence can be given of the want of energy in our governments than these disorders? If there exists not a power to check them, what security has a man for life, liberty, or property? To you, I am sure I need not add aught on this subject, the consequences of a lax, or inefficient government, are too obvious to be dwelt on. Thirteen Sovereignties pulling against each other, and all tugging at the foederal head will soon bring ruin on the whole; whereas a liberal, and energetic Constitution, well guarded and closely watched, to prevent incroachments, might restore us to that degree of respectability and consequence, to which we had a fair claim, and the brightest prospect of attaining. With sentiments of the sincerest esteem etc.

VIEWPOINT 6

"I hold it that a little rebellion now and then is a good thing, and as necessary in the political world as storms in the physical."

The Threat Posed by Shays's Rebellion Has Been Exaggerated

Thomas Jefferson (1743-1826)

In the years following the American Revolution, many impoverished farmers in several states resorted to mob violence in an effort to attain debt and tax relief. Shays's Rebellion in Massachusetts in 1786-1787 was one of the most serious of these insurrections. Many political leaders throughout America looked upon events in Massachusetts with alarm, believing them evidence that America was falling apart. Even after Shays's Rebellion was crushed in early 1787, historian Richard Bernstein writes, its influence was felt during the Constitutional Convention and ratification debates, and served "as a reliable propaganda device for proponents of the Constitution."

A different view of Shays's Rebellion comes from Thomas Jefferson, the author of the Declaration of Independence and future president of the United States. Jefferson was minister to France from 1785 to 1789; his role in the creation of the Constitution was limited to the correspondence he pursued with James Madison and others. Jefferson's views on developments in Massachusetts are revealed in two letters reprinted here. In the first, written to Edward Carrington, January 16, 1787, Jefferson maintains that the respect of America among European governments has not been

From *The Writings of Thomas Jefferson*, Paul L. Ford, ed. New York, 1892.

diminished by events in Massachusetts, and he compares favorably the independent state of people in America with the situation in Europe. In the second letter, written to James Madison on January 30, Jefferson argues that rebellions are necessary to preserve free government.

I

The tumults in America I expected would have produced in Europe an unfavorable opinion of our political state. But it has not. On the contrary, the small effect of these tumults seems to have given more confidence in the firmness of our governments. The interposition of the people themselves on the side of government has had a great effect on the opinion here. I am persuaded myself that the good sense of the people will always be found to be the best army. They may be led astray for a moment, but will soon correct themselves.

Inform the People

The people are the only censors of their governors; and even their errors will tend to keep these to the true principles of their institution. To punish these errors too severely would be to suppress the only safeguard of the public liberty. The way to prevent these irregular interpositions of the people is to give them full information of their affairs through the channel of the public papers, and to contrive that those papers should penetrate the whole mass of the people. The basis of our governments being the opinion of the people, the very first object should be to keep that right; and were it left to me to decide whether we should have a government without newspapers, or newspapers without a government, I should not hesitate a moment to prefer the latter. But I should mean that every man should receive those papers, and be capable of reading them.

I am convinced that those societies (as the Indians) which live without government enjoy in their general mass an infinitely greater degree of happiness than those who live under the European governments. Among the former, public opinion is in the place of law, and restrains morals as powerfully as laws ever did anywhere. Among the latter, under pretense of governing, they have divided their nations into two classes, wolves and sheep. I do not exaggerate.

This is a true picture of Europe. Cherish, therefore, the spirit of our people, and keep alive their intention. Do not be too severe upon their errors, but reclaim them by enlightening them. If once they become inattentive to the public affairs, you and I, and Congress and assemblies, judges and governors shall all become wolves. It seems to be the law of our general nature, in spite of individual exceptions; and experience declares that man is the only animal which devours his own kind; for I can apply no milder term to the governments of Europe, and to the general prey of the rich on the poor.

The name of Daniel Shays, one of the leaders of the Massachusetts farmers' rebellion, was mentioned often in the public and private writings of American political leaders in 1786 and 1787. The only contemporary picture of Shays (left) and his associate Job Shattuck appeared on the cover of the 1787 edition of Bickerstaff's Boston Almanack.

II

My last to you was of the 16th of December; since which, I have received yours of November 25 and December 4, which afforded me, as your letters always do, a treat on matters public, individual, and economical. I am impatient to learn your sentiments on the late troubles in the Eastern states. So far as I have yet seen, they do not appear to threaten serious consequences. Those states have suffered by the stoppage of the channels of their commerce, which have not yet found other issues. This must render money scarce and make the people uneasy. This uneasiness has produced acts absolutely unjustifiable; but I hope they will provoke no severities from their governments. A consciousness of those in power that their administration of the public affairs has been honest may, perhaps, produce too great a degree of indignation; and those characters, wherein fear predominates over hope, may apprehend too much from these instances of irregularity. They may conclude too hastily that nature has formed man insusceptible of any other government than that of force, a conclusion not founded in truth nor experience.

Societies exist under three forms, sufficiently distinguishable: (1) without government, as among our Indians; (2) under governments, wherein the will of everyone has a just influence, as is the case in England, in a slight degree, and in our states, in a great one; (3) under governments of force, as is the case in all other monarchies, and in most of the other republics.

To have an idea of the curse of existence under these last, they must be seen. It is a government of wolves over sheep. It is a problem, not clear in my mind, that the first condition is not the best. But I believe it to be inconsistent with any great degree of population. The second state has a great deal of good in it. The mass of mankind under that enjoys a precious degree of liberty and happiness. It has its evils, too, the principal of which is the turbulence to which it is subject. But weigh this against the oppressions of monarchy, and it becomes nothing. *Malo periculosam libertatem quam quietam servitutem* [I prefer liberty at risk to peaceful servitude]. Even this evil is productive of good. It prevents the degeneracy of government and nourishes a general attention to the public affairs.

I hold it that a little rebellion now and then is a good thing, and as necessary in the political world as storms in the physical. Unsuccessful rebellions, indeed, generally establish the encroachments on the rights of the people which have produced them. An observation of this truth should render honest republican governors so mild in their punishment of rebellions as not to discourage them too much. It is a medicine necessary for the sound health of government.

CHAPTER 2

The Convention Debates Rival Plans of Government

Chapter Preface

The Constitutional Convention that assembled in Philadelphia in May 1787 was the culmination of efforts and agitations by a relatively small group of political leaders convinced of the need for a stronger national government. Its origins can be traced to a convention held the previous year in Annapolis, Maryland. The Annapolis Convention, which was proposed by the Virginia state legislature, involved delegates' meeting to discuss and settle interstate commerce issues. It accomplished little since representatives from only five states attended. Alexander Hamilton, one of the convention participants who was a longtime critic of the Articles of Confederation, drafted a resolution calling delegates from the states to meet again in Philadelphia in 1787 "to take into consideration the situation of the United States, to devise such further provisions as shall appear to them necessary to render the Constitution of the federal government adequate to the exigencies of the Union." Influenced in part by Shays's Rebellion, the Continental Congress agreed to authorize the convention, although it limited its mandate to be "for the sole and express purpose of revising the Articles of Confederation."

Every state except Rhode Island selected delegates for the Constitutional Convention. Of the seventy-four men selected, only fifty-five attended all or part of the meeting. At the outset of their meeting the course they would take was unclear. Would the Convention limit itself to making amendments to the Articles of Confederation, as some delegates desired? Or would they scrap the Articles entirely and create a new national government? Historian Ralph Ketcham writes in *The Anti-Federalist Papers and the Constitutional Convention Debates* that the people who assembled in Philadelphia "had in mind generally to strengthen the Articles, but beyond that there was little agreement on how extensively and in what way to do that."

The following viewpoints are mostly taken from alternative plans presented at the Constitutional Convention and the debates surrounding them. They present differing views on the extent of changes required in the Articles of Confederation and the necessity of creating a new national government supreme over the states. Many of the debates and speeches excerpted here were preserved in the notes of Virginia delegate James Madison, who undertook the task of recording the proceedings of the Constitutional Convention (although he did not allow the publishing of his notes until after his death in 1836). Despite the fact that Madison was far more than a detached observer at the Convention, most historians have judged his notes to be generally fair and objective. As noted historian Clinton Rossiter writes in *1787: The Grand Convention:*

> Madison seems to have been a faithful and honest reporter. As one learns in comparing his notes with those of the other self-appointed but only part-time scribes, the record he left us is remarkably full, impartial, and accurate. Although we can never be entirely sure that what Madison wrote down was "history as it actually happened," we can have more confidence in his celebrated *Notes* than in almost any other unofficial document of the early years of the Republic.

Viewpoint 1

"There were many advantages, which the U.S. might acquire, which were not attainable under the confederation."

A New National Government Should Be Established (The Virginia Plan)

Edmund Randolph (1753-1813)

The Constitutional Convention was scheduled to start on May 14, 1787, but, due to travel difficulties and delays, did not have enough delegates to officially begin until May 25. The Virginia delegation, led by James Madison, took advantage of the delay to informally meet and plan a strategy for the upcoming Convention. They devised a set of fifteen resolutions that have become known to historians as the Virginia Plan. The resolutions, going beyond the official mandate of amending the Articles of Confederation, created a whole new national government with three branches: legislative, executive, and judiciary. Among the features of the proposed new government was a bicameral (two-house) legislature elected with proportional representation (unlike the Confederation in which each state got one vote), and a relatively weak national executive selected by the legislature for a seven-year term. By opening with these resolutions, Madison and the rest of the Virginia delegation were able to set the terms of the debate for the opening weeks of the Convention, and to place it on the course of establishing a new government.

The delegate chosen to introduce the plan was Edmund Randolph, the governor of Virginia. Randolph, a member of an elite Virginia family, had previously been an aide to George Washing-

From *Documents Illustrative of the Formation of the Union of the American States*, Charles C. Tansill, ed. Washington, DC: GPO, 1927.

ton in 1775, Virginia's first attorney general from 1776 to 1778, and a member of the Continental Congress from 1779 to 1782. His polished speaking and handsome profile were perhaps part of the reason he was called upon to introduce the Virginia Plan to the Convention on May 29. He introduced the fifteen resolutions with a prefatory speech attacking the Articles of Confederation, arguing that they had failed to establish a government that served the United States. Randoph's speech and resolutions, presented here, were preserved in James Madison's notes of the Convention.

Despite Randolph's strong involvement in the Constitutional Convention, he was, along with George Mason and Elbridge Gerry, one of three participating delegates who refused to sign the finished document, citing concerns about excessive national power. In Virginia's 1788 ratification convention, however, he changed his position and urged ratification. Randolph later served in President George Washington's cabinet as the nation's first attorney general and then as secretary of state before retiring to private life.

Mr. Randolph expressed his regret, that it should fall to him, rather than those, who were of longer standing in life and political experience, to open the great subject of their mission. But, as the convention had originated from Virginia, and his colleagues supposed that some proposition was expected from them, they had imposed this task on him.

He then commented on the difficulty of the crisis, and the necessity of preventing the fulfillment of the prophecies of the American downfall.

He observed that in revising the federal system we ought to inquire 1) into the properties, which such a government ought to possess, 2) the defects of the confederation, 3) the danger of our situation and 4) the remedy.

1. The Character of such a government ought to secure 1) against foreign invasion: 2) against dissentions between members of the Union, or seditions in particular states: 3) to procure to the several States, various blessings, of which an isolated situation was incapable: 4) to be able to defend itself against incroachment: and 5) to be paramount to the state constitutions.

Defects of the Confederation

2. In speaking of the defects of the confederation he professed a high respect for its authors, and considered them, as having done

all that patriots could do, in the then infancy of the science, of constitutions, and of confederacies,—when the inefficiency of requisitions was unknown—no commercial discord had arisen among any states—no rebellion had appeared as in Massachusetts—foreign debts had not become urgent—the havoc of paper money had not been foreseen—treaties had not been violated—and perhaps nothing better could be obtained from the jealousy of the states with regard to their sovereignty.

The Virginia Plan provided the basis for much of the Constitution. George Washington's handwritten copy is pictured here.

He then proceeded to enumerate the defects: 1) That the confederation produced no security against foreign invasion; congress not being permitted to prevent a war nor to support it by their own authority—Of this he cited many examples; most of which tended to show, that they could not cause infractions of treaties or of the law of nations, to be punished: that particular states might by their conduct provoke war without control; and that neither militia nor draughts being fit for defence on such occasions, inlistments only could be successful, and these could not be executed without money. 2) That the federal government could not check the quarrels between states, nor a rebellion in any, not having constitutional power nor means to interpose according to the exigency. 3) That there were many advantages, which the U. S. might acquire, which were not attainable under the confederation—such as a productive impost—counteraction of the commercial regulations of other nations—pushing of commerce ad libitum—etc. etc. 4) That the federal government could not defend itself against the incroachments from the states. 5) That it was not even paramount to the state constitutions, ratified, as it was in many of the states.

3. He next reviewed the danger of our situation, appealed to the sense of the best friends of the United States—the prospect of anarchy from the laxity of government everywhere; and to other considerations.

4. He then proceeded to the remedy; the basis of which he said must be the republican principle.

He proposed as conformable to his ideas the following resolutions, which he explained one by one.

Resolutions Proposed By Mr. Randolph in Convention

1. Resolved that the Articles of Confederation ought to be so corrected and enlarged as to accomplish the objects proposed by their institution; namely, "common defense, security of liberty and general welfare."

2. Resolved therefore that the rights of suffrage in the National Legislature ought to be proportioned to the Quotas of contribution, or to the number of free inhabitants, as the one or the other rule may seem best in different cases.

A Two-Branch Legislature

3. Resolved that the National Legislature ought to consist of two branches.

4. Resolved that the members of the first branch of the National Legislature ought to be elected by the people of the several States every   for the term of   ; to be of the age of   years at least, to receive liberal stipends by which they may be compensated for the devotion of their time to public service; to be ineligible to any office established by a particular State, or under the authority of the United States, except those peculiarly belonging to the functions of the first branch, during the term of service, and for the space of   after its expiration; to be incapable of re-election for the space of   after the expiration of their term of service, and to be subject to recall.

5. Resolved that the members of the second branch of the National Legislature ought to be elected by those of the first, out of a proper number of persons nominated by the individual Legisla-

tures, to be of the age of   years at least; to hold their offices for a term sufficient to ensure their independency; to receive liberal stipends, by which they may be compensated for the devotion of their time to public service; and to be ineligible to any office established by a particular State, or under the authority of the United States, except those peculiarly belonging to the functions of the second branch, during the term of service, and for the space of   after the expiration thereof.

6. Resolved that each branch ought to possess the right of originating Acts; that the National Legislature ought to be impowered to enjoy the Legislative Rights vested in Congress by the Confederation and moreover to legislate in all cases to which the separate States are incompetent, or in which the harmony of the United States may be interrupted by the exercise of individual Legislation; to negative all laws passed by the several States, contravening in the opinion of the National Legislature the articles of Union; and to call forth the force of the Union against any member of the Union failing to fulfill its duty under the articles thereof.

A National Executive and Judiciary

7. Resolved that a National Executive be instituted; to be chosen by the National Legislature for the term of   years to receive punctually at stated times, a fixed compensation for the services rendered, in which no increase or diminution shall be made so as to affect the Magistracy, existing at the time of increase or diminution, and to be ineligible a second time; and that besides a general authority to execute the National laws, it ought to enjoy the Executive rights vested in Congress by the Confederation.

8. Resolved that the Executive and a convenient number of the National Judiciary, ought to compose a Council of revision with authority to examine every act of the National Legislature before it shall operate, and every act of a particular Legislature before a Negative thereon shall be final; and that the dissent of the said Council shall amount to a rejection, unless the Act of the National Legislature be again passed, or that of a particular Legislature be again negatived by   of the members of each branch.

9. Resolved that a National Judiciary be established to consist of one or more supreme tribunals, and of inferior tribunals to be chosen by the National Legislature, to hold their offices during good behaviour; and to receive punctually at stated times fixed compensation for their services, in which no increase or diminution shall be made so as to affect the persons actually in office at the time of such increase or diminution. That the jurisdiction of the inferior tribunals shall be to hear and determine in the first instance, and of the supreme tribunal to hear and determine in the [last] resort, all piracies and felonies on the high seas, captures

from an enemy; cases in which foreigners or citizens of other States applying to such jurisdictions may be interested, or which respect the collection of the National revenue; impeachments of any National officers, and questions which may involve the national peace and harmony.

10. Resolved that provision ought to be made for the admission of States lawfully arising within the limits of the United States, whether from a voluntary junction of Government and Territory or otherwise, with the consent of a number of voices in the National Legislature less than the whole.

11. Resolved that a Republican Government and the territory of each State, except in the instance of a voluntary junction of Government and territory, ought to be guaranteed by the United States to each State.

12. Resolved that provision ought to be made for the continuance of Congress and their authorities and privileges, until a given day after the reform of the articles of Union shall be adopted, and for the completion of all their engagements.

13. Resolved that provision ought to be made for the amendment of the Articles of Union whensoever it shall seem necessary, and that the assent of the National Legislature ought not to be required thereto.

14. Resolved that the Legislative Executive and Judiciary powers within the several States ought to be bound by oath to support the articles of Union.

15. Resolved that the amendments which shall be offered to the Confederation, by the Convention ought at a proper time, or times, after the approbation of Congress to be submitted to an assembly or assemblies of Representatives, recommended by the several Legislatures to be expressly chosen by the people, to consider and decide thereon.

He concluded with an exhortation, not to suffer the present opportunity of establishing general peace, harmony, happiness and liberty in the U. S. to pass away unimproved.

VIEWPOINT 2

"Our powers were explicit and confined to the sole and express purpose of revising the Articles of Confederation."

The Convention Lacks the Authority to Establish a New National Government

Robert Yates (1738-1801) and John Lansing (1754-1829)

The first weeks of the Constitutional Convention were dominated by debate over the set of fifteen resolutions proposed by the Virginia delegation led by James Madison. The resolutions, known as the Virginia Plan, in effect would replace the Articles of Confederation with a new national government. Several delegates at the Convention objected that they were exceeding their legal authority—the Continental Congress had authorized this Convention to meet for "the sole and express purpose of revising the Articles of Confederation."

Two of the main opponents of the Virginia Plan were Robert Yates and John Lansing, delegates from New York. Yates and Lansing, both lawyers, were close political allies of George Clinton, the governor of New York, who strongly opposed giving new powers to the national government. In arguing against the Virginia Plan, Yates and Lansing cited the fact that the New York legislature specifically forbade them from doing more than proposing revisions to the Articles of Confederation. On July 10, believing that their arguments against creating a new national government were not going to prevail in Philadelphia, they left the Constitutional Convention.

On December 21, 1787, Yates and Lansing jointly wrote a letter

From *The Debates in the Several State Conventions on the Adoption of the Federal Constitution, etc., etc.*, Jonathan Elliot, ed. Philadelphia, 1861.

addressed to Governor Clinton. In the letter, excerpted here, they explain the reasons for their decision to desert the Convention, and restate their arguments against creating a more centralized national government. The letter was transmitted to the state legislature on January 11, 1788, and was reprinted in the *New York Journal* and other newspapers during the national ratification debates. Clinton, Lansing, and Yates all later participated in the 1788 New York ratifying convention, in which they unsuccessfully opposed ratification of the Constitution.

We do ourselves the honor to advise Your Excellency that in pursuance to concurrent resolutions of the honorable Senate and Assembly we have, together with Mr. Hamilton, attended the Convention appointed for revising the Articles of Confederation, and reporting amendments to the same.

It is with the sincerest concern we observe that, in the prosecution of the important objects of our mission, we have been reduced to the disagreeable alternative of either exceeding the powers delegated to us, and giving assent to measures which we conceive destructive to the political happiness of the citizens of the United States, or opposing our opinions to that of a body of respectable men to whom those citizens had given the most unequivocal proofs of confidence. Thus circumstanced, under these impressions, to have hesitated would have been to be culpable. We therefore gave the principles of the Constitution which has received the sanction of a majority of the Convention our decided and unreserved dissent; but we must candidly confess that we should have been equally opposed to any system, however modified, which had in object the consolidation of the United States into one government.

Reasons for Opposition

We beg leave, briefly, to state some cogent reasons which, among others, influenced us to decide against a consolidation of the states. These are reducible into two heads:

1. The limited and well-defined powers under which we acted and which could not, on any possible construction, embrace an idea of such magnitude as to assent to a general Constitution, in subversion of that of the state.

2. A conviction of the impracticability of establishing a general government, pervading every part of the United States, and extending essential benefits to all.

Our powers were explicit and confined to the sole and express purpose of revising the Articles of Confederation, and reporting such alterations and provisions therein as should render the federal Constitution adequate to the exigencies of government and the preservation of the Union.

Small States and the Virginia Plan

Maryland's attorney general, Luther Martin, was one of the most vociferous opponents of the Virginia Plan, which he believed unfairly advanced the power of the large states at the expense of small states like his own. In these passages taken from a June 27 speech at the Constitutional Convention, Martin criticizes the Virginia Plan and questions the Convention's authority to alter the Articles of Confederation. Martin's speech was preserved in the notes of New York delegate Robert Yates.

Unequal confederacies can never produce good effects. Apply this to the Virginia Plan. Out of the number 90, Virginia has 16 votes, Massachusetts 14, Pennsylvania 12—in all 42. Add to this a state having four votes, and it gives a majority in the general legislature. Consequently a combination of these states will govern the remaining nine or ten states. Where is the safety and independency of those states? Pursue this subject farther. The executive is to be appointed by the legislature, and becomes the executive in consequence of this undue influence. And hence flows the appointment of all your officers, civil, military, and judicial. The executive is also to have a negative on all laws. Suppose the possibility of a combination of ten states; he negatives a law; it is totally lost, because those states cannot form two-thirds of the legislature. I am willing to give up private interest for the public good, but I must be satisfied first that it is the public interest. Who can decide this point? A majority only of the union. . . .

I would rather confederate with any single state, than submit to the Virginia Plan. But we are already confederated, and no power on earth can dissolve it but by the consent of *all* the contracting powers, and four states, on this floor, have already declared their opposition to annihilate it. Is the old confederation dissolved because some of the states wish a new confederation?

From these expressions, we were led to believe that a system of consolidated government could not in the remotest degree have been in contemplation of the legislature of this state; for that so important a trust as the adopting measures which tended to deprive the state government of its most essential rights of sovereignty, and to place it in a dependent situation, could not have been confided by implication; and the circumstance, that the acts of the Convention were to receive a state approbation in the last resort, forcibly corroborated the opinion that our powers could not involve the subversion of a Constitution which, being immediately derived from the people, could only be abolished by their express consent, and not by a legislature possessing authority vested in them for its preservation. Nor could we suppose that, if it had been the intention of the legislature to abrogate the existing Confederation, they would, in such pointed terms, have directed the attention of their delegates to the revision and amendment of it in total exclusion of every other idea.

Reasoning in this manner, we were of opinion that the leading feature of every amendment ought to be the preservation of the individual states in their uncontrolled constitutional rights; and that, in reserving these, a mode might have been devised of granting to the Confederacy the moneys arising from a general system of revenue, the power of regulating commerce and enforcing the observance of foreign treaties, and other necessary matters of less moment.

Against Consolidated Government

Exclusive of our objections originating from the want of power, we entertained an opinion that a general government, however guarded by declarations of rights or cautionary provisions, must unavoidably, in a short time, be productive of the destruction of the civil liberty of such citizens who could be effectually coerced by it, by reason of the extensive territory of the United States, the dispersed situation of its inhabitants, and the insuperable difficulty of controlling or counteracting the views of a set of men (however unconstitutional and oppressive their acts might be) possessed of all the powers of government, and who, from their remoteness from their constituents, and necessary permanency of office, could not be supposed to be uniformly actuated by an attention to their welfare and happiness; that, however wise and energetic the principles of the general government might be, the extremities of the United States could not be kept in due submission and obedience to its laws, at the distance of many hundred miles from the seat of government; that, if the general legislature was composed of so numerous a body of men as to represent the interests of all the inhabitants of the United States in the usual and true ideas of representation, the expense of supporting it would become intolerably burdensome; and that if a few only were vested with a power of legislation, the interests of a great majority of the inhabitants of the United States must necessarily be unknown, or, if known, even in the first stages of the operations of the new government, unattended to.

These reasons were, in our opinion, conclusive against any system of consolidated government; to that recommended by the Convention, we suppose most of them very forcibly apply.

It is not our intention to pursue this subject further than merely to explain our conduct in the discharge of the trust which the honorable legislature reposed in us. Interested, however, as we are, in common with our fellow citizens, in the result, we cannot forbear to declare that we have the strongest apprehensions that a government so organized as that recommended by the Convention cannot afford that security to equal and permanent liberty which we wished to make an invariable object of our pursuit.

No Alternative but to Depart

We were not present at the completion of the new Constitution; but before we left the Convention, its principles were so well established as to convince us that no alteration was to be expected to conform it to our ideas of expediency and safety. A persuasion that our further attendance would be fruitless and unavailing rendered us less solicitous to return.

We have thus explained our motives for opposing the adoption of the national Constitution, which we conceived it our duty to communicate to Your Excellency, to be submitted to the consideration of the honorable legislature.

Viewpoint 3

"Let us, therefore, fairly try whether the confederation cannot be mended, and if it can, we shall do our duty, and I believe the people will be satisfied."

The Articles of Confederation Should Be Revised (The New Jersey Plan)

William Paterson (1745-1806)

The first days of the Constitutional Convention were focused on debating the fifteen resolutions known as the Virginia Plan. In its support James Madison and other sponsors of the plan had put together a coalition of the three largest states (Virginia, Pennsylvania, and Massachusetts) and the three states of the Deep South (North Carolina, South Carolina, and Georgia). This coalition favored a national government with a legislature in which the states would be represented in proportion to their population (a population that counted each slave as three-fifths of a person). The coalition was consistently able to outvote the five smaller states (New Jersey, New York, Maryland, Delaware, Connecticut) who feared that a government with proportional representation would be dominated by the larger states. (Of the remaining two states, New Hampshire's delegates arrived late, and Rhode Island refused to send a delegation to the Convention.)

By June 13 the provisions of the Virginia Plan had been separately passed with minor alterations. The following day William Paterson, a delegate from New Jersey, moved that the Convention be adjourned for a day so that an alternative plan could be prepared for the Convention's consideration. That plan, presented by Paterson on June 15, was a joint product of the delegations of

From *Documents Illustrative of the Formation of the Union of the American States*, Charles C. Tansill, ed. Washington, DC: GPO, 1927.

New Jersey, New York, Connecticut, and Delaware, but became known to historians as the New Jersey Plan.

The following excerpts from the Convention's debate over the New Jersey Plan are in two parts. Part I is the plan itself. It calls for revising the Articles of Confederation while preserving the sovereignty of the individual states, and giving each state an equal vote in the national legislature. Part II is taken from a speech made on June 16 by Paterson in support of the plan, in which he argues that the American people did not wish for a new national government. Paterson, who consistently voiced fears that a new centralized government would be detrimental to the interests of the small states, argues in his speech that revising the Articles of Confederation is sufficient and timely. His speech is taken from the notes of Robert Yates, a New York delegate who also supported the New Jersey Plan.

Paterson's plan was voted down by the Convention, but some of its ideas made it to the final version of the Constitution, including the provisions giving all states equal voting power in the Senate. Paterson signed the finished Constitution and later served as an associate justice of the U.S. Supreme Court from 1793 to 1806.

I

1. Resolved that the articles of Confederation ought to be so revised, corrected & enlarged, as to render the federal Constitution adequate to the exigencies of Government, & the preservation of the Union.

Powers of Congress

2. Resolved that in addition to the powers vested in the United States in Congress, by the present existing articles of Confederation, they be authorized to pass acts for raising a revenue, by levying a duty or duties on all goods or merchandizes of foreign growth or manufacture, imported into any part of the United States, by Stamps on paper, vellum or parchment, and by a postage on all letters or packages passing through the general post-office, to be applied to such federal purposes as they shall deem proper & expedient; to make rules & regulations for the collection thereof; and the same from time to time, to alter & amend in such manner as they shall think proper: to pass Acts for the regulation of trade & commerce as well with foreign nations as with each other: provided that all punishments, fines, forfeitures

& penalties to be incurred for contravening such acts rules and regulations shall be adjudged by the Common law Judiciaries of the State in which any offence contrary to the true intent & meaning of such Acts rules & regulations shall have been committed or perpetrated, with liberty of commencing in the first instance all suits & prosecutions for that purpose in the superior common law Judiciary in such State, subject nevertheless, for the correction of all errors, both in law & fact in rendering Judgment, to an appeal to the Judiciary of the United States.

William Paterson, the Irish-born son of a shopkeeper, became a successful lawyer and New Jersey's attorney general. He was a consistent advocate of the small states' interests.

Stock Montage, Inc.

3. Resolved that whenever requisitions shall be necessary, instead of the rule for making requisitions mentioned in the articles of Confederation, the United States in Congress be authorized to make such requisitions in proportion to the whole number of white & other free citizens & inhabitants of every age sex and condition including those bound to servitude for a term of years & three fifths of all other persons not comprehended in the foregoing description, except Indians not paying taxes; that if such requisitions be not complied with, in the time specified therein, to direct the collection thereof in the non complying States & for

that purpose to devise and pass acts directing & authorizing the same; provided that none of the powers hereby vested in the United States in Congress shall be exercised without the consent of at least   States, and in that proportion if the number of Confederated States should hereafter be increased or diminished.

4. Resolved that the United States in Congress be authorized to elect a federal Executive to consist of   persons, to continue in office for the term of   years, to receive punctually at stated times a fixed compensation for their services, in which no increase or diminution shall be made so as to affect the persons composing the Executive at the time of such increase or diminution, to be paid out of the federal treasury; to be incapable of holding any other office or appointment during their time of service and for   years thereafter; to be ineligible a second time, & removeable by Congress on application by a majority of the Executives of the several States; that the Executives besides their general authority to execute the federal acts ought to appoint all federal officers not otherwise provided for, & to direct all military operations; provided that none of the persons composing the federal Executive shall on any occasion take command of any troops, so as personally to conduct any enterprise as General or in other capacity.

The Judiciary

5. Resolved that a federal Judiciary be established to consist of a supreme Tribunal the Judges of which to be appointed by the Executive, & to hold their offices during good behaviour, to receive punctually at stated times a fixed compensation for their services in which no increase or diminution shall be made, so as to affect the persons actually in office at the time of such increase or diminution; that the Judiciary so established shall have authority to hear & determine in the first instance on all impeachments of federal officers, & by way of appeal in the dernier resort in all cases touching the rights of Ambassadors, in all cases of captures from an enemy, in all cases of piracies & felonies on the high Seas, in all cases in which foreigners may be interested, in the construction of any treaty or treaties, or which may arise on any of the Acts for regulation of trade, or the collection of the federal Revenue: that none of the Judiciary shall during the time they remain in office be capable of receiving or holding any other office or appointment during their time of service, or for thereafter.

6. Resolved that all Acts of the United States in Congress made by virtue & in pursuance of the powers hereby & by the articles of Confederation vested in them, and all Treaties made & ratified under the authority of the United States shall be the supreme law of the respective States so far forth as those Acts or Treaties shall relate to the said States or their Citizens, and that the Judiciary of

the several States shall be bound thereby in their decisions, any thing in the respective laws of the Individual States to the contrary notwithstanding; and that if any State, or any body of men in any State shall oppose or prevent the carrying into execution such acts or treaties, the federal Executive shall be authorized to call forth the power of the Confederated States, or so much thereof as may be necessary to enforce and compel an obedience to such Acts, or an observance of such Treaties.

7. Resolved that provision be made for the admission of new States into the Union.

8. Resolved the rule for naturalization ought to be the same in every State.

9. Resolved that a Citizen of one State committing an offence in another State of the Union, shall be deemed guilty of the same offence as if it had been committed by a Citizen of the State in which the offence was committed.

II

As I had the honor of proposing a new system of government for the union, it will be expected that I should explain its principles.

1st. The plan accords with our own powers.

2d. It accords with the sentiments of the people.

The Articles of Confederation

But if the subsisting confederation is so radically defective as not to admit of amendment, let us say so and report its insufficiency, and wait for enlarged powers. We must, in the present case, pursue our powers, if we expect the approbation of the people. I am not here to pursue my own sentiments of government, but of those who have sent me; and I believe that a little practical virtue is to be preferred to the finest theoretical principles, which cannot be carried into effect. Can we, as representatives of independent States, annihilate the essential powers of independency? Are not the votes of this convention taken on every question under the idea of independency? Let us turn to the 5th article of confederation—in this it is mutually agreed, that each State should have one vote—It is a fundamental principle arising from confederated governments. The 13th article provides for amendments; but they must be agreed to by every State—the dissent of one renders every proposal null. The confederation is in the nature of a compact; and can any State, unless by the consent of the whole, either in politics or law, withdraw their powers? Let it be said by Pennsylvania, and the other large States, that they, for the sake of peace, assented to the confederation; can she now resume her original right without the consent of the donee?

And although it is now asserted that the larger States reluctantly agreed to that part of the confederation which secures an equal suffrage to each, yet let it be remembered, that the smaller States were the last who approved the confederation.

On this ground representation must be drawn from the States to maintain their independency, and not from the people composing those States.

Comparing the Two Plans

The Convention debated the New Jersey Plan for several days following its introduction on June 15, 1787, by William Paterson. In comments made on June 16, New York delegate John Lansing compares the plan favorably with the Virginia Plan, arguing that the people do not want a consolidated government. Lansing's remarks were preserved in the notes of fellow New York delegate Robert Yates.

Mr. Lansing moved to have the first article of the last plan of government read; which being done, he observed, that this system is fairly contrasted with the one ready to be reported—the one federal, and the other national. In the first, the powers are exercised as flowing from the respective State governments—The second, deriving its authority from the people of the respective States—which latter must ultimately destroy or annihilate the State governments. To determine the powers on these grand objects with which we are invested, let us recur to the credentials of the respective States, and see what the views were of those who sent us. The language is there expressive—it is upon the revision of the present confederation, to alter and amend such parts as may appear defective, so as to give additional strength to the union. And he would venture to assert, that had the legislature of the State of New York, apprehended that their powers would have been construed to extend to the formation of a national government, to the extinguishment of their independency, no delegates would have here appeared on the part of that State. . . . It is in vain to adopt a mode of government which we have reason to believe the people gave us no power to recommend—as they will consider themselves on this ground authorized to reject it.

The doctrine advanced by a learned gentleman from Pennsylvania, that all power is derived from the people, and that in proportion to their numbers they ought to participate equally in the benefits and rights of government, is right in principle, but unfortunately for him, wrong in the application to the question now in debate.

When independent societies confederate for mutual defence, they do so in their collective capacity; and then each State, for those purposes, must be considered as *one* of the contracting parties. Destroy this balance of equality, and you endanger the rights of the *lesser* societies by the danger of usurpation in the greater.

Let us test the government intended to be made by the Virginia plan on these principles. The representatives in the national legislature are to be in proportion to the number of inhabitants in each State. So far it is right, upon the principles of equality, when State distinctions are done away; but those to certain purposes still exist. Will the government of Pennsylvania admit a participation of their common stock of land to the citizens of New Jersey? I fancy not. It therefore follows, that a national government upon the present plan, is unjust, and destructive of the common principles of reciprocity. Much has been said that this government is to operate on persons, not on States. This, upon examination, will be found equally fallacious; for the fact is, it will, in the quotas of revenue, be proportioned among the States, as States; and in this business Georgia will have one vote, and Virginia sixteen. The truth is, both plans may be considered to compel individuals to a compliance with their requisitions, although the requisition is made on the States.

Much has been said in commendation of two branches in a legislature, and of the advantages resulting from their being checks to each other. This may be true when applied to State governments, but will not equally apply to a national legislature, whose legislative objects are few and simple.

Whatever may be said of congress, or their conduct on particular occasions, the people in general are pleased with such a body, and in general wish an increase of their powers for the good government of the union. Let us now see the plan of the national government on the score of expense. The least the second branch of the legislature can consist of is 90 members—The first branch of at least 270. How are they to be paid in our present impoverished situation? Let us, therefore, fairly try whether the confederation cannot be mended, and if it can, we shall do our duty, and I believe the people will be satisfied.

VIEWPOINT 4

"The plan of Mr. Paterson, not giving even a negative on the acts of the States, left them as much at liberty as ever to execute their unrighteous projects against each other."

Revising the Articles of Confederation Will Accomplish Little

James Madison (1751-1836)

James Madison, the Virginia delegate who was perhaps the single most important participant in the Constitutional Convention, was one of several delegates who spoke out against the plan presented on June 15, 1787, by William Paterson of New Jersey. Paterson had presented his New Jersey Plan as an alternative to the Virginia Plan sponsored by Madison, and the Convention faced an important vote in determining which of the two plans to embrace. Madison presented his arguments before the Convention on June 19. In his speech, which was recorded in his own notes of the Convention, Madison argues that Paterson's New Jersey Plan to simply revise and strengthen the Articles of Confederation would not "remedy the evils" the Confederation has caused America. The problems that Madison cites include treaty violations, encroachments on federal authority, and the threat of insurrection by armed minorities. Madison argues that the United States might dissolve into separate states or into two or more confederacies, which would then leave the smaller states in worse condition than that created by the Virginia Plan.

From *Documents Illustrative of the Formation of the Union of the American States*, Charles C. Tansill, ed. Washington, DC: GPO, 1927.

Madison's speech was successful in that the Convention voted by states seven to three to adhere to the Virginia Plan and drop the New Jersey Plan. However, some of the issues raised by the debate over the New Jersey Plan would continue to bedevil the Convention.

Much stress had been laid by some gentlemen on the want of power in the Convention to propose any other than a *federal* plan. To what had been answered by others, he would only add, that neither of the characteristics attached to a *federal* plan would support this objection. One characteristic, was that in a *federal* Government, the power was exercised not on the people individually; but on the people *collectively*, on the *States*. Yet in some instances as in piracies, captures etc. the existing Confederacy, and in many instances, the amendments to it proposed by Mr. Paterson, must operate immediately on individuals. The other characteristic was that a *federal* Government derived its appointments not immediately from the people, but from the States which they respectively composed. Here too were facts on the other side. In two of the States, Connecticut and Rhode Island, the delegates to Congress were chosen, not by the Legislatures, but by the people at large; and the plan of Mr. Paterson intended no change in this particular.

The Nature of the Confederation

It had been alleged [by Mr. Paterson], that the Confederation having been formed by unanimous consent, could be dissolved by unanimous Consent only. Does this doctrine result from the nature of compacts? Does it arise from any particular stipulation in the articles of Confederation? If we consider the federal union as analagous to the fundamental compact by which individuals compose one Society, and which must in its theoretic origin at least, have been the unanimous act of the component members, it can not be said that no dissolution of the compact can be effected without unanimous consent. A breach of the fundamental principles of the compact by a part of the Society would certainly absolve the other part from their obligations to it. If the breach of *any* article by *any* of the parties, does not set the others at liberty, it is because, the contrary is *implied* in the compact itself, and particularly by that law of it, which gives an indefinite authority to the majority to bind the whole in all cases. This latter circumstance shows that we are not to consider the federal Union as analagous to the social compact of individuals: for if it were so, a

Majority would have a right to bind the rest, and even to form a new Constitution for the whole, which the Gentleman from New Jersey would be among the last to admit. If we consider the federal Union as analogous not to the social compacts among individual men: but to the conventions among individual States. What is the doctrine resulting from these conventions? Clearly, according to the Expositors of the law of Nations, that a breach of any one article, by any one party, leaves all the other parties at liberty, to consider the whole convention as dissolved, unless they choose rather to compel the delinquent party to repair the breach. In some treaties indeed it is expressly stipulated that a violation of particular articles shall not have this consequence, and even that particular articles shall remain in force during war, which in general is understood to dissolve all subsisting Treaties. But are there any exceptions of this sort to the Articles of confederation? So far from it that there is not even an express stipulation that force shall be used to compel an offending member of the Union to discharge its duty. He observed that the violations of the federal articles had been numerous and notorious. Among the most notorious was an act of New Jersey herself; by which she *expressly refused* to comply with a constitutional requisition of Congress and yielded no farther to the expostulations of their deputies, than barely to rescind her vote of refusal without passing any positive act of compliance. He did not wish to draw any rigid inferences from these observations. He thought it proper however that the true nature of the existing confederacy should be investigated, and he was not anxious to strengthen the foundations on which it now stands.

Examining the New Jersey Plan

Proceeding to the consideration of Mr. Paterson's plan, he stated the object of a proper plan to be twofold. 1. To preserve the Union. 2. To provide a Government that will remedy the evils felt by the States both in their united and individual capacities. Examine Mr. Paterson's plan, and say whether it promises satisfaction in these respects.

1. Will it prevent those violations of the law of nations and of Treaties which if not prevented must involve us in the calamities of foreign wars? The tendency of the States to these violations has been manifested in sundry instances. The files of Congress contain complaints already, from almost every nation with which treaties have been formed. Hitherto indulgence has been shown to us. This can not be the permanent disposition of foreign nations. A rupture with other powers is among the greatest of national calamities. It ought therefore to be effectually provided that no part of a nation shall have it in its power to bring them on the whole. The existing

Confederacy does not sufficiently provide against this evil. The proposed amendment to it does not supply the omission. It leaves the will of the States as uncontrolled as ever.

The Need for Substantial Reform

Edmund Randolph was the presenter of the Virginia Plan. In remarks made June 16, 1787, while debating the New Jersey Plan, Randolph reiterated his belief that the Convention should seize the opportunity to go beyond revising the Articles of Confederation, which he held could not be repaired.

Mr. Randolph, was not scrupulous on the point of power. When the salvation of the Republic was at stake, it would be treason to our trust, not to propose what we found necessary. He painted in strong colours, the imbecility of the existing Confederacy, and the danger of delaying a substantial reform. In answer to the objection drawn from the sense of our Constituents as denoted by their acts relating to the Convention and the objects of their deliberation, he observed that as each State acted separately in the case, it would have been indecent for it to have charged the existing Constitution with all the vices which it might have perceived in it. The first State that set on foot this experiment would not have been justified in going so far, ignorant as it was of the opinion of others, and sensible as it must have been of the uncertainty of a successful issue to the experiment. There are certainly seasons of a peculiar nature where the ordinary cautions must be dispensed with; and this is certainly one of them. He would not as far as depended on him leave any thing that seemed necessary, undone. The present moment is favorable, and is probably the last that will offer.

2. Will it prevent encroachments on the federal authority? A tendency to such encroachments has been sufficiently exemplified, among ourselves, as well in every other confederated republic ancient and Modern. By the federal articles, transactions with the Indians appertain to Congress. Yet in several instances, the States have entered into treaties and wars with them. In like manner no two or more States can form among themselves any treaties etc. without the consent of Congress. Yet Virginia and Maryland in one instance—Pennsylvania and New Jersey in another, have entered into compacts, without previous application or subsequent apology. No State again can of right raise troops in time of peace without the like consent. Of all cases of the league, this seems to require the most scrupulous observance. Has not Massachusetts, notwithstanding, the most powerful member of the Union, already raised a body of troops? Is she not now augmenting them, without having even deigned to apprise Congress

of Her intention? In fine—Have we not seen the public land dealt out to Connecticut to bribe her acquiescence in the decree constitutionally awarded against her claim on the territory of Pennsylvania for no other possible motive can account for the policy of Congress in that measure?—If we recur to the examples of other confederacies, we shall find in all of them the same tendency of the parts to encroach on the authority of the whole. He then reviewed the Amphyctionic and Achæan confederacies among the ancients, and the Helvetic, Germanic and Belgic among the moderns, tracing their analogy to the United States—in the constitution and extent of their federal authorities—in the tendency of the particular members to usurp on these authorities; and to bring confusion and ruin on the whole.—He observed that the plan of Mr. Paterson besides omitting a control over the States as a general defence of the federal prerogatives was particularly defective in two of its provisions. 1. Its ratification was not to be by the people at large, but by the *legislatures*. It could not therefore render the Acts of Congress in pursuance of their powers, even legally *paramount* to the Acts of the States. 2. It gave to the federal Tribunal an appellate jurisdiction only—even in the criminal cases enumerated. The necessity of any such provision supposed a danger of undue acquittals in the State tribunals. Of what avail could an appellate tribunal be, after an acquittal? Besides in most if not all of the States, the Executives have by their respective *Constitutions* the right of pardoning. How could this be taken from them by a *legislative* ratification only?

Preventing Conflicts Between States

3. Will it prevent trespasses of the States on each other? Of these enough has been already seen. He instanced Acts of Virginia and Maryland which give a preference to their own Citizens in cases where the Citizens of other States are entitled to equality of privileges by the Articles of Confederation. He considered the emissions of paper money and other kindred measures as also aggressions. The States relatively to one another being each of them either Debtor or Creditor; The creditor States must suffer unjustly from every emission by the debtor States. We have seen retaliating acts on this subject which threatened danger not to the harmony only, but the tranquility of the Union. The plan of Mr. Paterson, not giving even a negative on the acts of the States, left them as much at liberty as ever to execute their unrighteous projects against each other.

4. Will it secure the internal tranquility of the States themselves? The insurrections in Massachusetts admonished all the States of the danger to which they were exposed. Yet the plan of Mr. Paterson contained no provisions for supplying the defect of the Con-

federation on this point. According to the Republican theory indeed, Right and power being both vested in the majority, are held to be synonimous. According to fact and experience, a minority may in an appeal to force be an overmatch for the majority. 1. If the minority happen to include all such as possess the skill and habits of military life, with such as possess the great pecuniary resources, one third may conquer the remaining two thirds. 2. one third of those who participate in the choice of rulers may be rendered a majority by the accession of those whose poverty disqualifies them from a suffrage, and who for obvious reasons may be more ready to join the standard of sedition than that of the established Government. 3. where slavery exists, the Republican Theory becomes still more fallacious.

The Powers of the Convention

Pennsylvania delegate James Wilson, an advocate of strong national government, was one of the most influential delegates at the 1787 Constitutional Convention. In remarks made on June 16 while debating the New Jersey and Virginia Plans, Wilson addresses two fundamental issues: the authority of the Convention to go beyond merely revising the Articles of Confederation, and the sentiments of the American people concerning national government. Wilson's comments were preserved in the notes of James Madison.

With regard to the *power of the Convention*, he conceived himself authorized to *conclude nothing*, but to be at liberty to *propose any thing*. In this particular he felt himself perfectly indifferent to the two plans.

With *regard to the sentiments of the people*, he conceived it difficult to know precisely what they are. Those of the particular circle in which one moved, were commonly mistaken for the general voice. He could not persuade himself that the State Governments and Sovereignties were so much the idols of the people, nor a National Government so obnoxious to them, as some supposed. Why should a National Government be unpopular? Has it less dignity? Will each Citizen enjoy under it less liberty or protection? Will a Citizen of *Delaware* be degraded by becoming a Citizen of the *United States?* Where do the people look at present for relief from the evils of which they complain? Is it from an internal reform of their Governments? No, Sir. It is from the National Councils that relief is expected. For these reasons he did not fear, that the people would not follow us into a national Government and it will be a further recommendation of Mr. Edmund Randolph's plan that it is to be submitted to *them*, and not to the *Legislatures*, for ratification.

5. Will it secure a good internal legislation and administration to the particular States? In developing the evils which vitiate the

political system of the United States it is proper to take into view those which prevail within the States individually as well as those which affect them collectively: Since the former indirectly affect the whole; and there is great reason to believe that the pressure of them had a full share in the motives which produced the present Convention. Under this head he enumerated and animadverted on 1. the multiplicity of the laws passed by the several States. 2. the mutability of their laws. 3. the injustice of them. 4. the impotence of them: observing that Mr. Paterson's plan contained no remedy for this dreadful class of evils, and could not therefore be received as an adequate provision for the exigencies of the Community.

6. Will it secure the Union against the influence of foreign powers over its members? He pretended not to say that any such influence had yet been tried; but it was naturally to be expected that occasions would produce it. As lessons which claimed particular attention, he cited the intrigues practised among the Amphyctionic Confederates first by the Kings of Persia, and afterwards fatally by Philip of Macedon: among the Achæans, first by Macedon and afterwards no less fatally by Rome: among the Swiss by Austria, France and the lesser neighbouring powers: among the members of the Germanic Body by France, England, Spain and Russia—: and in the Belgic Republic, by all the great neighbouring powers. The plan of Mr. Paterson, not giving to the general Councils any negative on the will of the particular States, left the door open for the like pernicious machinations among ourselves.

Addressing the Smaller States

7. He begged the smaller States which were most attached to Mr. Paterson's plan to consider the situation in which it would leave them. In the first place they would continue to bear the whole expence of maintaining their Delegates in Congress. It ought not to be said that if they were willing to bear this burden, no others had a right to complain. As far as it led the small States to forbear keeping up a representation, by which the public business was delayed, it was evidently a matter of common concern. An examination of the minutes of Congress would satisfy every one that the public business had been frequently delayed by this cause; and that the States most frequently unrepresented in Congress were not the larger States. He reminded the convention of another consequence of leaving on a small State the burden of maintaining a Representation in Congress. During a considerable period of the War, one of the Representatives of Delaware, in whom alone before the signing of the Confederation the entire vote of that State and after that event one half of its vote, frequently resided, was a Citizen and Resident of Pennsylvania and

81

held an office in his own State incompatible with an appointment from it to Congress. During another period, the same State was represented by three delegates two of whom were citizens of Pennsylvania and the third a Citizen of New Jersey. These expedients must have been intended to avoid the burden of supporting delegates from their own State. But whatever might have been the cause, was not in effect the vote of one State doubled, and the influence of another increased by it? In the second place the coercion, on which the efficacy of the plan depends, can never be exerted but on themselves. The larger States will be impregnable, the smaller only can feel the vengeance of it. He illustrated the position by the history of the Amphyctionic Confederates: and the ban of the German Empire. It was the cobweb which could entangle the weak, but would be the sport of the strong.

8. He begged them to consider the situation in which they would remain in case their pertinacious adherence to an inadmissible plan, should prevent the adoption of any plan. The contemplation of such an event was painful; but it would be prudent to submit to the task of examining it at a distance, that the means of escaping it might be the more readily embraced. Let the Union of the States be dissolved, and one of two consequences must happen. Either the States must remain individually independent and sovereign; or two or more Confederacies must be formed among them. In the first event would the small States be more secure against the ambition and power of their larger neighbours, than they would be under a general Government pervading with equal energy every part of the Empire, and having an equal interest in protecting every part against every other part? In the second, can the smaller expect that their larger neighbours would confederate with them on the principle of the present confederacy, which gives to each member, an equal suffrage; or that they would exact less severe concessions from the smaller States, than are proposed in the scheme of Mr. Randolph?

The Issue of Representation

The great difficulty lies in the affair of Representation; and if this could be adjusted, all others would be surmountable. It was admitted by both the gentlemen from New Jersey, [Mr. David Brearly and Mr. Paterson] that it would not be *just to allow Virginia* which was 16 times as large as Delaware an equal vote only. Their language was that it would not be *safe for Delaware* to allow Virginia 16 times as many votes. The expedient proposed by them was that all the States should be thrown into one mass and a new partition be made into 13 equal parts. Would such a scheme be practicable? The dissimilarities existing in the rules of property, as well as in the manners, habits and prejudices of the different

82

States, amounted to a prohibition of the attempt. It had been found impossible for the power of one of the most absolute princes in Europe [King of France] directed by the wisdom of one of the most enlightened and patriotic Ministers [Mr. Jacques Neckar] that any age has produced to equalize in some points only the different usages and regulations of the different provinces. But admitting a general amalgamation and repartition of the States to be practicable, and the danger apprehended by the smaller States from a proportional representation to be real; would not a particular and voluntary coalition of these with their neighbours, be less inconvenient to the whole community, and equally effectual for their own safety. If New Jersey or Delaware conceived that an advantage would accrue to them from an equalization of the States, in which case they would necessarily form a junction with their neighbours, why might not this end be attained by leaving them at liberty by the Constitution to form such a junction whenever they pleased? And why should they wish to obtrude a like arrangement on all the States, when it was, to say the least, extremely difficult, would be obnoxious to many of the States, and when neither the inconveniency, nor the benefit of the expedient to themselves, would be lessened, by confining it to themselves.—The prospect of many new States to the Westward was another consideration of importance. If they should come into the Union at all, they would come when they contained but few inhabitants. If they should be entitled to vote according to their proportions of inhabitants, all would be right and safe. Let them have an equal vote, and a more objectionable minority than ever might give law to the whole.

VIEWPOINT 5

"He had no scruple in declaring ... that the British Government was the best in the world: ... he doubted much whether any thing short of it would do in America."

A New National Government Should Emulate the British System

Alexander Hamilton (1755-1804)

Alexander Hamilton was a noted statesman and political figure in America's formative years. Born in the West Indies, he moved to America in 1772. While studying at King's College (now Columbia University) in New York, Hamilton gained fame for his pro-patriot writings and speeches. His distinguished military career during the Revolutionary War, his close association with Gen. George Washington, and his marriage into a prominent New York family helped cement his social standing and his strong nationalist and elitist political views.

Hamilton was a New York delegate to the Constitutional Convention, but his main contributions to the creation of the Constitution were before and after that meeting. His writings and organizing efforts helped persuade the Continental Congress to authorize the Convention, and his speeches and pamphlets were largely responsible for New York's ratification of the Constitution in 1788. Hamilton's influence at the Constitutional Convention itself was relatively limited. His two fellow New York delegates, John Lansing and Robert Yates, were consistent opponents of any new national government, and carried New York's vote against

From *Documents Illustrative of the Formation of the Union of the American States*, Charles C. Tansill, ed. Washington, DC: GPO, 1927.

Hamilton's preferences at almost every turn. In frustration Hamilton left the Convention on June 30. Yates and Lansing themselves left the Convention July 10, and Hamilton returned to Philadelphia August 13. Although still without an effective vote (Lansing and Yates's departure having left New York without an official quorum), he helped to write the Constitution as a member of the Committee on Style, and signed the finished document.

Hamilton's own views on what the new national government should ideally be are best revealed in a long speech he gave on June 18, 1787, which was recorded in abbreviated form by James Madison. The Convention was debating the relative merits of two plans: the Virginia Plan, which created a new national government, and the New Jersey Plan, which revised the Articles of Confederation and preserved the powers of the separate states. In his speech, which lasted around six hours, Hamilton criticized both the New Jersey and Virginia plans, arguing that neither went far enough to establish the strong national government Hamilton believed was necessary. Hamilton outlined plans for a new government based on the British system, which Hamilton praised as the best in the world. His plan included a Senate with members indirectly elected for life, and a national executive, indirectly elected by the people, who also served for life. State governors would be appointed by the national government and would have an absolute veto on state legislation. Hamilton's plan was not officially taken up by the Convention. In the words of Connecticut delegate William Samuel Johnson, the plan, so radically different from all that had been debated before, was "praised by everybody . . . [but] supported by none."

Mr. Hamilton, had been hitherto silent on the business before the Convention, partly from respect to others whose superior abilities age and experience rendered him unwilling to bring forward ideas dissimilar to theirs, and partly from his delicate situation with respect to his own State, to whose sentiments as expressed by his Colleagues, he could by no means accede. The crisis however which now marked our affairs, was too serious to permit any scruples whatever to prevail over the duty imposed on every man to contribute his efforts for the public safety and happiness. He was obliged therefore to declare himself unfriendly to both plans. He was particularly opposed to that from New Jersey, being fully convinced, that no amendment of the Confederation, leaving the States in possession of their Sovereignty could possibly answer the purpose. On the other hand he confessed he was much discouraged by the amazing extent of the Country in expecting the desired blessings from any general sovereignty that could be substituted.—As to the powers of the Convention, he thought the doubts started on that subject had arisen from distinctions and reasonings too subtle. A *federal* Government he conceived to mean an association of independent Communities into one. Different Confederacies have different powers, and exercise them in different ways. In some instances the powers are exercised over collective bodies; in others over individuals, as in the German Diet [council of princes]—and among ourselves in cases of piracy. Great latitude therefore must be given to the signification of the term. The plan last proposed departs itself from the *federal* idea, as understood by some, since it is to operate eventually on individuals. He agreed moreover with the Honorable gentleman from Virginia [Edmund Randolph] that we owed it to our Country, to do on this emergency whatever we should deem essential to its happiness. The States sent us here to provide for the exigences of the Union. To rely on and propose any plan not adequate to these exigences, merely because it was not clearly within our powers, would be to sacrifice the means to the end. It may be said that the *States* can not *ratify* a plan not within the purview of the article of Confederation providing for alterations and amendments. But may not the States themselves in which no constitutional authority equal to this purpose exists in the Legislatures, have had in view a reference to the people at large. In the Senate of New York, a proviso was moved, that no act of the Convention should be binding untill it should be referred to the people and ratified; and the motion was lost by a single voice only, the reason assigned against it being, that it might possibly be found an inconvenient shackle.

Examining the Virginia and New Jersey Plans

The great question is what provision shall we make for the happiness of our Country? He would first make a comparative examination of the two plans—prove that there were essential defects in both—and point out such changes as might render a *national one*, efficacious.—The great and essential principles necessary for the support of Government are 1. An active and constant interest in supporting it. This principle does not exist in the States in favor of the federal Government. They have evidently in a high degree, the esprit de corps. They constantly pursue internal interests adverse to those of the whole. They have their particular debts—their particular plans of finance etc. All these when opposed to, invariably prevail over the requisitions and plans of Congress. 2. The love of power. Men love power. The same remarks are applicable to this principle. The States have constantly shown a disposition rather to regain the powers delegated by them than to part with more, or to give effect to what they had parted with. The ambition of their demagogues is known to hate the control of the General Government. It may be remarked too that the Citizens have not that anxiety to prevent a dissolution of the General Government as of the particular Governments. A dissolution of the latter would be fatal; of the former would still leave the purposes of Government attainable to a considerable degree. Consider what such a State as Virginia will be in a few years, a few compared with the life of nations. How strongly will it feel its importance and self-sufficiency? 3. An habitual attachment of the people. The whole force of this tie is on the side of the State Government. Its sovereignty is immediately before the eyes of the people: its protection is immediately enjoyed by them. From its hand distributive justice, and all those acts which familiarize and endear Government to a people, are dispensed to them. 4. *Force* by which may be understood a *coertion of laws* or *coertion of arms*. Congress have not the former except in few cases. In particular States, this coercion is nearly sufficient; though he held it in most cases, not entirely so. A certain portion of military force is absolutely necessary in large communities. Massachusetts is now feeling this necessity and making provision for it. But how can this force be exerted on the States collectively. It is impossible. It amounts to a war between the parties. Foreign powers also will not be idle spectators. They will interpose, the confusion will increase, and a dissolution of the Union ensue. 5. *Influence.* He did not mean corruption, but a dispensation of those regular honors and emoluments, which produce an attachment to the Government. Almost all the weight of these is on the side of the States; and must continue so as long as the States continue to exist. All the passions then we see, of avarice, ambition, interest, which govern most individuals, and all public bodies, fall into the current of the States, and do not flow in the stream of the General Government. The former therefore will generally be an overmatch for the General Government and render any confederacy, in its very nature precarious. Theory is in this case fully confirmed by experience. . . .

The New Jersey Plan

How then are all these evils to be avoided? Only by such a compleat sovereignty in the general Government as will turn all the strong principles and passions above mentioned on its side. Does the scheme of New Jersey produce this effect? Does it afford any substantial remedy whatever? On the contrary it labors under great defects, and the defect of some of its provisions will destroy the efficacy of others. It gives a direct revenue to Congress but this will not be sufficient. The balance can only be supplied by requisitions: which experience proves can not be relied on. If States are to deliberate on the mode, they will also deliberate on the object of the supplies, and will grant or not grant as they approve or disapprove of it. The delinquency of one will invite and countenance it in others. . . . Another destructive ingredient in the

The Public Supports Strong Government

Discouraged by the lack of reception to his ideas, Alexander Hamilton left the Constitutional Convention June 30, 1787. In a letter written on July 3 to George Washington, Hamilton argues that public opinion may be more favorable toward a strong national government than those at the Constitutional Convention realize. He worries that in trying to placate people's fears of creating too autocratic a government, the Convention might waste an opportunity to save the "American empire."

In my passage through the Jerseys and since my arrival here I have taken particular pains to discover the public sentiment and I am more and more convinced that this is the critical opportunity for establishing the prosperity of this country on a solid foundation. I have conversed with men of information not only of this City but from different parts of the state; and they agree that there has been an astonishing revolution for the better in the minds of the people. The prevailing apprehension among thinking men is that the Convention, from a fear of shocking the popular opinion, will not go far enough. They seem to be convinced that a strong well mounted government will better suit the popular palate than one of a different complexion. Men in office are indeed taking all possible pains to give an unfavourable impression of the Convention; but the current seems to be running strongly the other way. . . .

These appearances though they will not warrant a conclusion that the people are yet ripe for such a plan as I advocate, yet serve to prove that there is no reason to despair of their adopting one equally energetic, if the Convention should think proper to propose it. They serve to prove that we ought not to allow too much weight to objections drawn from the supposed repugnancy of the people to an efficient constitution. . . .

I own to you Sir that I am seriously and deeply distressed at the aspect of the Councils which prevailed when I left Philadelphia. I fear that we shall let slip the golden opportunity of rescuing the American empire from disunion anarchy and misery. No motley or feeble measure can answer the end or will finally receive the public support. Decision is true wisdom and will be not less reputable to the Convention than salutary to the community.

I shall of necessity remain here ten or twelve days; if I have reason to believe that my attendance at Philadelphia will not be mere waste of time, I shall after that period rejoin the Convention.

plan, is that equality of suffrage which is so much desired by the small States. It is not in human nature that Virginia and the large States should consent to it, or if they did that they should long abide by it. It shocks too much the ideas of Justice, and every human feeling. Bad principles in a Government though slow are sure in their operation, and will gradually destroy it. A doubt has been raised whether Congress at present have a right to keep Ships or troops in time of peace. He leans to the negative. Mister Paterson's plan provides no remedy.—If the powers proposed were adequate, the organization of Congress is such that they could never be properly and effectually exercised. The members of Congress being chosen by the States and subject to recall, represent all the local prejudices. Should the powers be found effectual, they will from time to time be heaped on them, till a tyrannic sway shall be established. The general power whatever be its form if it preserves itself, must swallow up the State powers. Otherwise it will be swallowed up by them. It is against all the principles of a good Government to vest the requisite powers in such a body as Congress. Two Sovereignties can not co-exist within the same limits. Giving powers to Congress must eventuate in a bad Government or in no Government.

What Is to Be Done?

The plan of New Jersey therefore will not do. What then is to be done? Here he was embarrassed. The extent of the Country to be governed, discouraged him. The expense of a general Government was also formidable; unless there were a diminution of expense on the side of the State Government as the case would admit. If they were extinguished, he was persuaded that great œconomy might be obtained by substituting a general Government. He did not mean however to shock the public opinion by proposing such a measure. On the other hand he saw no *other* necessity for declining it. They are not necessary for any of the great purposes of commerce, revenue, or agriculture. Subordinate authorities he was aware would be necessary. There must be district tribunals: corporations for local purposes. But cui bono [for what purpose?], the vast and expensive apparatus now appertaining to the States. The only difficulty of a serious nature which occurred to him, was that of drawing representatives from the extremes to the center of the Community. What inducements can be offered that will suffice? The moderate wages for the first branch would only be a bait to little demagogues. Three dollars or thereabouts he supposed would be the utmost. The Senate he feared from a similar cause, would be filled by certain undertakers who wish for particular offices under the Government. This view of the subject almost led him to despair that a Republican Government could be established over so great an extent. He was sensible at the same time that it would be unwise to propose one of any other form. In his private opinion he had no scruple in declaring, supported as he was by the opinions of so many of the wise and good, that the British Government was the best in the world: and that he doubted much whether any thing short of it would do in America. He hoped Gentlemen of different opinions would bear with him in this, and begged them to recollect the change of opinion on this subject which had taken place and was still going on. It was once thought that the power of Congress was amply sufficient to secure the end of their institution. The error was now seen by every one. The members most tenacious of republicanism, he observed, were as loud as any in declaiming against the vices of democracy. This progress of the public mind led him to anticipate the time, when others as well as himself would join in the praise bestowed by Mr. [Jacques] Neckar on the British Constitution, namely, that it is the only Government in the world "which unites public strength with individual security."—In every community where industry is encouraged, there will be a division of it into the few and the many. Hence separate interests will arise. There will be debtors and creditors etc. Give all power to the many, they will oppress the few. Both therefore ought to have power, that each may defend itself against the other. To the want of this check we owe our paper money, instalment laws etc. To the proper adjustment of it the British owe the excellence of their Constitution. Their house of Lords is a most noble institution. Having nothing to hope for by a change, and a sufficient interest by means of their property, in being faithful to the interest, they form a permanent barrier against every pernicious innovation, whether attempted on the part of the Crown or of the Commons. No temporary Senate will have firmness enough to answer the purpose. The Senate [of Maryland] which seems to be so much appealed to, has not yet been sufficiently tried. Had the people been unanimous and eager, in the late appeal to them on the subject of a paper emission they would have yielded to the torrent. Their acquiescing in such an appeal is a proof of it.—Gentlemen differ in their opinions concerning the necessary checks, from the different estimates they form of the human passions. They suppose seven years a sufficient period to give the senate an adequate firmness, from not duly considering the amazing violence and turbulence of the democratic spirit. When a great object of Government is pursued, which seizes the popular passions, they spread like wild fire, and become irresistable. He appealed to the gentlemen from the New England States whether experience had not there verified the remark.

As to the Executive, it seemed to be admitted that no good

A Gloomy Assessment

George Washington was elected by the delegates to serve as president of the Constitutional Convention. Because he participated little in the debates, and scrupulously kept to the rule of secrecy and divulged little of the Convention in his writings while it was in session, there are few records of Washington's views on the evolving arguments surrounding the Constitution's creation. One exception is a July 10, 1787, letter to Alexander Hamilton, the New York delegate who had left the Convention on June 30. Responding to a Hamilton letter written a week earlier, Washington pleads with him to return to Philadelphia, and reiterates his own desires for a strong national government.

I thank you for your communication of the 3d. When I refer you to the State of the Councils which prevailed at the period you left this city—and add, that they are now, if possible, in a worse train than ever; you will find that little ground on which the hope of a good establishment can be formed. In a word, I *almost* dispair of seeing a favourable issue to the proceedings of the Convention, and do therefore repent having had any agency in the business.

The Men who oppose a strong & energetic government are, in my opinion, narrow minded politicians, or are under the influence of local views. The apprehension expressed by them that the *people* will not accede to the form proposed is the *ostensible*, not the *real* cause of the opposition—but admitting that the present sentiment is as they prognosticate, the question ought nevertheless to be, is it or is it not, the best form? If the former, recommend it, and it will assuredly obtain mauger opposition.

I am sorry you went away. I wish you were back. The crisis is equally important and alarming, and no opposition under such circumstances should discourage exertions till the signature is fixed. I will not, at this time trouble you with more than my best wishes and sincere regards.

could be established on Republican principles. Was not this giving up the merits of the question: for can there be a good Government without a good Executive. The English model was the only good one on this subject. The Hereditary interest of the King was so interwoven with that of the Nation, and his personal emoluments so great, that he was placed above the danger of being corrupted from abroad—and at the same time was both sufficiently independent and sufficiently controled, to answer the purpose of the institution at home. One of the weak sides of Republics was their being liable to foreign influence and corruption. Men of little character, acquiring great power become easily the tools of intermedling Neighbors. Sweden was a striking instance. The French and English had each their parties during the late Revolution which was affected by the predominant influence of the former.

What is the inference from all these observations? That we ought to go as far in order to attain stability and permanency, as republican principles will admit. Let one branch of the Legislature hold their places for life or at least during good behaviour. Let the Executive also be for life. He appealed to the feelings of the members present whether a term of seven years, would induce the sacrifices of private affairs which an acceptance of public trust would require, so as to ensure the services of the best Citizens. On this plan we should have in the Senate a permanent will, a weighty interest, which would answer essential purposes. But is this a Republican Government, it will be asked? Yes if all the magistrates are appointed, and vacancies are filled, by the people, or a process of election originating with the people. He was sensible that an Executive constituted as he proposed would have in fact but little of the power and independence that might be necessary. On the other plan of appointing him for 7 years, he thought the Executive ought to have but little power. He would be ambitious, with the means of making creatures; and as the object of his ambition would be to *prolong* his power, it is probable that in case of a war, he would avail himself of the emergence, to evade or refuse a degradation from his place. An Executive for life has not this motive for forgetting his fidelity, and will therefore be a safer depository of power. It will be objected probably, that such an Executive will be an *elective Monarch*, and will give birth to the tumults which characterize that form of Government. He would reply that *Monarch* is an indefinite term. It marks not either the degree or duration of power. If this Executive Magistrate would be a monarch for life—the other proposed by the Report from the Committee of the whole, would be a monarch for seven years. The circumstance of being elective was also applicable to both. It had been observed by judicious writers that elective monarchies would be the best if they could be guarded against the *tumults* excited by the ambition and intrigues of competitors. He was not sure that tumults were an inseparable evil. He rather thought this character of Elective Monarchies had been taken rather from particular cases than from general principles. The election of Roman Emperors was made by the *Army*. In *Poland* the election is made by great rival *princes* with independent power, and ample means, of raising commotions. In the German Empire, the appointment is made by the Electors and Princes, who have equal motives and means, for exciting cabals and parties. Might not such a mode of election be devised among ourselves as will defend the community against these effects in any dangerous degree? Having made these observations he would read to the Committee a sketch of a plan which he should prefer to either of those under consideration. He was aware that it went beyond the ideas of most members. But will such a plan be adopted out of doors? In return he would ask will the people adopt the other plan? At present they will adopt neither. But he sees the Union dissolving or already dissolved—he sees evils operating in the States which must soon cure the people of their fondness for democracies—he sees that a great progress has been already made and is still going on in the public mind. He thinks therefore that the people will in time be unshackled from their prejudices; and whenever that happens, they will themselves not be satisfied at stopping where the plan of Mr. Randolph would place them, but be ready to go as far at least as he proposes. He did not mean to offer the paper he had sketched as a proposition to the Committee. It was meant only to give a more correct view of his ideas, and to suggest the amendments which he should probably propose to the plan of Mr. Randolph in the proper stages of its future discussion. He read his sketch in the words following, to wit:

Hamilton's Plan

I. The Supreme Legislative power of the United States of America to be vested in two different bodies of men; the one to be called the Assembly, the other the Senate who together shall form the Legislature of the United States with power to pass all laws whatsoever subject to the Negative hereafter mentioned.

II. The Assembly to consist of persons elected by the people to serve for three years.

III. The Senate to consist of persons elected to serve during good behaviour; their election to be made by electors chosen for that purpose by the people: in order to do this the States to be divided into election districts. On the death, removal or resignation of any Senator his place to be filled out of the district from which he came.

IV. The supreme Executive authority of the United States to be vested in a Governor to be elected to serve during good behaviour—the election to be made by Electors chosen by the people in the Election Districts aforesaid—The authorities and functions of the Executive to be as follows: to have a negative on all laws about to be passed, and the execution of all laws passed; to have the direction of war when authorized or begun; to have with the advice and approbation of the Senate the power of making all treaties; to have the sole appointment of the heads or chief officers of the departments of Finance, War and Foreign Affairs; to have the nomination of all other officers (Ambassadors to foreign Nations included) subject to the approbation or rejection of the Senate; to have the power of pardoning all offences except Treason; which he shall not pardon without the approbation of the Senate.

V. On the death resignation or removal of the Governor his authorities to be exercised by the President of the Senate till a Successor be appointed.

VI. The Senate to have the sole power of declaring war, the power of advising and approving all Treaties, the power of approving or rejecting all appointments of officers except the heads or chiefs of the departments of Finance War and Foreign Affairs.

VII. The supreme Judicial authority to be vested in   Judges to hold their offices during good behaviour with adequate and permanent salaries. This Court to have original jurisdiction in all causes of capture, and an appelative jurisdiction in all causes in which the revenues of the general Government or the Citizens of foreign Nations are concerned.

VIII. The Legislature of the United States to have power to Institute Courts in each State for the determination of all matters of general concern.

IX. The Governor Senators and all officers of the United States to be liable to impeachment for mal- and corrupt conduct; and upon conviction to be removed from office, and disqualified for holding any place of trust or profit—All impeachments to be tried by a Court to consist of the Chief [Justice] or Judge of the superior Court of Law of each State, provided such Judge shall hold his place during good behavior, and have a permanent salary.

X. All laws of the particular States contrary to the Constitution or laws of the United States to be utterly void; and the better to prevent such laws being passed, the Governor or president of each State shall be appointed by the General Government and shall have a negative upon the laws about to be passed in the State of which he is Governor or President.

XI. No State to have any forces land or Naval; and the Militia of all the States to be under the sole and exclusive direction of the United States, the officers of which to be appointed and commissioned by them.

VIEWPOINT 6

"Much has been said of the Constitution of Great Britain. . . . I am confident it is one that will not or can not be introduced into this Country."

The United States Should Create Its Own System of Government

Charles Pinckney (1757-1824)

At twenty-nine, Charles Pinckney was one of the youngest members of the Constitutional Convention. His prominent and wealthy South Carolina family supplied two representatives to the Convention; his cousin, Charles Cotesworth Pinckney, was a fellow delegate. On May 29, 1787, Charles Pinckney submitted his own plan of government alongside Edmund Randolph's Virginia Plan. Although Pinckney's plan was not taken up officially by the Convention, many of its ideas made their way to the final document.

On June 25, 1787, Pinckney made a significant speech to the Convention that was in part a rebuttal to Alexander Hamilton's address extolling the virtues of the British constitution. Pinckney questioned whether Britain's system could work in America, arguing that American society, with its greater equality and lack of an aristocracy, was distinctly different from that of Great Britain. Historians and writers Christopher Collier and James Lincoln Collier write in *Decision in Philadelphia*:

> The essence of Pinckney's reply [to Hamilton] was that the United States was different from any other place on earth, and that the delegates could therefore look to no other system for

From *Documents Illustrative of the Formation of the Union of the American States*, Charles C. Tansill, ed. Washington, DC: GPO, 1927.

answers to the American problem. Charles Warren writes, "Into the debates, which had so largely turned on devotion to the States, Pinckney now breathed a spirit of Americanism."

Pinckney gave a copy of his address to James Madison to be recorded in the Virginia delegate's notes, and the material presented below is taken from Madison's work. Following the Convention Pinckney successfully worked for the Constitution's ratification in South Carolina. His future political career included several terms as South Carolina governor as well as service in the Senate and House of Representatives.

In order to form a right judgment in the case, it will be proper to examine the situation of this Country more accurately than it has yet been done. The people of the United States are perhaps the most singular of any we are acquainted with. Among them there are fewer distinctions of fortune & less of rank, than among the inhabitants of any other nation. Every freeman has a right to the same protection & security; and a very moderate share of property entitles them to the possession of all the honors and privileges the public can bestow: hence arises a greater equality, than is to be found among the people of any other country, and an equality which is more likely to continue—I say this equality is likely to continue, because in a new Country, possessing immense tracts of uncultivated lands, where every temptation is offered to emigration & where industry must be rewarded with competency, there will be few poor, and few dependent—Every member of the Society almost, will enjoy an equal power of arriving at the supreme offices & consequently of directing the strength & sentiments of the whole Community. None will be excluded by birth, & few by fortune, from voting for proper persons to fill the offices of Government—the whole community will enjoy in the fullest sense that kind of political liberty which consists in the power the members of the State reserve to themselves, of arriving at the public offices, or at least, of having votes in the nomination of those who fill them.

If this State of things is true & the prospect of its continuing probable, it is perhaps not politic to endeavour too close an imitation of a Government calculated for a people whose situation is, & whose views ought to be extremely different.

The British Constitution

Much has been said of the Constitution of Great Britain. I will confess that I believe it to be the best Constitution in existence;

but at the same time I am confident it is one that will not or can not be introduced into this Country, for many centuries.—If it were proper to go here into a historical dissertation on the British Constitution, it might easily be shewn that the peculiar excellence, the distinguishing feature of that Government can not possibly be introduced into our System—that its balance between the Crown & the people can not be made a part of our Constitution.—that we neither have or can have the members to compose it, nor the rights, privileges & properties of so distinct a class of Citizens to guard.—that the materials for forming this balance or check do not exist, nor is there a necessity for having so permanent a part of our Legislative, until the Executive power is so constituted as to have something fixed & dangerous in its principle— By this I mean a sole, hereditary, though limited Executive.

A wealthy and politically ambitious South Carolina aristocrat, at twenty-nine Charles Pinckney was one of the youngest delegates at the Constitutional Convention.

That we cannot have a proper body for forming a Legislative balance between the inordinate power of the Executive and the people, is evident from a review of the accidents & circumstances which gave rise to the peerage of Great Britain—I believe it is well ascertained that the parts which compose the British Constitution arose immediately from the forests of Germany; but the antiquity of the establishment of nobility is by no means clearly defined. Some authors are of opinion that [it] was derived from the old Roman to the German Empire; while others are of opinion that they existed among the Germans long before the Romans were acquainted with them. The institution however of nobility is immemorial among the nations who may probably be termed the ancestors of Britain.—At the time they were summoned in England to become a part of the National Council, and the circumstances which have contributed to make them a constituent part of that constitution, must be well known to all gentlemen who have had industry & curiosity enough to investigate the subject— The nobles with their possessions & dependents composed a body permanent in their nature and formidable in point of power. They had a distinct interest both from the King and the people; an interest which could only be represented by themselves, and the guardianship could not be safely intrusted to others.—At the time they were originally called to form a part of the National Council, necessity perhaps as much as other cause, induced the Monarch to look up to them. It was necessary to demand the aid of his subjects in personal & pecuniary services. The power and possessions of the Nobility would not permit taxation from any assembly of which they were not a part: & the blending the deputies of the Commons with them, & thus forming what they called their parler-ment was perhaps as much the effect of chance as of any thing else. The Commons were at that time compleatly subordinate to the nobles, whose consequence & influence seem to have been the only reasons for their superiority; a superiority; so degrading to the Commons that in the first Summons we find the peers are called upon to consult, the commons to consent. From this time the peers have composed a part of the British Legislature, and notwithstanding their power and influence have diminished & those of the Commons have increased, yet still they have always formed an excellent balance against either the encroachments of the Crown or the people.

Equality in the United States

I have said that such a body cannot exist in this Country for ages, and that untill the situation of our people is exceedingly changed no necessity will exist for so permanent a part of the Legislature. To illustrate this I have remarked that the people of the United States are more equal in their circumstances than the people of any other Country—that they have very few rich men among them,—by rich men I mean those whose riches may have a dangerous influence, or such as are esteemed rich in Europe— perhaps there are not one hundred such on the Continent; that it is not probable this number will be greatly increased: that the genius of the people, their mediocrity of situation & the prospects which are afforded their industry in a Country which must be a new one for centuries are unfavorable to the rapid distinction of ranks. The destruction of the right of primogeniture & the equal division of the property of Intestates will also have an effect to preserve this mediocrity; for laws invariably affect the manners of a people. On the other hand that vast extent of unpeopled territory which opens to the frugal & industrious a sure road to competency & independence will effectually prevent for a considerable time the increase of the poor or discontented, and be the means of preserving that equality of condition which so eminently distinguishes us.

The Pinckney Plan

On May 29, 1787, the same day the Virginia Plan was introduced, Charles Pinckney submitted his own plan for a constitution to the Convention. Unfortunately, the original manuscript has been lost, and historians still debate over the contents of Pinckney's original plan. Many believe Pinckney gave himself too much credit while writing of his plan after the Convention was over. The only surviving record from the Convention itself is a summary of the plan by James Wilson, made while he was serving on the Committee of Detail. Portions of his notes appear below.

A Confederation between the free and independent States of N.H. [New Hampshire] &c. is hereby solemnly made uniting them together under one general superintending Government for their common Benefit and for their Defense and Security against all Designs and Leagues that may be injurious to their Interests and against all Forc[e] and Attacks offered to or made upon them or any of them. . . .

Two Branches of the Legislature—Senate—House of Delegates—together the U.S. in Congress assembled

H.D. to consist of one Member for every   thousand Inhabitants ⅗ of Blacks included

Senate to be elected from four Districts—to serve by Rotation of four Years—to be elected by the H.D. either from among themselves or the People at large. . . .

The Senate and H.D. shall by joint Ballot annually chuse the Presidt. U.S. from among themselves or the People at large.—In the Presidt. the executive Authority of the U.S. shall be vested.—His Powers and Duties—He shall have a Right to advise with the Heads of the different Departments as his Council. . . .

No State to make Treaties—lay interfering Duties—keep a naval or land Force.

If equality is as I contend the leading feature of the United States, where then are the riches & wealth whose representation & protection is the peculiar province of this permanent body. Are they in the hands of the few who may be called rich; in the possession of less than a hundred citizens? certainly not. They are in the great body of the people, among whom there are no men of wealth, and very few of real poverty.—Is it probable that a change will be created, and that a new order of men will arise? If under the British Government, for a century no such change was probable, I think it may be fairly concluded it will not take place while even the semblance of Republicanism remains.—How is this change to be effected? Where are the sources from whence it is to flow? From the landed interest? No. That is too unproductive & too much divided in most of the States. From the Monied interest? If such exists at present, little is to be apprehended from that source. Is it to spring from commerce? I believe it would be the first instance in which a nobility sprang from merchants. Besides, Sir, I apprehend that on this point the policy of the United States has been much mistaken. We have unwisely considered ourselves as the inhabitants of an old instead of a new country. We have adopted the maxims of a State full of people & manufactures & established in credit. We have deserted our true interest, and instead of applying closely to those improvements in domestic policy which would have ensured the future importance of our commerce, we have rashly & prematurely engaged in schemes as extensive as they are imprudent. This however is an error which daily corrects itself & I have no doubt that a few more severe trials will convince us, that very different commercial principles ought to govern the conduct of these States.

The people of this country are not only very different from the inhabitants of any State we are acquainted with in the modern world; but I assert that their situation is distinct from either the people of Greece or Rome, or of any State we are acquainted with among the antients.—Can the orders introduced by the institution of Solon, can they be found in the United States? Can the military habits & manners of Sparta be resembled to our habits & manners? Are the distinctions of Patrician & Plebeian known among us? Can the Helvetic or Belgic confederacies, or can the unwieldy, unmeaning body called the Germanic Empire, can they be said to possess either the same or a situation like ours? I apprehend not.—They are perfectly different, in their distinctions of rank, their Constitutions, their manners & their policy.

Our true situation appears to me to be this.—a new extensive Country containing within itself the materials for forming a Government capable of extending to its citizens all the blessings of civil & religious liberty—capable of making them happy at home. This is the great end of Republican Establishments. We mistake the object of our Government, if we hope or wish that it is to make us respectable abroad. Conquest or superiority among other powers is not or ought not ever to be the object of republican systems. If they are sufficiently active & energetic to rescue us from contempt & preserve our domestic happiness & security, it is all we can expect from them,—it is more than almost any other Government ensures to its citizens.

I believe this observation will be found generally true:—that no two people are so exactly alike in their situation or circumstances as to admit the exercise of the same Government with equal benefit: that a system must be suited to the habits & genius of the people it is to govern, and must grow out of them.

Classes of American People

The people of the U.S. may be divided into three classes—*Professional men* who must from their particular pursuits always have a considerable weight in the Government while it remains popular—*Commercial men*, who may or may not have weight as a wise or injudicious commercial policy is pursued.—If that commercial policy is pursued which I conceive to be the true one, the merchants of this Country will not or ought not for a considerable time to have much weight in the political scale.—The third is the *landed interest*, the owners and cultivators of the soil, who are and ought ever to be the governing spring in the system.—These three classes, however distinct in their pursuits are individually equal in the political scale, and may be easily proved to have but one interest. The dependence of each on the other is mutual. The merchant depends on the planter. Both must in private as well as public affairs be connected with the professional men; who in their turn must in some measure depend upon them. Hence it is clear from this manifest connection, & the equality which I before stated exists, & must for the reasons then assigned, continue, that after all there is one, but one great & equal body of citizens composing the inhabitants of this Country among whom there are no distinctions of rank, and very few or none of fortune.

For a people thus circumstanced are we then to form a government & the question is what kind of Government is best suited to them.

Will it be the British Government? No. Why? Because Great Britain contains three orders of people distinct in their situation, their possessions & their principles.—These orders combined form the great body of the Nation, and as in national expences the wealth of the whole community must contribute, so ought each component part to be properly & duly represented—No other combination of power could form this due representation, but the one that exists.—Neither the peers or the people could represent the royalty, nor could the Royalty & the people form a proper representation for the Peers.—Each therefore must of necessity be represented by itself, or the sign of itself; and this accidental mixture has certainly formed a Government admirably well balanced.

But the United States contain but one order that can be assimilated to the British Nation,—this is the order of Commons. They will not surely then attempt to form a Government consisting of three branches, two of which shall have nothing to represent. They will not have an Executive & Senate [hereditary] because the King & Lords of England are so. The same reasons do not exist and therefore the same provisions are not necessary.

We must as has been observed suit our Government to the people it is to direct. These are I believe as active, intelligent & susceptible of good Government as any people in the world. The Confusion which has produced the present relaxed State is not owing to them. It is owing to the weakness & [defects] of a Government incapable of combining the various interests it is intended to unite, and destitute of energy.—All that we have to do then is to distribute the powers of Government in such a manner, and for such limited periods, as while it gives a proper degree of permanency to the Magistrate, will reserve to the people, the right of election they will not or ought not frequently to part with.—I am of opinion that this may be easily done; and that with some amendments the propositions before the Committee will fully answer this end.

CHAPTER 3

Creating a Republican Government

Chapter Preface

The delegates to the Constitutional Convention as well as those who participated in the ratification debates disagreed on many things. Most, however, professed a common goal: the creation of a successful republican government. They disagreed on whether the Constitution succeeded in this goal.

A Mixed Government

One important feature of any republican government, most educated Americans believed, was that it be in a "mixed" form. Many pamphlets on the Constitution focused on whether it created a successfully "mixed" form of government. In examining this issue it is necessary to be familiar with the classical political theories of Aristotle and other philosophers of ancient Greece and Rome, which had over the centuries been interpreted and refined by political theoreticians including Niccolò Machiavelli of Renaissance Italy, John Milton of seventeenth-century England, and American contemporary John Adams. Richard B. Bernstein in *Are We to Be a Nation?* describes some of these ideas that influenced American thinking on republicanism:

> Going back to Aristotle, classical political theory had identified three "pure" forms of government, each linked to a discrete order or segment of society and aspect of human nature: *monarchy*, or rule by one man; *aristocracy*, or rule by an elite of powerful men; and *democracy*, or rule by the people. Each of these pure forms contained the seeds of degeneration and would undergo a cyclical process of decline and fall—a monarchy would become a tyranny, an aristocracy would slide into oligarchy, and a democracy would collapse into mob rule. Only a "mixed" or "balanced" government, commingling all three pure forms and the segments of society they represented, would have any hope of resisting the otherwise inevitable cycle of decay and decline.

Many of the pamphlets on and debates over the Constitution focused on whether such a "balance" was achieved. In other words, did it create a government that would not degenerate into rule by a tyranny, an oligarchic elite, or the mob as exemplified by the Massachusetts farmers of Shays's Rebellion? Defenders of the Constitution such as James Madison argued that it had. Its intricate system of checks and balances and its methods of representing the people, he and others argued, successfully preserved Americans from the evils both of despotic government and excessive democracy. But many attackers of the Constitution argued that it went too far in diluting the democratic powers of the people. The Constitution, argued James Lincoln in South Carolina's ratifying convention, created an "aristocratic government" that would surely degenerate into "tyrannical monarchy." The viewpoints in this chapter examine the question of whether the Constitution succeeded in its republican aims.

VIEWPOINT 1

"A free republic cannot succeed over a country of such immense extent, containing such a number of inhabitants ... as that of the whole United States."

A Republic Must Be Small and Uniform to Survive

"Brutus"

The Constitution that emerged from the 1787 Constitutional Convention proposed the creation of a new republican government whose authority would be binding upon all of the states. This in itself was a revolutionary and controversial goal. The conventional wisdom of that time held that republics were practical only in communities where the population was manageably small and homogeneous. America at the time was already far larger than most other countries, stretching 1200 miles from north to south and 200 miles inland from the Atlantic Ocean. Its population (not counting American Indians) of roughly three and a half million, while not as multiculturally diverse as today, had significant divisions in nationality, wealth, and race. (One-sixth of the population was black, most of whom were slaves living south of Pennsylvania.) Historical writer Charles L. Mee writes in *The Genius of the American People:*

> Although the greatest number of these Americans were of English descent, a wide range of nationalities and religions and languages could be already found among them, and a wide variety of experiences of daily life.

Many anti-federalist writers cited the size and diversity of America as grounds for asserting that a national regime could not effectively govern without sacrificing the personal freedoms and liberties Americans valued. A persuasive example of this argu-

"Brutus," *New York Journal*, October 18, 1787.

ment comes from "Brutus," the pseudonym for an author of sixteen anti-federalist essays published in the *New York Journal* between October 1787 and April 1788 and widely reprinted elsewhere. Some historians have suggested that the author was Robert Yates (1738-1801), a New York delegate to the Constitutional Convention who opposed and refused to sign the Constitution. The following viewpoint is taken from the first article of the series, which appeared in the *Journal* October 18, 1787. "Brutus" criticizes the proposed Constitution for greatly centralizing powers in the national government. A few days after its publication, James Madison wrote in a letter that "a new Combatant . . . with considerable address & plausibility, strikes at the foundation" of the proposed new government. Madison responded to the arguments found here in the first of his contributions to *The Federalist*, the famous No. 10.

The first question that presents itself on the subject is, whether a confederated government be the best for the United States or not? Or in other words, whether the thirteen United States should be reduced to one great republic, governed by one legislature, and under the direction of one executive and judicial; or whether they should continue thirteen confederated republics, under the direction and controul of a supreme federal head for certain defined national purposes only?

This enquiry is important, because, although the government reported by the convention does not go to a perfect and entire consolidation, yet it approaches so near to it, that it must, if executed, certainly and infallibly terminate in it.

A National Government with Absolute Power

This government is to possess absolute and uncontroulable power, legislative, executive and judicial, with respect to every object to which it extends, for by the last clause of section 8th, article 1st, it is declared "that the Congress shall have power to make all laws which shall be necessary and proper for carrying into execution the foregoing powers, and all other powers vested by this constitution, in the government of the United States; or in any department or office thereof." And by the 6th article, it is declared "that this constitution, and the laws of the United States, which shall be made in pursuance thereof, and the treaties made, or which shall be made, under the authority of the United States, shall be the supreme law of the land; and the judges in every state shall be bound thereby, any thing in the constitution, or law of any state to the contrary notwithstanding." It appears from these articles that there is no need of any intervention of the state governments, between the Congress and the people, to execute any one power vested in the general government, and that the constitution and laws of every state are nullified and declared void, so far as they are or shall be inconsistent with this constitution, or the laws made in pursuance of it, or with treaties made under the authority of the United States. . . .

A House Divided

In the third of his seven letters, "Cato" argues that the Constitution cannot achieve the objectives listed in its preamble because of the size and extent of the United States. The essay appeared in the New York Journal *of October 25, 1787.*

The freedom, equality, and independence which you enjoyed by nature, induced you to consent to a political power. The same principles led you to examine the errors and vices of a British superintendence, to divest yourselves of it, and to reassume a new political shape. It is acknowledged that there are defects in this, and another is tendered to you for acceptance; the great question then, that arises on this new political principle, is, whether it will answer the ends for which it is said to be offered to you, and for which all men engage in political society, to wit, the mutual preservation of their lives, liberties, and estates.

The recital, or premises on which this new form of government is erected, declares a consolidation or union of all the thirteen parts, or states, into one great whole, under the firm of the United States, for all the various and important purposes therein set forth.—But whoever seriously considers the immense extent of territory comprehended within the limits of the United States, together with the variety of its climates, productions, and commerce, the difference of extent, and number of inhabitants in all; the dissimilitude of interests, morals, and policies, in almost every one, will receive it as an intuitive truth, that a consolidated republican form of government therein, can never *form a perfect union, establish justice, insure domestic tranquility, promote the general welfare, and secure the blessings of liberty to you and your posterity,* for to these objects it must be directed: this unkindred legislature therefore, composed of interests opposite and dissimilar in their nature, will in its exercise, emphatically be, like a house divided against itself.

The legislature of the United States are vested with the great and uncontroulable powers, of laying and collecting taxes, duties, imposts, and excises; of regulating trade, raising and supporting armies, organizing, arming, and disciplining the militia, instituting courts, and other general powers. And are by this clause invested with the power of making all laws, *proper and necessary*, for carrying all these into execution; and they may so exercise this power as entirely to annihilate all the state governments, and reduce this country to one single government. And if they may do it, it is pretty certain they will; for it will be found that the power retained by individual states, small as it is, will be a clog upon the wheels of the government of the United States; the latter therefore will be naturally inclined to remove it out of the way. Besides, it is a truth confirmed by the unerring experience of ages, that every man, and every body of men, invested with power, are ever disposed to increase it, and to acquire a superiority over every thing that stands in their way. This disposition, which is implanted in human nature, will operate in the federal legislature to lessen and ultimately to subvert the state authority, and having such advantages, will most certainly succeed, if the federal government succeeds at all. It must be very evident then, that what this constitution wants of being a complete consolidation of the several parts of the union into one complete government, possessed of perfect legislative, judicial, and executive powers, to all intents and purposes, it will necessarily acquire in its exercise and operation.

Can a Government Be Large and Free?

Let us now proceed to enquire, as I at first proposed, whether it be best the thirteen United States should be reduced to one great republic, or not? It is here taken for granted, that all agree in this, that whatever government we adopt, it ought to be a free one; that it should be so framed as to secure the liberty of the citizens of America, and such an one as to admit of a full, fair, and equal representation of the people. The question then will be, whether a government thus constituted, and founded on such principles, is practicable, and can be exercised over the whole United States, reduced into one state?

If respect is to be paid to the opinion of the greatest and wisest men who have ever thought or wrote on the science of government, we shall be constrained to conclude, that a free republic cannot succeed over a country of such immense extent, containing such a number of inhabitants, and these encreasing in such rapid progression as that of the whole United States. Among the many illustrious authorities which might be produced to this point, I shall content myself with quoting only two. The one is the baron [Charles-Louis] de Montesquieu, spirit of laws, chap. xvi. vol. I [book VIII]. "It is natural to a republic to have only a small territory, otherwise it cannot long subsist. In a large republic there are men of large fortunes, and consequently of less moderation;

there are trusts too great to be placed in any single subject; he has interest of his own; he soon begins to think that he may be happy, great and glorious, by oppressing his fellow citizens; and that he may raise himself to grandeur on the ruins of his country. In a large republic, the public good is sacrificed to a thousand views; it is subordinate to exceptions, and depends on accidents. In a small one, the interest of the public is easier perceived, better understood, and more within the reach of every citizen; abuses are of less extent, and of course are less protected." Of the same opinion is the marquis Beccarari [Cesare di Beccaria].

History furnishes no example of a free republic, any thing like the extent of the United States. The Grecian republics were of small extent; so also was that of the Romans. Both of these, it is true, in process of time, extended their conquests over large territories of country; and the consequence was, that their governments were changed from that of free government to those of the most tyrannical that ever existed in the world.

Not only the opinion of the greatest men, and the experience of mankind, are against the idea of an extensive republic, but a variety of reasons may be drawn from the reason and nature of things, against it. In every government, the will of the sovereign is the law. In despotic governments, the supreme authority being lodged in one, his will is law, and can be as easily expressed to a large extensive territory as to a small one. In a pure democracy the people are the sovereign, and their will is declared by themselves; for this purpose they must all come together to deliberate, and decide. This kind of government cannot be exercised, therefore, over a country of any considerable extent; it must be confined to a single city, or at least limited to such bounds as that the people can conveniently assemble, be able to debate, understand the subject submitted to them, and declare their opinion concerning it.

The Consent of the People

In a free republic, although all laws are derived from the consent of the people, yet the people do not declare their consent by themselves in person, but by representatives, chosen by them, who are supposed to know the minds of their constituents, and to be possessed of integrity to declare this mind.

In every free government, the people must give their assent to the laws by which they are governed. This is the true criterion between a free government and an arbitrary one. The former are ruled by the will of the whole, expressed in any manner they may agree upon; the latter by the will of one, or a few. If the people are to give their assent to the laws, by persons chosen and appointed by them, the manner of the choice and the number chosen, must be such, as to possess, be disposed, and consequently qualified to declare the sentiments of the people; for if they do not know, or are not disposed to speak the sentiments of the people, the people do not govern, but the sovereignty is in a few. Now, in a large extended country, it is impossible to have a representation, possessing the sentiments, and of integrity, to declare the minds of the people, without having it so numerous and unwieldy, as to be subject in great measure to the inconveniency of a democratic government.

The territory of the United States is of vast extent; it now contains near three millions of souls, and is capable of containing much more than ten times that number. Is it practicable for a country, so large and so numerous as they will soon become, to elect a representation, that will speak their sentiments, without their becoming so numerous as to be incapable of transacting public business? It certainly is not.

The Diversity of the United States

In a republic, the manners, sentiments, and interests of the people should be similar. If this be not the case, there will be a constant clashing of opinions; and the representatives of one part will be continually striving against those of the other. This will retard the operations of government and prevent such conclusions as will promote the public good. If we apply this remark to the condition of the United States, we shall be convinced that it forbids that we should be one government. The United States includes a variety of climates. The productions of the different parts of the union are very variant, and their interests, of consequence, diverse. Their manners and habits differ as much as their climates and productions; and their sentiments are by no means coincident. The laws and customs of the several states are, in many respects, very diverse, and in some opposite; each would be in favor of its own interests and customs, and, of consequence, a legislature, formed of representatives from the respective parts, would not only be too numerous to act with any care or decision, but would be composed of such heterogenous and discordant principles, as would constantly be contending with each other.

The laws cannot be executed in a republic, of an extent equal to that of the United States, with promptitude.

The magistrates in every government must be supported in the execution of the laws, either by an armed force, maintained at the public expence for that purpose; or by the people turning out to aid the magistrate upon his command, in case of resistance.

In despotic governments, as well as in all the monarchies of Europe, standing armies are kept up to execute the commands of the prince or the magistrate, and are employed for this purpose when occasion requires: But they have always proved the destruction of liberty, and abhorrent to the spirit of a free republic. In England, where they depend upon the parliament for their annual support, they have always been complained of as oppressive and unconstitutional, and are seldom employed in executing of the laws; never except on extraordinary occasions, and then under the direction of a civil magistrate.

An Absurd Idea

The third of eighteen essays by "Agrippa" appeared in the Massachusetts Gazette *on December 3, 1787. Most historians believe the author to have been judge and college teacher James Winthrop. In this excerpt, Winthrop makes the commonly used argument that America with its six million "white inhabitants" is too large for the creation of a true republican government, and adds some disparaging remarks on the southern states.*

It is the opinion of the ablest writers on the subject, that no extensive empire can be governed upon republican principles, and that such a government will degenerate to a despotism, unless it be made up of a confederacy of small states, each having the full powers of internal regulation. This is precisely the principle which has hitherto preserved our freedom. No instance can be found of any free government of considerable extent which has been supported upon any other plan. Large and consolidated empires may indeed dazzle the eyes of a distant spectator with their splendour, but if examined more nearly are always found to be full of misery. The reason is obvious. In large states the same principles of legislation will not apply to all the parts. The inhabitants of warmer climates are more dissolute in their manners, and less industrious, than in colder countries. A degree of severity is, therefore, necessary with one which would cramp the spirit of the other. . . .

The idea of an uncompounded republick, on an average one thousand miles in length, and eight hundred in breadth, and containing six millions of white inhabitants all reduced to the same standard of morals, of habits, and of laws, is in itself an absurdity, and contrary to the whole experience of mankind.

A free republic will never keep a standing army to execute its laws. It must depend upon the support of its citizens. But when a government is to receive its support from the aid of the citizens, it must be so constructed as to have the confidence, respect, and affection of the people. Men who, upon the call of the magistrate, offer themselves to execute the laws, are influenced to do it either by affection to the government, or from fear; where a standing army is at hand to punish offenders, every man is actuated by the latter principle, and therefore, when the magistrate calls, will obey: but, where this is not the case, the government must rest for its support upon the confidence and respect which the people have for their government and laws. The body of the people being attached, the government will always be sufficient to support and execute its laws, and to operate upon the fears of any faction which may be opposed to it, not only to prevent an opposition to the execution of the laws themselves, but also to compel the most of them to aid the magistrate; but the people will not be likely to have such confidence in their rulers, in a republic so extensive as the United States, as necessary for these purposes. The confidence which the people have in their rulers, in a free republic, arises from their knowing them, from their being responsible to them for their conduct, and from the power they have of displacing them when they misbehave: but in a republic of the extent of this continent, the people in general would be acquainted with very few of their rulers: the people at large would know little of their proceedings, and it would be extremely difficult to change them. The people in Georgia and New-Hampshire would not know one another's mind, and therefore could not act in concert to enable them to effect a general change of representatives. The different parts of so extensive a country could not possibly be made acquainted with the conduct of their representatives, nor be informed of the reasons upon which measures were founded. The consequence will be, they will have no confidence in their legislature, suspect them of ambitious views, be jealous of every measure they adopt, and will not support the laws they pass. Hence the government will be nerveless and inefficient, and no way will be left to render it otherwise, but by establishing an armed force to execute the laws at the point of the bayonet—a government of all others the most to be dreaded.

In a republic of such vast extent as the United States, the legislature cannot attend to the various concerns and wants of its different parts. It cannot be sufficiently numerous to be acquainted with the local condition and wants of the different districts, and if it could, it is impossible it should have sufficient time to attend to and provide for all the variety of cases of this nature, that would be continually arising.

The Abuse of Power

In so extensive a republic, the great officers of government would soon become above the controul of the people, and abuse their power to the purpose of aggrandizing themselves, and oppressing them. The trust committed to the executive offices, in a country of the extent of the United States, must be various and of magnitude. The command of all the troops and navy of the republic, the appointment of officers, the power of pardoning offences, the collecting of all the public revenues, and the power of expending them, with a number of other powers, must be lodged and exercised in every state, in the hands of a few. When these are attended with great honor and emolument, as they always will be in large states, so as greatly to interest men to pursue them, and to be proper objects for ambitious and designing men, such men will be ever restless in their pursuit after them. They will use the power, when they have acquired it, to the purposes of gratifying their own interest and ambition, and it is scarcely possible, in a very large republic, to call them to account for their misconduct, or to prevent their abuse of power.

These are some of the reasons by which it appears, that a free republic cannot long subsist over a country of the great extent of these states. If then this new constitution is calculated to consolidate the thirteen states into one, as it evidently is, it ought not to be adopted.

"The extent of the Union gives it the most palpable advantage."

A Viable Republic Can Be Large and Diverse

James Madison (1751-1836)

James Madison's contributions to the creation of the Constitution extended well beyond his significant role in the 1787 Constitutional Convention. During the ratification debates he wrote numerous articles, letters, and pamphlets urging ratification of the Constitution. His most noteworthy and lasting writings in this debate are the famous *Federalist Papers*, a series of newspaper articles coauthored with Alexander Hamilton and John Jay under the pseudonym "Publius."

The articles were originally published in several New York newspapers between October 27, 1787, and May 28, 1788, and were initiated by Hamilton as part of a campaign urging ratification of the Constitution in New York. Madison, a resident of Virginia, was in New York as a delegate to the Continental Congress and thus available to help when Hamilton enlisted him. Political scientist Garry Wills writes:

> Though the *Federalist* "Numbers" would all be addressed to New Yorkers, one of the men addressing his fellow citizens was actually from Virginia. And this member of the Publius team wrote almost forty percent of the final product. He could not have done so, he assures us, but for his preparations before the convention in Philadelphia and his participation in its debates. Along with Hamilton, Madison had studied the history of leagues, ancient and modern, to prove that a loose confederation could not possibly address itself to challenging times with any efficiency. The notes taken in Philadelphia supplied him with a text for the New York campaign.

"Publius," open letter "To the People of the State of New York" (*Federalist* no. 10), New York *Daily Advertiser*, November 22, 1787.

The Federalist No. 10, Madison's first and most famous contribution to the series, was originally published November 22, 1787, in the New York *Daily Advertiser*. He was responding in part to arguments made by "Brutus" and others that republican governments were viable only in smaller communities where the "interests of the people should be similar." Madison argues that republican governments in such situations are vulnerable to the problem of "factions"—the ability of local majorities motivated by selfish concerns to dominate the government, create bad law, and tyrannize the minority. Creating a government over a larger territory, Madison contends, can "extend the sphere" and prevent a single faction from gaining control over the government. Madison concludes that the Constitution, in creating a representative government over the whole United States, creates "a Republican remedy for the diseases most incident to Republican government."

To the People of the State of New York:

Among the numerous advantages promised by a well-constructed Union, none deserves to be more accurately developed than its tendency to break and control the violence of faction. The friend of popular governments never finds himself so much alarmed for their character and fate, as when he contemplates their propensity to this dangerous vice. He will not fail, therefore, to set a due value on any plan which, without violating the principles to which he is attached, provides a proper cure for it. The instability, injustice, and confusion introduced into the public councils, have, in truth, been the mortal diseases under which popular governments have everywhere perished; as they continue to be the favorite and fruitful topics from which the adversaries to liberty derive their most specious declamations. The valuable improvements made by the American constitutions on the popular models, both ancient and modern, cannot certainly be too much admired; but it would be an unwarrantable partiality, to contend that they have as effectually obviated the danger on this side, as was wished and expected. Complaints are everywhere heard from our most considerate and virtuous citizens, equally the friends of public and private faith, and of public and personal liberty, that our governments are too unstable, that the public good is disregarded in the conflicts of rival parties, and that measures are too often decided, not according to the rules of justice and the rights of the minor party, but by the superior force of an interested and overbearing majority. However anxiously we may wish that these complaints had no foundation, the evidence of known facts will not permit us to deny that they are in some degree true. It will be found, indeed, on a candid review of our situation, that some of the distresses under which we labor have been erroneously charged on the operation of our governments; but it will be found, at the same time, that other causes will not alone account for many of our heaviest misfortunes; and, particularly, for that prevailing and increasing distrust of public engagements, and alarm for private rights, which are echoed from one end of the continent to the other. These must be chiefly, if not wholly, effects of the unsteadiness and injustice with which a factious spirit has tainted our public administrations.

➤➤➤✦◆◆◆

The FŒDERALIST, No. 10.

To the People of the State of New-York.

AMONG the numerous advantages promised by a well constructed Union, none deserves to be more accurately developed than its tendency to break and control the violence of faction. The friend of popular governments, never finds himself so much alarmed for their character and fate, as when he contemplates their propensity to this dangerous vice. He will not fail therefore to set a due value on any plan which, without violating the principles to which he is attached, provides a proper cure for it. The instability, injustice and confusion introduced into the public councils, have in truth been the mortal diseases under which popular governments have every where perished; as they continue to be the favorite and fruitful topics from which the adversaries to liberty derive their most specious declamations. The valuable improvements made by the American Constitutions on the popular models, both ancient and modern, cannot certainly

James Madison's famous Federalist No. 10 appeared in the New-York Packet, November 23, 1787, one day after its first printing in the Daily Advertiser.

By a faction, I understand a number of citizens, whether amounting to a majority or minority of the whole, who are united and actuated by some common impulse of passion, or of interest, adverse to the rights of other citizens, or to the permanent and aggregate interests of the community.

There are two methods of curing the mischiefs of faction: the one, by removing its causes; the other, by controlling its effects.

There are again two methods of removing the causes of faction: the one, by destroying the liberty which is essential to its existence; the other, by giving to every citizen the same opinions, the same passions, and the same interests.

It could never be more truly said than of the first remedy, that it was worse than the disease. Liberty is to faction what air is to fire, an aliment without which it instantly expires. But it could not be less folly to abolish liberty, which is essential to political life, because it nourishes faction, than it would be to wish the annihilation of air, which is essential to animal life, because it imparts to fire its destructive agency.

The second expedient is as impracticable as the first would be unwise. As long as the reason of man continues fallible, and he is at liberty to exercise it, different opinions will be formed. As long as the connection subsists between his reason and his self-love, his opinions and his passions will have a reciprocal influence on each other: and the former will be objects to which the latter will attach themselves. The diversity in the faculties of men, from which the rights of property originate, is not less an insuperable obstacle to a uniformity of interests. The protection of these faculties is the first object of government. From the protection of different and unequal faculties of acquiring property, the possession of different degrees and kinds of property immediately results; and from the influence of these on the sentiments and views of the respective proprietors, ensues a division of the society into different interests and parties.

The Causes of Faction

The latent causes of faction are thus sown in the nature of man; and we see them everywhere brought into different degrees of activity, according to the different circumstances of civil society. A zeal for different opinions concerning religion, concerning government, and many other points, as well of speculation as of practice; an attachment to different leaders ambitiously contending for pre-eminence and power; or to persons of other descriptions whose fortunes have been interesting to the human passions, have, in turn, divided mankind into parties, inflamed them with mutual animosity, and rendered them much more disposed to vex and oppress each other than to co-operate for their common good. So strong is this propensity of mankind to fall into mutual animosities, that where no substantial occasion presents itself, the most frivolous and fanciful distinctions have been sufficient to kindle their unfriendly passions and excite their most violent conflicts. But the most common and durable source of factions has been the various and unequal distribution of property. Those who hold and those who are without property have ever formed distinct interests in society. Those who are creditors, and those who are debtors, fall under a like discrimination. A landed interest, a manufacturing interest, a mercantile interest, a moneyed interest, with many lesser interests, grow up of necessity in civilized nations, and divide them into different classes, actuated by different sentiments and views. The regulation of these various and interfering interests forms the principal task of modern legislation, and involves the spirit of party and faction in the necessary and ordinary operations of the government.

No man is allowed to be a judge in his own cause, because his interest would certainly bias his judgment, and, not improbably, corrupt his integrity. With equal, nay with greater reason, a body of men are unfit to be both judges and parties at the same time; yet what are many of the most important acts of legislation, but so many judicial determinations, not indeed concerning the rights of single persons, but concerning the rights of large bodies of citizens? And what are the different classes of legislators but advocates and parties to the causes which they determine? Is a law proposed concerning private debts? It is a question to which the creditors are parties on one side and the debtors on the other. Justice ought to hold the balance between them. Yet the parties are, and must be, themselves the judges; and the most numerous party, or, in other words, the most powerful faction must be expected to prevail. Shall domestic manufactures be encouraged, and in what degree, by restrictions on foreign manufactures? are questions which would be differently decided by the landed and the manufacturing classes, and probably by neither with a sole regard to justice and the public good. The apportionment of taxes on the various descriptions of property is an act which seems to require the most exact impartiality; yet there is, perhaps, no legislative act in which greater opportunity and temptation are given to a predominant party to trample on the rules of justice. Every shilling with which they overburden the inferior number, is a shilling saved to their own pockets.

It is in vain to say that enlightened statesmen will be able to adjust these clashing interests, and render them all subservient to the public good. Enlightened statesmen will not always be at the helm. Nor, in many cases, can such an adjustment be made at all without taking into view indirect and remote considerations, which will rarely prevail over the immediate interest which one party may find in disregarding the rights of another or the good of the whole.

The inference to which we are brought is, that the *causes* of faction cannot be removed, and that relief is only to be sought in the means of controlling its *effects*.

If a faction consists of less than a majority, relief is supplied by the republican principle, which enables the majority to defeat its sinister views by regular vote. It may clog the administration, it may convulse the society; but it will be unable to execute and mask its violence under the forms of the Constitution. When a majority is included in a faction, the form of popular government, on the other hand, enables it to sacrifice to its ruling passion or interest both the public good and the rights of other citizens. To secure the public good and private rights against the danger of such a faction, and at the same time to preserve the spirit and the form of popular government, is then the great object to which our inquiries are directed. Let me add that it is the great desideratum by which this form of government can be rescued from the opprobrium under which it has so long labored, and be recommended to the esteem and adoption of mankind.

By what means is this object attainable? Evidently by one of two only. Either the existence of the same passion or interest in a majority at the same time must be prevented, or the majority, having such coexistent passion or interest, must be rendered, by their number and local situation, unable to concert and carry into effect schemes of oppression. If the impulse and the opportunity be suffered to coincide, we well know that neither moral nor religious motives can be relied on as an adequate control. They are not found to be such on the injustice and violence of individuals, and lose their efficacy in proportion to the number combined together, that is, in proportion as their efficacy becomes needful.

Comparing Republics and Democracies

From this view of the subject it may be concluded that a pure democracy, by which I mean a society consisting of a small number of citizens, who assemble and administer the government in person, can admit of no cure for the mischiefs of faction. A common passion or interest will, in almost every case, be felt by a majority of the whole; a communication and concert result from the form of government itself; and there is nothing to check the inducements to sacrifice the weaker party or an obnoxious individual. Hence it is that such democracies have ever been spectacles of turbulence and contention; have ever been found incompatible with personal security or the rights of property; and have in general been as short in their lives as they have been violent in their deaths. Theoretic politicians, who have patronized this species of government, have erroneously supposed that by reducing mankind to a perfect equality in their political rights, they would, at the same time, be perfectly equalized and assimilated in their possessions, their opinions, and their passions.

A republic, by which I mean a government in which the scheme of representation takes place, opens a different prospect, and promises the cure for which we are seeking. Let us examine the points in which it varies from pure democracy, and we shall comprehend both the nature of the cure and the efficacy which it must derive from the Union.

The two great points of difference between a democracy and a

Extensive Territory Is Not a Bar to Good Government

Many critics of the Constitution cited the French political philosopher Charles-Louis de Montesquieu in arguing that republican government could not survive over an extended territory. The Virginia governor Edmund Randolph, in a June 6, 1788, speech at the Virginia ratifying convention, attempted to turn the tables by quoting Montesquieu while arguing against the notion that a small territory was necessary.

It is objected by the Honorable Gentleman over the way (Mr. *George Mason*) that a republican Government is impracticable in an extensive territory, and the extent of the United States is urged as a reason for the rejection of this Constitution. Let us consider the definition of a republican Government, as laid down by a man who is highly esteemed. Montesquieu, so celebrated among politicians, says, "That a republican Government is that in which the body, or only a part of the people, is possessed of the supreme power; a monarchical, that in which a single person governs by fixed and established laws; a despotic Government, that in which a single person, without law, and without rule, directs every thing by his own will and caprice." This author has not distinguished a republican Government from a monarchy, by the extent of its boundaries, but by the nature of its principles. He, in another place, contradistinguishes it, as a government of laws, in opposition to others which he denominates a government of men. The empire or Government of laws, according to that phrase, is that in which the laws are made with the free will of the people; hence then, if laws be made by the assent of the people, the Government may be deemed free. When laws are made with integrity, and executed with wisdom, the question is, whether a great extent of country will tend to abridge the liberty of the people. If defensive force be necessary in proportion to the extent of country, I conceive that in a judiciously constructed Government, be the country ever so extensive, its inhabitants will be proportionably numerous and able to defend it. Extent of country, in my conception, ought to be no bar to the adoption of a good Government. No extent on earth seems to me too great, provided the laws be wisely made and executed.

republic are: first, the delegation of the government, in the latter, to a small number of citizens elected by the rest; secondly, the greater number of citizens, and greater sphere of country, over which the latter may be extended.

The effect of the first difference is, on the one hand, to refine and enlarge the public views, by passing them through the medium of a chosen body of citizens, whose wisdom may best discern the true interest of their country, and whose patriotism and love of justice will be least likely to sacrifice it to temporary or partial considerations. Under such a regulation, it may well happen that the public voice, pronounced by the representatives of the people, will be more consonant to the public good than if pronounced by the people themselves, convened for the purpose. On the other hand, the effect may be inverted. Men of factious tempers, of local prejudices, or of sinister designs, may, by intrigue, by corruption, or by other means, first obtain the suffrages, and then betray the interests, of the people. The question resulting is, whether small or extensive republics are more favorable to the election of proper guardians of the public weal; and it is clearly decided in favor of the latter by two obvious considerations:

In the first place, it is to be remarked that, however small the republic may be, the representatives must be raised to a certain number, in order to guard against the cabals of a few; and that, however large it may be, they must be limited to a certain number, in order to guard against the confusion of a multitude. Hence, the number of representatives in the two cases not being in proportion to that of the two constituents, and being proportionally greater in the small republic, it follows that, if the proportion of fit characters be not less in the large than in the small republic, the former will present a greater option, and consequently a greater probability of a fit choice.

In the next place, as each representative will be chosen by a greater number of citizens in the large than in the small republic, it will be more difficult for unworthy candidates to practise with success the vicious arts by which elections are too often carried; and the suffrages of the people being more free, will be more likely to centre in men who possess the most attractive merit and the most diffusive and established characters.

It must be confessed that in this, as in most other cases, there is a mean, on both sides of which inconveniences will be found to lie. By enlarging too much the number of electors, you render the representative too little acquainted with all their local circumstances and lesser interests; as by reducing it too much, you render him unduly attached to these, and too little fit to comprehend and pursue great and national objects. The federal Constitution forms a happy combination in this respect; the great and aggregate interests being referred to the national, the local and particular to the State legislatures.

Extending the Sphere

The other point of difference is, the greater number of citizens and extent of territory which may be brought within the compass of republican than of democratic government; and it is this circumstance principally which renders factious combinations less to be dreaded in the former than in the latter. The smaller the society, the fewer probably will be the distinct parties and interests composing it; the fewer the distinct parties and interests, the more frequently will a majority be found of the same party; and the smaller the number of individuals composing a majority, and the smaller the compass within which they are placed, the most easily will they concert and execute their plans of oppression. Extend the sphere, and you take in a greater variety of parties and interests; you make it less probable that a majority of the whole will have a common motive to invade the rights of other citizens; or if such a common motive exists, it will be more difficult for all who feel it to discover their own strength, and to act in unison with each other. Besides other impediments, it may be remarked that, where there is a consciousness of unjust or dishonorable purposes, communication is always checked by distrust in proportion to the number whose concurrence is necessary.

Hence, it clearly appears, that the same advantage which a republic has over a democracy, in controlling the effects of faction, is enjoyed by a large over a small republic,—is enjoyed by the Union over the States composing it. Does the advantage consist in the substitution of representatives whose enlightened views and virtuous sentiments render them superior to local prejudices and to schemes of injustice? It will not be denied that the representation of the Union will be most likely to possess these requisite endowments. Does it consist in the greater security afforded by a greater variety of parties, against the event of any one party being able to outnumber and oppress the rest? In an equal degree does the increased variety of parties comprised within the Union, increase this security. Does it, in fine, consist in the greater obstacles opposed to the concert and accomplishment of the secret wishes of an unjust and interested majority? Here, again, the extent of the Union gives it the most palpable advantage.

The influence of factious leaders may kindle a flame within their particular States, but will be unable to spread a general conflagration through the other States. A religious sect may degenerate into a political faction in a part of the Confederacy; but the variety of sects dispersed over the entire face of it must secure the national councils against any danger from that source. A rage for paper money, for an abolition of debts, for an equal division of property, or for any other improper or wicked project, will be less apt to pervade the whole body of the Union than a particular member of it; in the same proportion as such a malady is more likely to taint a particular county or district, than an entire State.

In the extent and proper structure of the Union, therefore, we behold a republican remedy for the diseases most incident to republican government. And according to the degree of pleasure and pride we feel in being republicans, ought to be our zeal in cherishing the spirit and supporting the character of Federalists.

VIEWPOINT 3

"Ambition must be made to counteract ambition."

Checks and Balances Can Assure a Republican Form of Government

James Madison (1751-1836)

Creating a government with enough power to govern effectively, yet not powerful enough to corrupt officials, endanger freedoms, or become unanswerable to the people, was a fundamental quandary facing the makers of the Constitution. A part of the solution they proposed was the idea that power be shared between three distinct branches of government—the legislative, executive, and judiciary. Not only were the three branches to have separate powers and duties, but they were to function in a system of "checks and balances" under which the branches directly or indirectly affected each other, and prevented one single branch from gaining too much power.

An analysis and defense of the Constitution based on the idea of checks and balances is found in *The Federalist* No. 51, written by James Madison and first published in the February 6, 1788, edition of the New York *Independent Journal* and in other newspapers. James Madison played a prominent role in the creation of the Constitution, both as a Virginia delegate to the Constitutional Convention and as the writer of many of the *Federalist Papers*, a series of articles explaining the meaning of the Constitution and arguing for its ratification.

"Publius," open letter "To the People of the State of New York" (*Federalist* no. 51), New York *Independent Journal*, February 6, 1788.

To the People of the State of New York.

To what expedient then shall we finally resort for maintaining in practice the necessary partition of power among the several departments, as laid down in the constitution? The only answer that can be given is, that as all these exterior provisions are found to be inadequate, the defect must be supplied, by so contriving the interior structure of the government, as that its several constituent parts may, by their mutual relations, be the means of keeping each other in their proper places. Without presuming to undertake a full developement of this important idea, I will hazard a few general observations, which may perhaps place it in a clearer light, and enable us to form a more correct judgment of the principles and structure of the government planned by the convention.

In order to lay a due foundation for that separate and distinct exercise of the different powers of government, which to a certain extent, is admitted on all hands to be essential to the preservation of liberty, it is evident that each department should have a will of its own; and consequently should be so constituted, that the members of each should have as little agency as possible in the appointment of the members of the others. Were this principle rigorously adhered to, it would require that all the appointments for the supreme executive, legislative, and judiciary magistracies, should be drawn from the same fountain of authority, the people, through channels, having no communication whatever with one another. Perhaps such a plan of constructing the several departments would be less difficult in practice than it may in contemplation appear. Some difficulties however, and some additional expence, would attend the execution of it. Some deviations therefore from the principle must be admitted. In the constitution of the judiciary department in particular, it might be inexpedient to insist rigorously on the principle; first, because peculiar qualifications being essential in the members, the primary consideration ought to be to select that mode of choice, which best secures these qualifications; secondly, because the permanent tenure by which the appointments are held in that department, must soon destroy all sense of dependence on the authority conferring them.

It is equally evident that the members of each department should be as little dependent as possible on those of the others, for the emoluments annexed to their offices. Were the executive magistrate, or the judges, not independent of the legislature in this particular, their independence in every other would be merely nominal.

But the great security against a gradual concentration of the several powers in the same department, consists in giving to those

125

who administer each department, the necessary constitutional means, and personal motives, to resist encroachments of the others. The provision for defence must in this, as in all other cases, be made commensurate to the danger of attack. Ambition must be made to counteract ambition. The interest of the man must be connected with the constitutional rights of the place. It may be a reflection on human nature, that such devices should be necessary to controul the abuses of government. But what is government itself but the greatest of all reflections on human nature? If men were angels, no government would be necessary. If angels were to govern men, neither external nor internal controuls on government would be necessary. In framing a government which is to be administered by men over men, the great difficulty lies in this: You must first enable the government to controul the governed; and in the next place, oblige it to controul itself. A dependence on the people is no doubt the primary controul on the government; but experience has taught mankind the necessity of auxiliary precautions.

For his work prior to, during, and after the Constitutional Convention, James Madison is considered by many historians to be the single most influential participant in the creation of the Constitution.

This policy of supplying by opposite and rival interests, the defect of better motives, might be traced through the whole system of human affairs, private as well as public. We see it particularly displayed in all the subordinate distributions of power; where the constant aim is to divide and arrange the several offices in such a manner as that each may be a check on the other; that the private interest of every individual, may be a centinel over the public rights. These inventions of prudence cannot be less requisite in the distribution of the supreme powers of the state.

But it is not possible to give to each department an equal power of self defence. In republican government the legislative authority, necessarily, predominates. The remedy for this inconveniency is, to divide the legislature into different branches; and to render them by different modes of election, and different principles of action, as little connected with each other, as the nature of their common functions, and their common dependence on the society, will admit. It may even be necessary to guard against dangerous encroachments by still further precautions. As the weight of the legislative authority requires that it should be thus divided, the weakness of the executive may require, on the other hand, that it should be fortified. An absolute negative, on the legislature, appears at first view to be the natural defence with which the executive magistrate should be armed. But perhaps it would be neither altogether safe, nor alone sufficient. On ordinary occasions, it might not be exerted with the requisite firmness; and on extraordinary occasions, it might be perfidiously abused. May not this defect of an absolute negative be supplied, by some qualified connection between this weaker department, and the weaker branch of the stronger department, by which the latter may be led to support the constitutional rights of the former, without being too much detached from the rights of its own department?

If the principles on which these observations are founded be just, as I persuade myself they are, and they be applied as a criterion, to the several state constitutions, and to the federal constitution, it will be found, that if the latter does not perfectly correspond with them, the former are infinitely less able to bear such a test.

There are moreover two considerations particularly applicable to the federal system of America, which place that system in a very interesting point of view.

First. In a single republic, all the power surrendered by the people, is submitted to the administration of a single government; and usurpations are guarded against by a division of the government into distinct and separate departments. In the compound republic of America, the power surrendered by the people, is first divided between two distinct governments, and then the portion allotted to each, subdivided among distinct and separate departments. Hence a double security arises to the rights of the people. The different governments will controul each other; at the same time that each will be controuled by itself.

Second. It is of great importance in a republic, not only to guard the society against the oppression of its rulers; but to guard one

The Dangers of Arbitrary Power

Benjamin Rush was a noted physician who wrote several essays in support of the Constitution. The passage excerpted here is taken from an article printed in several newspapers, including the Columbian Herald *in Charleston, South Carolina, on April 19, 1788.*

I have the same opinion with the antifederalists of the danger of trusting arbitrary power to any single body of men; but no such power will be committed to our new rulers. Neither the house of representatives, the senate, or the president can perform a single legislative act by themselves. An hundred principles in man will lead them to watch, to check and to oppose each other, should an attempt be made by either of them upon the liberties of the people. If we may judge of their conduct, by what we have so often observed in all the state governments, the members of the federal legislature will much oftener injure their constituents by voting agreeably to their inclinations, than *against* them.

part of the society against the injustice of the other part. Different interests necessarily exist in different classes of citizens. If a majority be united by a common interest, the rights of the minority will be insecure. There are but two methods of providing against this evil: The one by creating a will in the community independent of the majority, that is, of the society itself; the other by comprehending in the society so many separate descriptions of citizens, as will render an unjust combination of a majority of the whole, very improbable, if not impracticable. The first method prevails in all governments possessing an hereditary or self appointed authority. This at best is but a precarious security; because a power independent of the society may as well espouse the unjust views of the major, as the rightful interests, of the minor party, and may possibly be turned against both parties. The second method will be exemplified in the federal republic of the United States. Whilst all authority in it will be derived from and dependent on the society, the society itself will be broken into so many parts, interests and classes of citizens, that the rights of individuals or of the minority, will be in little danger from interested combinations of the majority. In a free government, the security for civil rights must be the same as for religious rights. It consists in the one case in the multiplicity of interests, and in the other, in the multiplicity of sects. The degree of security in both cases will depend on the number of interests and sects; and this may be presumed to depend on the extent of country and number of people comprehended under the same government. This view of the subject must particularly recommend a proper federal system to all the sincere and considerate friends of republican government: Since it shews that in exact proportion as the territory of the union may be formed into more circumscribed confederacies or states, oppressive combinations of a majority will be facilitated, the best security under the republican form, for the rights of every class of citizens, will be diminished; and consequently, the stability and independence of some member of the government, the only other security, must be proportionally increased. Justice is the end of government. It is the end of civil society. It ever has been, and ever will be pursued, until it be obtained, or until liberty be lost in the pursuit. In a society under the forms of which the stronger faction can readily unite and oppress the weaker, anarchy may as truly be said to reign, as in a state of nature where the weaker individual is not secured against the violence of the stronger: And as in the latter state even the stronger individuals are prompted by the uncertainty of their condition, to submit to a government which may protect the weak as well as themselves: So in the former state, will the more powerful factions or parties be gradually induced by a like motive, to wish for a government which will protect all parties, the weaker as well as the more powerful. It can be little doubted, that if the state of Rhode Island was separated from the confederacy, and left to itself, the insecurity of rights under the popular form of government within such narrow limits, would be displayed by such reiterated oppressions of factious majorities, that some power altogether independent of the people would soon be called for by the voice of the very factions whose misrule had proved the necessity of it. In the extended republic of the United States, and among the great variety of interests, parties and sects which it embraces, a coalition of a majority of the whole society could seldom take place on any other principles than those of justice and the general good; and there being thus less danger to a minor from the will of the major party, there must be less pretext also, to provide for the security of the former, by introducing into the government a will not dependent on the latter; or in other words, a will independent of the society itself. It is no less certain than it is important, notwithstanding the contrary opinions which have been entertained, that the larger the society, provided it lie within a practicable sphere, the more duly capable it will be of self government. And happily for the *republican cause*, the practicable sphere may be carried to a very great extent, by a judicious modification and mixture of the *federal principle*.

VIEWPOINT 4

"If the administrators of every government are actuated by... ambition, how is the welfare... of the community to be the result of such jarring adverse interests?"

Checks and Balances Cannot Assure a Republican Form of Government

Samuel Bryan (1759-1821)

On October 5, 1787, one of the first of eighteen articles by "Centinel" appeared in the Philadelphia *Independent Gazetteer*. The essay, one of the earliest and harshest attacks on the Constitution, was believed by many to have been written by George Bryan, a Pennsylvania supreme court judge who led the anti-federalist opposition to the Constitution in Pennsylvania. Historians now generally attribute the "Centinel" essays to his son, Samuel Bryan, who possibly wrote them in collaboration with his father.

Bryan writes as a strong supporter of Pennsylvania's existing state constitution. That constitution, created in 1776, differed greatly from other state constitutions and from the U.S. Constitution created in 1787. Instead of creating a complicated system of "checks and balances" in which a strong executive would check the legislature and the legislature itself was divided into two parts, Pennsylvania created a simple structure with an emphasis on accountability and democracy. Historian Richard B. Bernstein writes in *Are We to Be a Nation?*:

> The Pennsylvania constitution concentrated all powers of government in the hands of a popularly elected, unicameral

"Centinel," open letter "To the Freemen of Pennsylvania," Philadelphia *Independent Gazetteer*, October 5, 1787.

General Assembly; the members of the General Assembly elected a twelve-member Supreme Executive Council whose president was the functional equivalent of the chairman of a board of directors of a modern business corporation.

The Pennsylvania constitution is far superior to the complex and divided system created by the Constitution, Bryan argues. Bryan attacks the ideas of John Adams, then the American minister to Great Britain, who wrote several books defending the concept of balanced government in which the different interests checked each other. A system of checks and balances will not protect liberty, Bryan argues, but rather prevent people from holding their rulers accountable for corruption or tyranny. This, along with a lack of a bill of rights, makes the Constitution a dangerous threat to people's liberty, Bryan concludes.

To the Freemen of Pennsylvania.

Friends, Countrymen and Fellow Citizens,

Permit one of yourselves to put you in mind of certain *liberties* and *privileges* secured to you by the constitution of this commonwealth, and to beg your serious attention to his uninterested opinion upon the plan of federal government submitted to your consideration, before you surrender these great and valuable privileges up forever. Your present frame of government, secures to you a right to hold yourselves, houses, papers and possessions free from search and seizure, and therefore warrants granted without oaths or affirmations first made, affording sufficient foundation for them, whereby any officer or messenger may be commanded or required to search your houses or seize your persons or property, not particularly described in such warrant, shall not be granted. Your constitution further provides "that in controversies respecting property, and in suits between man and man, the parties have a right *to trial by jury, which ought to be held sacred.*" It also provides and declares, "*that the people have a right of* FREEDOM OF SPEECH, *and of* WRITING *and* PUBLISHING *their sentiments, therefore* THE FREEDOM OF THE PRESS OUGHT NOT TO BE RESTRAINED." The constitution of Pennsylvania is *yet* in existence, *as yet* you have the right to *freedom of speech*, and of *publishing your sentiments*. How long those rights will appertain to you, you yourselves are called upon to say, whether your *houses* shall continue to be your *castles*; whether your *papers*, your *persons* and your *property*, are to be held sacred and free from *general warrants*, you are now to determine. Whether the *trial by jury* is to continue as

131

your birth-right, the freemen of Pennsylvania, nay, of all America, are now called upon to declare.

Without presuming upon my own judgement, I cannot think it an unwarrantable presumption to offer my private opinion, and call upon others for their's; and if I use my pen with the boldness of a freeman, it is because I know that *the liberty of the press yet remains unviolated,* and *juries yet are judges.*

The Scourge of Despotic Power

In the ninth of his "Centinel" letters, Samuel Bryan warns Pennsylvanians that their local system of government is threatened by the new Constitution.

To the People of Pennsylvania. *Fellow Citizens,*
You have the peculiar felicity of living under the most perfect system of local government in the world; prize then this invaluable blessing as it deserves. Suffer it not to be wrested from you, and the scourge of despotic power substituted in its place, under the specious pretence of vesting the general government of the United States with necessary power; that this would be the inevitable consequence of the establishment of the new constitution, the least consideration of its nature and tendency is sufficient to convince every unprejudiced mind.

The late Convention have submitted to your consideration a plan of a new federal government—The subject is highly interesting to your future welfare—Whether it be calculated to promote the great ends of civil society, *viz.* the happiness and prosperity of the community; it behoves you well to consider, uninfluenced by the authority of names. Instead of that frenzy of enthusiasm, that has actuated the citizens of Philadelphia, in their approbation of the proposed plan, before it was possible that it could be the result of a rational investigation into its principles; it ought to be dispassionately and deliberately examined, and its own intrinsic merit the only criterion of your patronage. If ever free and unbiassed discussion was proper or necessary, it is on such an occasion.—All the blessings of liberty and the dearest privileges of freemen, are now at stake and dependent on your present conduct. Those who are competent to the task of developing the principles of government, ought to be encouraged to come forward, and thereby the better enable the people to make a proper judgment; for the science of government is so abstruse, that few are able to judge for themselves; without such assistance the people are too apt to yield an implicit assent to the opinions of those characters, whose abilities are held in the highest esteem, and to those in whose integrity and patriotism they can confide; not considering that the love of domination is generally in proportion to talents, abilities, and superior acquirements; and that the men of the greatest purity of intention may be made instruments of despotism in the hands of the *artful and designing*. If it were not for the stability and attachment which time and habit gives to forms of government, it would be in the power of the enlightened and aspiring few, if they should combine, at any time to destroy the best establishments, and even make the people the instruments of their own subjugation.

The late revolution having effaced in a great measure all former habits, and the present institutions are so recent, that there exists not that great reluctance to innovation, so remarkable in old communities, and which accords with reason, for the most comprehensive mind cannot foresee the full operation of material changes on civil polity; it is the genius of the common law to resist innovation.

The wealthy and ambitious, who in every community think they have a right to lord it over their fellow creatures, have availed themselves, very successfully, of this favorable disposition; for the people thus unsettled in their sentiments, have been prepared to accede to any extreme of government; all the distresses and difficulties they experience, proceeding from various causes, have been ascribed to the impotency of the present confederation, and thence they have been led to expect full relief from the adoption of the proposed system of government; and in the other event, immediately ruin and annihilation as a nation. These characters flatter themselves that they have lulled all distrust and jealousy of their new plan, by gaining the concurrence of the two men in whom America has the highest confidence, and now triumphantly exult in the completion of their long meditated schemes of power and aggrandisement. I would be very far from insinuating that the two illustrious personages alluded to, have not the welfare of their country at heart; but that the unsuspecting goodness and zeal of the one, has been imposed on, in a subject of which he must be necessarily inexperienced, from his other arduous engagements; and that the weakness and indecision attendant on old age, has been practised on in the other.

The Misleading Ideas of John Adams

I am fearful that the principles of government inculcated in Mr. [John] Adams's treatise [*Defence of the Constitutions of Government of the United States*], and enforced in the numerous essays and paragraphs in the newspapers, have misled some well designing members of the late Convention. . . .

I have been anxiously expecting that some enlightened patriot would, ere this, have taken up the pen to expose the futility, and counteract the baneful tendency of such principles. Mr. Adams's *sine qua non* of a good government is three balancing powers, whose repelling qualities are to produce an equilibrium of interests, and thereby promote the happiness of the whole community. He asserts that the administrators of every government, will ever be actuated by views of private interest and ambition, to the prejudice of the public good; that therefore the only effectual method to secure the rights of the people and promote their welfare, is to create an opposition of interests between the members of two distinct bodies, in the exercise of the powers of government, and balanced by those of a third. This hypothesis supposes human wisdom competent to the task of instituting three co-equal orders in government, and a corresponding weight in the community to enable them respectively to exercise their several parts, and whose views and interests should be so distinct as to prevent a coalition of any two of them for the destruction of the third. Mr. Adams, although he has traced the constitution of every form of government that ever existed, as far as history affords materials, has not been able to adduce a single instance of such a government; he indeed says that the British constitution is such in theory, but this is rather a confirmation that his principles are chimerical and not to be reduced to practice. If such an organization of power were practicable, how long would it continue? not a day—for there is so great a disparity in the talents, wisdom and industry of mankind, that the scale would presently preponderate to one or the other body, and with every accession of power the means of further increase would be greatly extended. The state of society in England is much more favorable to such a scheme of government than that of America. There they have a powerful hereditary nobility, and real distinctions of rank and interests; but even there, for want of that perfect equallity of power and distinction of interests, in the three orders of government, they exist but in name; the only operative and efficient check, upon the conduct of administration, is the sense of the people at large.

Suppose a government could be formed and supported on such principles, would it answer the great purposes of civil society; if the administrators of every government are actuated by views of private interest and ambition, how is the welfare and happiness of the community to be the result of such jarring adverse interests?

A Republican Government Needs Virtuous People

Therefore, as different orders in government will not produce the good of the whole, we must recur to other principles. I believe it will be found that the form of government, which holds those entrusted with power, in the greatest responsibility to their constitutents, the best calculated for freemen. A republican, or free government, can only exist where the body of the people are virtuous, and where property is pretty equally divided[;] in such a government the people are the sovereign and their sense or opinion is the criterion of every public measure; for when this ceases to be the case, the nature of the government is changed, and an aristocracy, monarchy or despotism will rise on its ruin. The highest responsibility is to be attained, in a simple structure of government, for the great body of the people never steadily attend to the operations of government, and for want of due information are liable to be imposed on—If you complicate the plan by various orders, the people will be perplexed and divided in their sentiments about the source of abuses or misconduct, some will impute it to the senate, others to the house of representatives, and so on, that the interposition of the people may be rendered imperfect or perhaps wholly abortive. But if, imitating the constitution of Pennsylvania, you vest all the legislative power in one body of men (separating the executive and judicial) elected for a short period, and necessarily excluded by rotation from permanency, and guarded from precipitancy and surprise by delays imposed on its proceedings, you will create the most perfect responsibility for then, whenever the people feel a grievance they cannot mistake the authors, and will apply the remedy with certainty and effect, discarding them at the next election. This tie of responsibility will obviate all the dangers apprehended from a single legislature, and will the best secure the rights of the people. . . .

The proposed plan of government . . . has none of the essential requisites of a free government; . . . it is neither founded on those balancing restraining powers, recommended by Mr. Adams and attempted in the British constitution, or possessed of that responsibility to its constituents, which, in my opinion, is the only effectual security for the liberties and happiness of the people; but on the contrary, that it is a most daring attempt to establish a despotic aristocracy among freemen, that the world has ever witnessed.

VIEWPOINT 5

"Can the liberties of three millions of people be securely trusted in the hands of 24 men? . . . Reason revolts at the idea."

The People Are Not Adequately Represented by Congress in the Constitution

Melancton Smith (1744-1798)

The question of how the people should be represented in the national government was a controversial issue, both during the Constitutional Convention and in the debates over ratification that followed. Regarding representation, the Constitution differed from existing state constitutions in several significant respects. Historian Paul Goodman writes in *The American Constitution:*

> Popularly elected legislative bodies that accurately mirrored the interests of citizens were regarded as the cornerstones of republican government. The state constitutions framed during the Revolution attempted to achieve this by keeping constituencies relatively small and socially uniform so that all the particular interests in the state had a voice in the assembly. Annual elections further made sure that legislators faithfully represented those who elected them or faced prompt removal. The Federal Constitution significantly departed from these practices. Members of the House of Representatives, the popularly elected branch of the Federal legislature, had two-year terms and their constituencies were large and relatively diverse.

The ability of the House of Representatives to reflect the wishes of the people is questioned here by Melancton Smith in arguments excerpted from a speech given on June 21, 1788, at the

From *Debates and Proceedings of the Convention of the State of New York*, Francis Childs, ed. New York, 1788.

New York ratifying convention. Smith, a New York merchant, politician, and veteran of the Revolutionary War, argues that the number of people in Congress is too small to adequately represent the people of America. He argues that the system proposed by the Constitution would not represent America's "middling class" and would lead to government corruption.

An honorable gentleman [Alexander Hamilton] has observed that it is a problem that cannot be solved, what the proper number is which ought to compose the house of representatives, and calls upon me to fix the number. I admit this is a question that will not admit of a solution with mathematical certainty—few political questions will—yet we may determine with certainty that certain numbers are too small or too large. We may be sure that ten is too small and a thousand too large a number—every one will allow that the first number is too small to possess the sentiments, be influenced by the interests of the people, or secure against corruption: A thousand would be too numerous to be capable of deliberating.

Who Should Be Represented?

To determine whether the number of representatives proposed by this Constitution is sufficient, it is proper to examine the qualifications which this house ought to possess, in order to exercise their powers discreetly for the happiness of the people. The idea that naturally suggests itself to our minds, when we speak of representatives is, that they resemble those they represent; they should be a true picture of the people; possess the knowledge of their circumstances and their wants; sympathize in all their distresses, and be disposed to seek their true interests. The knowledge necessary for the representatives of a free people, not only comprehends extensive political and commercial information, such as is acquired by men of refined education, who have leisure to attain to high degrees of improvement, but it should also comprehend that kind of acquaintance with the common concerns and occupations of the people, which men of the middling class of life are in general much better competent to, than those of a superior class. To understand the true commercial interests of a country, not only requires just ideas of the general commerce of the world, but also, and principally, a knowledge of the productions of your own country and their value, what your soil is capable of producing, the nature of your manufactures, and the capacity of the country to increase both. To exercise the power of laying taxes, duties and excises with discretion requires something more than an acquaintance with the abstruse parts of the system of finance. It calls for a knowledge of the circumstances and ability of the people in general, a discernment how the burdens imposed will bear upon the different classes.

The Meaning of Representation

In the third of sixteen essays by "Brutus" published in the New York Journal *between October 1787 and April 1788, the author argues that because of its small size, the House of Representatives fails to adequately represent the American people.*

The very term, representative, implies, that the person or body chosen for this purpose, should resemble those who appoint them—a representation of the people of America, if it be a true one, must be like the people. It ought to be so constituted, that a person, who is a stranger to the country, might be able to form a just idea of their character, by knowing that of their representatives. They are the sign—the people are the thing signified. It is absurd to speak of one thing being the representative of another, upon any other principle. The ground and reason of representation, in a free government, implies the same thing. Society instituted government to promote the happiness of the whole, and this is the great end always in view in the delegation of powers. It must then have been intended, that those who are placed instead of the people, should possess their sentiments and feelings, and be governed by their interests, or, in other words, should bear the strongest resemblance of those in whose room they are substituted. It is obvious, that for an assembly to be a true likeness of the people of any country, they must be considerably numerous.—One man, or a few men, cannot possibly represent the feelings, opinions, and characters of a great multitude. In this respect, the new constitution is radically defective.—The house of assembly, which is intended as a representation of the people of America, will not, nor cannot, in the nature of things, be a proper one—sixty-five men cannot be found in the United States, who hold the sentiments, possess the feelings, or are acquainted with the wants and interests of this vast country. This extensive continent is made up of a number of different classes of people; and to have a proper representation of them, each class ought to have an opportunity of choosing their best informed men for the purpose; but this cannot possibly be the case in so small a number.

From these observations results this conclusion that the number of representatives should be so large, as that while it embraces men of the first class, it should admit those of the middling class of life. I am convinced that this Government is so constituted, that the representatives will generally be composed of the first class in the community, which I shall distinguish by the name of the natural aristocracy of the country. I do not mean to give offence by using this term. I am sensible this idea is treated by many gentlemen as chimerical. I shall be asked what is meant by the natural aristocracy—and told that no such distinction of classes of men exists among us. It is true it is our singular felicity that we have no legal or hereditary distinctions of this kind; but still there are real differences: Every society naturally divides itself into classes. The author of nature has bestowed on some greater capacities than on others—birth, education, talents and wealth, create distinctions among men as visible and of as much influence as titles, stars and garters. In every society, men of this class will command a superior degree of respect—and if the government is so constituted as to admit but few to exercise the powers of it, it will, according to the natural course of things, be in their hands. Men in the middling class, who are qualified as representatives, will not be so anxious to be chosen as those of the first. When the number is so small the office will be highly elevated and distinguished—the stile in which the members live will probably be high—circumstances of this kind, will render the place of a representative not a desirable one to sensible, substantial men, who have been used to walk in the plain and frugal paths of life.

Government Will Fall into the Hands of the Wealthy

Besides, the influence of the great will generally enable them to succeed in elections—it will be difficult to combine a district of country containing 30 or 40,000 inhabitants, frame your election laws as you please, in any one character; unless it be in one of conspicuous, military, popular, civil or legal talents. The great easily form associations; the poor and middling class form them with difficulty. If the elections be by plurality, as probably will be the case in this state, it is almost certain, none but the great will be chosen—for they easily unite their interest—The common people will divide, and their divisions will be promoted by the others. There will be scarcely a chance of their uniting, in any other but some great man, unless in some popular demagogue, who will probably be destitute of principle. A substantial yeoman of sense and discernment, will hardly ever be chosen. From these remarks it appears that the government will fall into the hands of the few and the great. This will be a government of oppression. I do not mean to declaim against the great, and charge them indiscriminately with want of principle and honesty.—The same passions and prejudices govern all men. The circumstances in which men are placed in a great measure give a cast to the human character.

Those in middling circumstances, have less temptation—they are inclined by habit and the company with whom they associate, to set bounds to their passions and appetites—if this is not sufficient, the want of means to gratify them will be a restraint—they are obliged to employ their time in their respective callings—hence the substantial yeomanry of the country are more temperate, of better morals and less ambition than the great. The latter do not feel for the poor and middling class; the reasons are obvious—they are not obliged to use the pains and labour to procure property as the other.—They feel not the inconveniences arising from the payment of small sums. The great consider themselves above the common people—entitled to more respect—do not associate with them—they fancy themselves to have a right of pre-eminence in every thing. In short, they possess the same feelings, and are under the influence of the same motives, as an hereditary nobility. I know the idea that such a distinction exists in this country is ridiculed by some—But I am not the less apprehensive of danger from their influence on this account—Such distinctions exist all the world over—have been taken notice of by all writers on free government—and are founded in the nature of things. It has been the principal care of free governments to guard against the encroachments of the great. Common observation and experience prove the existence of such distinctions. Will any one say, that there does not exist in this country the pride of family, of wealth, of talents; and that they do not command influence and respect among the common people? Congress, in their address to the inhabitants of the province of Quebec, in 1775, state this distinction in the following forcible words quoted from the Marquis Beccaria. "In every human society, there is an essay continually tending to confer on one part the height of power and happiness, and to reduce the other to the extreme of weakness and misery. The intent of good laws is to oppose this effort, and to diffuse their influence universally and equally." We ought to guard against the government being placed in the hands of this class—They cannot have that sympathy with their constituents which is necessary to connect them closely to their interest: Being in the habit of profuse living, they will be profuse in the public expences. They find no difficulty in paying their taxes, and therefore do not feel public burthens: Besides if they govern, they will enjoy the emoluments of the government. The middling class, from their frugal habits, and feeling themselves the public burdens, will be careful how they increase them.

But I may be asked, would you exclude the first class in the community, from any share in legislation? I answer by no means—they would be more dangerous out of power than in it—they would be factious—discontented and constantly disturb-

Inadequate Representation

After Pennsylvania ratified the Constitution on December 12, 1787, the minority of delegates at the ratifying convention who opposed it published their reasons for dissent. Their statement of opposition, first published on December 18, was widely reprinted across the country. In this excerpt, they question whether the people are truly represented by the legislature and executive established by the Constitution.

The house of representatives is to consist of 65 members; that is one for about every 50,000 inhabitants, to be chosen every two years. Thirty-three members will form a quorum for doing business; and 17 of these, being the majority, determine the sense of the house.

The senate, the other constituent branch of the legislature, consists of 26 members being *two* from each state, appointed by their legislatures every six years—fourteen senators make a quorum; the majority of whom, eight, determines the sense of that body. . . .

The president is to have the control over the enacting of laws, so far as to make the concurrence of *two* thirds of the representatives and senators present necessary, if he should object to the laws.

Thus it appears that the liberties, happiness, interests, and great concerns of the whole United States, may be dependent upon the integrity, virtue, wisdom, and knowledge of 25 or 26 men—How unadequate and unsafe a representation! Inadequate, because the sense and views of 3 or 4 millions of people diffused over so extensive a territory comprising such various climates, products, habits, interests, and opinions, cannot be collected in so small a body; and besides, it is not a fair and equal representation of the people even in proportion to its number, for the smallest state has as much weight in the senate as the largest, and from the smallness of the number to be chosen for both branches of the legislature; and from the mode of election and appointment, which is under the control of Congress; and from the nature of the thing, men of the most elevated rank in life, will alone be chosen. The other orders in the society, such as farmers, traders, and mechanics, who all ought to have a competent number of their best informed men in the legislature, will be totally unrepresented.

ing the government—it would also be unjust—they have their liberties to protect as well as others—and the largest share of property. But my idea is, that the Constitution should be so framed as to admit this class, together with a sufficient number of the middling class to control them. You will then combine the abilities and honesty of the community—a proper degree of information, and a disposition to pursue the the public good. A representative body, composed principally of respectable yeomanry is the best possible security to liberty.—When the interest of this part of the community is pursued, the public good is pursued, because the body of every nation consists of this class. And because the interest of both the rich and the poor are involved in that of the middling class. No burden can be laid on the poor, but what will sensibly affect the middling class. Any law rendering property insecure, would be injurious to them.—When therefore this class of society pursue their own interest, they promote that of the public, for it is involved in it.

The Danger of Corruption

In so small a number of representatives, there is great danger from corruption and combination. A great politician has said that every man has his price. I hope this is not true in all its extent— But I ask the gentlemen to inform, what government there is, in which it has not been practised? Notwithstanding all that has been said of the defects in the Constitution of the antient Confederacies of the Grecian Republics, their destruction is to be imputed more to this cause than to any imperfection in their forms of government. This was the deadly poison that effected their dissolution. This is an extensive country, increasing in population and growing in consequence. Very many lucrative offices will be in the grant of the government, which will be the object of avarice and ambition. How easy will it be to gain over a sufficient number, in the bestowment of these offices, to promote the views and purposes of those who grant them! Foreign corruption is also to be guarded against. A system of corruption is known to be the system of government in Europe. It is practised without blushing. And we may lay it to our account it will be attempted amongst us. The most effectual as well as natural security against this, is a strong democratic branch in the legislature frequently chosen, including in it a number of the substantial, sensible yeomanry of the country. Does the house of representatives answer this description? I confess, to me they hardly wear the complexion of a democratic branch—they appear the mere shadow of representation. The whole number in both houses amounts to 91—Of these 46 make a quorum; and 24 of those being secured, may carry any point. Can the liberties of three millions of people be securely trusted in the hands of 24 men? Is it prudent to commit to so small a number the decision of the great questions which will come before them? Reason revolts at the idea.

The honorable gentleman from New York has said that 65 members in the house of representatives are sufficient for the present situation of the country, and taking it for granted that they will increase as one for 30,000, in 25 years they will amount to 200. It is admitted by this observation that the number fixed in the Constitution, is not sufficient without it is augmented. It is not declared that an increase shall be made, but is left to the discretion of the legislature, by the gentleman's own concession; therefore the Constitution is imperfect. We certainly ought to fix in the Constitution those things which are essential to liberty. If any thing falls under this description, it is the number of the legislature. To say, as this gentleman does, that our security is to depend upon the spirit of the people, who will be watchful of their liberties, and not suffer them to be infringed, is absurd. It would equally prove that we might adopt any form of government. I believe were we to create a despot, he would not immediately dare to act the tyrant; but it would not be long before he would destroy the spirit of the people, or the people would destroy him. If our people have a high sense of liberty, the government should be congenial to this spirit—calculated to cherish the love of liberty, while yet it had sufficient force to restrain licentiousness. Government operates upon the spirit of the people, as well as the spirit of the people operates upon it—and if they are not comformable to each other, the one or the other will prevail. In a less time than 25 years, the government will receive its tone. What the spirit of the country may be at the end of that period, it is impossible to foretel: Our duty is to frame a government friendly to liberty and the rights of mankind, which will tend to cherish and cultivate a love of liberty among our citizens. If this government becomes oppressive it will be by degrees: It will aim at its end by disseminating sentiments of government opposite to republicanism; and proceed from step to step in depriving the people of a share in the government. A recollection of the change that has taken place in the minds of many in this country in the course of a few years, ought to put us upon our guard. Many who are ardent advocates for the new system, reprobate republican principles as chimerical and such as ought to be expelled from society. Who would have thought ten years ago, that the very men who risqued their lives and fortunes in support of republican principles, would now treat them as the fictions of fancy?—A few years ago we fought for liberty—We framed a general government on free principles—We placed the state legislatures, in whom the people have a full and fair representation, between Congress and the people. We were then, it is true, too cautious; and too much restricted the powers of the general government. But now it is proposed to go into the contrary, and a more dangerous extreme; to remove all barriers; to give the New Government free access to our pockets, and ample command of our persons; and that without providing for a genuine and fair representation of the people. No one can say what the progress of the change of sentiment may be in 25 years. The same men who now cry up the necessity of an energetic government, to induce a compliance with this system, may in much less time reprobate this in as severe terms as they now do the con-

143

federation, and may as strongly urge the necessity of going as far beyond this, as this is beyond the Confederation.—Men of this class are increasing—they have influence, talents and industry— It is time to form a barrier against them. And while we are willing to establish a government adequate to the purposes of the union, let us be careful to establish it on the broad basis of equal liberty.

"Why will not ninety-one be an adequate and safe representation? This at present appears to be the proper medium."

The People Are Adequately Represented by Congress in the Constitution

Alexander Hamilton (1755-1804)

Alexander Hamilton, former military aide to George Washington in the Revolutionary War and New York delegate to the 1787 Constitutional Convention, led the fight for getting the Constitution ratified in New York. Hamilton succeeded in part through his arguments, both written and oral, and in part through delaying tactics that prolonged the ratifying convention. By the time the question of ratification came up for a vote on July 26, 1788, the minimum nine states had already ratified the Constitution. This put the Constitution into effect, leaving New York and the three other remaining states with the choice of ratification or withdrawing from the United States.

The following is excerpted from a June 21 debate with Melancton Smith, the leader of the anti-federalist forces at the New York ratifying convention. Hamilton answers Smith's criticisms that there are too few legislators in the proposed Congress to give the people adequate representation. He defends the relatively large congressional districts, attacks the idea of pure democracy, argues that the president will also be a representative of the people, and defends the Constitution as "a genuine specimen of representative and republican government."

From *Debates and Proceedings of the Convention of the State of New York*, Francis Childs, ed. New York, 1788.

M<small>r.</small> *Hamilton* then reassumed his argument. When, said he, I had the honor to address the committee yesterday, I gave a history of the circumstances which attended the Convention, when forming the Plan before you. I endeavored to point out to you the principles of accommodation, on which this arrangement was made; and to shew that the contending interests of the States led them to establish the representation as it now stands. In the second place I attempted to prove, that, in point of number, the representation would be perfectly secure.

People Will Regulate the Representatives

Sir, no man agrees more perfectly than myself to the main principle for which the gentlemen contend. I agree that there should be a broad democratic branch in the national legislature. But this matter, Sir, depends on circumstances; It is impossible, in the first instance to be precise and exact with regard to the number; and it is equally impossible to determine to what point it may be proper in future to increase it. On this ground I am disposed to acquiesce. In my reasonings on the subject of government, I rely more on the interests and the opinions of men, than on any speculative parchment provisions whatever. I have found, that Constitutions are more or less excellent as they are more or less agreeable to the natural operation of things—I am therefore disposed not to dwell long on curious speculations, or pay much attention to modes and forms; but to adopt a system, whose principles have been sanctioned by experience; adapt it to the real state of our country; and depend on probable reasonings for its operation and result. I contend that sixty-five and twenty-six in two bodies afford perfect security, in the present state of things; and that the regular progressive enlargement, which was in the contemplation of the General Convention, will leave not an apprehension of danger in the most timid and suspicious mind. It will be the interest of the large states to increase the representation: This will be the standing instruction to their delegates.—But, say the gentlemen, the Members of Congress will be interested not to increase the number, as it will diminish their relative influence. In all their reasoning upon the subject, there seems to be this fallacy:—They suppose that the representative will have no motive of action, on the one side, but a sense of duty; or on the other, but corruption:—They do not reflect, that he is to return to the community; that he is dependent on the will of the people, and that it cannot be his interest to oppose their wishes. Sir, the general sense of the people will regulate the conduct of their representatives. I admit that there are exceptions to this rule: There are certain conjunctures, when it may be necessary and proper to disregard the opinions which the majority of the people have formed: But in the general course of things, the popular views and even prejudices will direct the actions of the rulers.

All governments, even the most despotic, depend, in a great degree, on opinion. In free republics, it is most peculiarly the case: In these, the will of the people makes the essential principle of the government; and the laws which control the community, receive their tone and spirit from the public wishes. It is the fortunate situation of our country, that the minds of the people are exceedingly enlightened and refined: Here then we may expect the laws to be proportionably agreeable to the standard of perfect policy; and the wisdom of public measures to consist with the most intimate conformity between the views of the representative and his constituent. If the general view of the people be for an increase, it undoubtedly must take place: They have it in their power to instruct their representatives; and the State Legislatures, which appoint the Senators, may enjoin it also upon them. Sir, if I believed that the number would remain at sixty-five, I confess I should give my vote for an amendment; though in a different form from the one proposed.

The Proper Ratio

The amendment proposes a ratio of one for twenty thousand: I would ask, by what rule or reasoning it is determined, that one man is a better representative for twenty than thirty thousand? At present we have three millions of people; in twenty-five years, we shall have six millions; and in forty years, nine millions: And this is a short period, as it relates to the existence of States. Here then, according to the ratio of one for thirty thousand, we shall have, in forty years, three hundred representatives. If this be true, and if this be a safe representation, why be dissatisfied? why embarrass the Constitution with amendments, that are merely speculative and useless. I agree with the gentleman [Melancton Smith], that a very small number might give some colour for suspicion: I acknowledge, that ten would be unsafe; on the other hand, a thousand would be too numerous. But I ask him, why will not ninety-one be an adequate and safe representation? This at present appears to be the proper medium. Besides, the President of the United States will be himself the representative of the people. From the competition that ever subsists between the branches of government, the President will be induced to protect their rights, whenever they are invaded by either branch. On whatever side we view this subject, we discover various and powerful checks to the encroachments of Congress. The true and permanent interests of the members are opposed to corruption: Their number is vastly

147

A Sufficient Number

Robert R. Livingston, who in 1776 helped draft the Declaration of Independence, was one of the strongest supporters of the Constitution at the New York ratifying convention. On June 23, 1788, following the heated debates between Melancton Smith and Alexander Hamilton on the issue of representation, he gave his own views on the matter.

Much has been said, Sir, about the number which ought to compose the house of representatives, and the question has been debated with great address by the gentlemen on both sides of the house. It is agreed, that the representative body should be so small, as to prevent the disorder inseparable from the deliberations of a mob; and yet sufficiently numerous, to represent the interests of the people; and to be a safe depository of power. There is, unfortunately, no standard, by which we can determine this matter. Gentlemen who think that a hundred may be the medium, in which the advantages of regular deliberation, and the safety of the people are united, will probably be disposed to support the plan as it stands; others, who imagine that no number less than three or four hundred can ensure the preservation of liberty, will contend for an alteration. Indeed, these effects depend so much upon contingency, and upon circumstances totally unconnected with the idea of number; that we ought not to be surprized at the want of a standing criterion. On so vague a subject, it is very possible that the opinions of no two gentlemen in this assembly, if they were governed by their own original reflections, would entirely coincide. I acknowledge myself one of those who suppose the number expressed in the constitution to be about the proper medium; and yet future experience may induce me to think it too small or too large. When I consider the objects and powers of the general government, I am of an opinion that one hundred men may at all times be collected, of sufficient information and integrity, to manage well the affairs of the union. Some gentlemen suppose, that to understand and provide for the general interests of commerce and manufactures, our legislatures ought to know how all commodities are produced, from the first principle of vegetation to the last polish of mechanical labour; that they ought to be minutely acquainted with all the process of all the arts: if this were true, it would be necessary, that a great part of the British house of commons should be woolen drapers: Yet, we seldom find such characters in that celebrated assembly.

too large for easy combination: The rivalship between the houses will forever prove an insuperable obstacle: The people have an obvious and powerful protection in their own State governments: Should any thing dangerous be attempted, these bodies of perpetual observation, will be capable of forming and conducting plans of regular opposition. Can we suppose the people's love of liberty will not, under the incitement of their legislative leaders, be roused into resistance, and the madness of tyranny be extinguished at a blow? Sir, the danger is too distant; it is beyond all rational calculations.

It has been observed by an honorable gentleman [John Williams], that a pure democracy, if it were practicable, would be the most perfect government. Experience has proved, that no position in politics is more false than this. The ancient democracies, in which the people themselves deliberated, never possessed one feature of good government.—Their very character was tyranny; their figure deformity:—When they assembled, the field of debate presented an ungovernable mob, not only incapable of deliberation, but prepared for every enormity. In these assemblies, the enemies of the people brought forward their plans of ambition systematically. They were opposed by their enemies of another party; and it became a matter of contingency, whether the people subjected themselves to be led blindly by one tyrant or by another.

It was remarked yesterday, that a numerous representation was necessary to obtain the confidence of the people. This is not generally true. The confidence of the people will easily be gained by a good administration. This is the true touchstone. I could illustrate the position, by a variety of historical examples, both ancient and modern. In Sparta, the Ephori were a body of magistrates, instituted as a check upon the senate, and representing the people. They consisted of only five men: But they were able to protect their rights, and therefore enjoyed their confidence and attachment. In Rome, the people were represented by three Tribunes, who were afterwards increased to ten. Every one acquainted with the history of that republic, will recollect how powerful a check to the senatorial encroachments, this small body proved; how unlimited a confidence was placed in them by the people whose guardians they were; and to what a conspicuous station in the government, their influence at length elevated the Plebians. Massachusetts has three hundred representatives; New-York has sixty-five. Have the people in this state less confidence in their representation, than the people of that? Delaware has twenty-one. Do the inhabitants of New York feel a higher confidence than those of Delaware? I have stated these examples, to prove that the gentleman's principle is not just. The popular confidence depends on circumstances very distinct from considerations of number. Probably the public attachment is more strongly secured by a train of prosperous events, which are the result of wise deliberation and vigorous execution, and to which large bodies are much less competent than small ones. If the representative conducts with propriety, he will necessarily enjoy the good will of the constituent. It appears then, if my reasoning be just, that the clause is perfectly proper, upon the principles of the gentleman who contends for the amendment: as there is in it the greatest degree of present security, and a moral certainty of an increase equal to our utmost wishes.

Not All Interests Should Be Represented

It has been farther, by the gentlemen in opposition, observed, that a large representation is necessary to understand the interests of the people—This principle is by no means true in the extent to which the gentleman seems to carry it. I would ask, why may not a man understand the interests of thirty as well as of twenty? The position appears to be made upon the unfounded presumption, that all the interests of all parts of the community must be represented. No idea is more erroneous than this. Only such interests are proper to be represented, as are involved in the powers of the General Government. These interests come compleatly under the observation of one, or a few men; and the requisite information is by no means augmented in proportion to the increase of number. What are the objects of the Government? Commerce, taxation, &c. In order to comprehend the interests of commerce, is it necessary to know how wheat is raised, and in what proportion it is produced in one district and in another? By no means. Neither is this species of knowledge necessary in general calculations upon the subject of taxation. The information necessary for these purposes, is that which is open to every intelligent enquirer; and of which, five men may be as perfectly possessed as fifty. In royal governments, there are usually particular men to whom the business of taxation is committed. These men have the forming of systems of finance; and the regulation of the revenue. I do not mean to recommend this practice. It proves however, this point; that a few individuals may be competent to these objects; and that large numbers are not necessary to perfection in the science of taxation. But, granting for a moment, that this minute and local knowledge the gentlemen contend for, is necessary, let us see, if under the New Constitution, it will not probably be found in the representation. The natural and proper mode of holding elections, will be to divide the state into districts, in proportion to the number to be elected. This state will consequently be divided at first into six. One man from each district will probably possess all the knowledge the gentlemen can desire. Are the senators of this state more ignorant of the interests of the people, than the assembly? Have they not ever enjoyed their confidence as much? Yet, instead of six districts, they are elected in four; and the chance of their being collected from the smaller divisions of the state consequently diminished. Their number is but twenty-four; and their powers are co-extensive with those of the assembly, and reach objects, which are most dear to the people—life, liberty and property.

Sir, we hear constantly a great deal, which is rather calculated to awake our passions, and create prejudices, than to conduct us to truth, and teach us our real interests.—I do not suppose this to be the design of the gentlemen.—Why then are we told so often of an aristocracy? For my part, I hardly know the meaning of this word as it is applied. If all we hear be true, this government is really a very bad one. But who are the aristocracy among us? Where do we find men elevated to a perpetual rank above their fellow citizens; and possessing powers entirely independent of them? The arguments of the gentlemen only go to prove that there are men who are rich, men who are poor, some who are wise, and others who are not—That indeed every distinguished man is an aristocrat.—This reminds me of a description of the aristocrats, I have seen in a late publication, styled the Federal Farmer.—The author reckons in the aristocracy, all governors of states, members of Congress, chief magistrates, and all officers of the militia.—This description, I presume to say, is ridiculous.— The image is a phantom. Does the new government render a rich man more eligible than a poor one? No. It requires no such qualification. It is bottomed on the broad and equal principle of your state constitution.

Sir, if the people have it in their option, to elect their most meritorious men; is this to be considered as an objection? Shall the constitution oppose their wishes, and abridge their most invaluable privilege? While property continues to be pretty equally divided, and a considerable share of information pervades the community; the tendency of the people's suffrages, will be to elevate merit even from obscurity—As riches increase and accumulate in few hands;—as luxury prevails in society; virtue will be in a greater degree considered as only a graceful appendage of wealth, and the tendency of things will be to depart from the republican standard. This is the real disposition of human nature: It is what, neither the honorable member nor myself can correct—It is a common misfortune, that awaits our state constitution, as well as all others.

Advantages of Large Districts

There is an advantage incident to large districts of election, which perhaps the gentlemen, amidst all their apprehensions of influence and bribery, have not adverted to. In large districts, the corruption of the electors is much more difficult:—Combinations for the purposes of intrigue are less easily formed: Factions and cabals are little known. In a small district, wealth will have a more complete influence; because the people in the vicinity of a great

151

man, are more immediately his dependants, and because this influence has fewer objects to act upon. It has been remarked, that it would be disagreeable to the middle class of men to go to the seat of the new government. If this be so, the difficulty will be enhanced by the gentleman's proposal. If his arguments be true, it proves that the larger the representation is, the less will be your choice of having it filled. But, it appears to me frivolous to bring forward such arguments as these. It has answered no other purpose, than to induce me, by way of reply, to enter into discussions, which I consider as useless, and not applicable to our subject.

Although he expressed much disagreement with other delegates at the Constitutional Convention where the Constitution was written, Alexander Hamilton led the fight for its ratification in New York.

It is a harsh doctrine, that men grow wicked in proportion as they improve and enlighten their minds. Experience has by no means justified us in the supposition, that there is more virtue in one class of men than in another. Look through the rich and the poor of the community; the learned and the ignorant.—Where does virtue predominate? The difference indeed consists, not in the quantity but kind of vices, which are incident to the various classes; and here the advantage of character belongs to the wealthy. Their vices are probably more favorable to the prosperity of the state, than those of the indigent; and partake less of moral depravity.

After all, Sir, we must submit to this idea, that the true principle of a republic is, that the people should choose whom they please to govern them. Representation is imperfect, in proportion as the current of popular favour is checked.—This great source of free government, popular election, should be perfectly pure, and the most unbounded liberty allowed. Where this principle is adhered to; where, in the organization of the government, the legislative, executive and judicial branches are rendered distinct; where again the legislative is divided into separate houses, and the operations of each are controuled by various checks and balances, and above all, by the vigilance and weight of the state governments; to talk of tyranny, and the subversion of our liberties, is to speak the language of enthusiasm. This balance between the national and the state governments ought to be dwelt on with peculiar attention, as it is of the utmost importance.—It forms a double security to the people. If one encroaches on their rights, they will find a powerful protection in the other.—Indeed they will both be prevented from overpassing their constitutional limits, by a certain rivalship, which will ever subsist between them.—I am persuaded, that a firm union is as necessary to perpetuate our liberties, as it is to make us respectable; and experience will probably prove, that the national government will be as natural a guardian of our freedom, as the state legislatures themselves.

Suggestions, Sir, of an extraordinary nature, have been frequently thrown out in the course of the present political controversy. It gives me pain to dwell on topics of this kind; and I wish they might be dismissed. We have been told, that the old Confederation has proved inefficacious, only because intriguing and powerful men, aiming at a revolution, have been forever instigating the people, and rendering them disaffected with it. This, Sir, is a false insinuation—The thing is impossible. I will venture to assert, that no combination of designing men under Heaven, will be capable of making a government unpopular, which is in its principles a wise and good one; and vigorous in its operations.

A Genuine Republic

The Confederation was framed amidst the agitation and tumult of society.—It was composed of unsound materials put together in haste. Men of intelligence discovered the feebleness of the structure, in the first stages of its existence; but the great body of the people, too much engrossed with their distresses, to contemplate any but the immediate causes of them, were ignorant of the defects of their Constitution.—But, when the dangers of war were removed, they saw clearly what they had suffered, and what they had yet to suffer from a feeble form of government. There was no need of discerning men to convince the people of their unhappy situation—the complaint was co-extensive with the evil, and both were common to all classes of the community. We have been told, that the spirit of patriotism and love of liberty are almost extin-

153

guished among the people; and that it has become a prevailing doctrine, that republican principles ought to be hooted out of the world. Sir, I am confident that such remarks as these are rather occasioned by the heat of argument, than by a cool conviction of their truth and justice. As far as my experience has extended, I have heard no such doctrine, nor have I discovered any diminution of regard for those rights and liberties, in defence of which, the people have fought and suffered. There have been, undoubtedly, some men who have had speculative doubts on the subject of government; but the principles of republicanism are founded on too firm a basis to be shaken by a few speculative and sceptical reasoners. Our error has been of a very different kind. We have erred through excess of caution, and a zeal false and impracticable. Our counsels have been destitute of consistency and stability. I am flattered with a hope, Sir, that we have now found a cure for the evils under which we have so long labored. I trust, that the proposed Constitution affords a genuine specimen of representative and republican government—and that it will answer, in an eminent degree, all the beneficial purposes of society.

VIEWPOINT 7

"The Society implore[s] the present Convention to make the Suppression of the African trade in the United States, a part of their important deliberations."

The Constitution Should Prohibit the Slave Trade

Pennsylvania Society for the Abolition of Slavery

Slavery was a controversial and divisive topic at the Constitutional Convention. At the time several northern states had already taken steps to abolish slavery. Slavery remained entrenched in the southern states, however, where more than 600,000 slaves formed an important part of the economy and society.

Some people saw the creation of the Constitution as an opportunity to take steps to abolish slavery in the United States. The following viewpoint is taken from an address to the Constitutional Convention written by the Pennsylvania Society for the Abolition of Slavery. The organization, started in 1775 and revived in 1784, was the nation's first abolitionist organization. Its president in 1787 was Benjamin Franklin, who was one of Pennsylvania's delegates to the Constitutional Convention. On June 2, 1787, the society submitted a petition for Franklin to present to the Convention. It deplored the slave trade and called for the Convention to suppress it. Franklin, however, perhaps mindful of the divisions it would cause, never introduced the petition. Delegates from the South were adamant in their position that the Constitution should not jeopardize the institution of slavery. Despite the antislavery leanings of Franklin and other delegates, the Constitution included a clause which would prevent the national government from legislating any slave trade restrictions until 1808.

Address of the Pennsylvania Society for the Abolition of Slavery, June 2, 1787. Philadelphia: Historical Society of Pennsylvania.

To the honorable the Convention of the United States of America now assembled in the City of Philadelphia. The memorial of the Pennsylvania Society for promoting the Abolition of Slavery and the releif of free Negroes unlawfully held in bondage.

The Pennsylvania Society for promoting the Abolition of Slavery and the releif of free Negroes unlawfully held in Bondage rejoice with their fellow Citizens in beholding a Convention of the States assembled for the purpose of amending the federal Constitution.

They recollect with pleasure, that among the first Acts of the illustrious [Continental] Congress of the Year 1774 was a resolution for prohibiting the Importation of African Slaves.

It is with deep distress they are forced to observe that the peace was scarcely concluded before the African Trade was revived and American Vessels employed in transporting the Inhabitants of Africa to cultivate as Slaves the soil of America before it had drank in all the blood which had been shed in her struggle for liberty.

To the revival of this trade the Society ascribe part of the Obloquy with which foreign Nations have branded our infant States. In vain will be their Pretentions to a love of liberty or a regard for national Character, while they share in the profits of a Commerce that can only be conducted upon Rivers of human tears and Blood.

By all the Attributes, therefore, of the Deity which are offended by this inhuman traffic—by the Union of our whole species in a common Ancestor and by all the Obligations which result from

The Constitution explicitly protected the slave trade from legislative repeal until 1808, the year this engraving of slaves just arrived from Africa was published.

it—by the apprehensions and terror of the righteous Vengeance of God in national Judgements—by the certainty of the great and awful day of retribution—by the efficacy of the Prayers of good Men, which would only insult the Majesty of Heaven, if offered up in behalf of our Country while the Iniquity we deplore continues among us—by the sanctity of the Christian Name—by the Pleasures of domestic Connections and the pangs which attend there Dissolutions—by the Captivity and Sufferings of our *American* bretheren in Algiers which seem to be intended by divine Providence to awaken us to a Sense of the Injustice and Cruelty of dooming our *African* Bretheren to perpetual Slavery and Misery—by a regard to the consistency of principles and Conduct which should mark the Citizens of Republics—by the magnitude and intensity of our desires to promote the happiness of those millions of intelligent beings who will probably cover this immense Continent with rational life—and by every other consideration that religion Reason Policy and Humanity can suggest the Society implore the present Convention to make the Suppression of the African trade in the United States, a part of their important deliberations.

Signed by order of the Society

June the 2 1787

Jonathan Penrose Vice President

VIEWPOINT 8

"By this article after the year 1808, the congress will have power to prohibit such importation. . . . I consider this as laying the foundation for banishing slavery."

Continuing the Slave Trade Was a Necessary Compromise

James Wilson (1742-1798)

The issue of slavery provoked several intense debates in the Constitutional Convention and in the subsequent debates over ratification. Delegates from North and South Carolina and Georgia argued that their states would never accept the Constitution if slavery was threatened. The Convention eventually formulated a complex compromise, part of which stated that the national government could not prohibit the slave trade until after the year 1808.

This compromise came under attack at several of the state ratifying conventions, including the Pennsylvania convention, which met from November 20 to December 15, 1787. The following viewpoint is taken from a speech made by James Wilson on December 3, in which he defends the slave trade clause of the Constitution. Wilson, a Constitutional Convention delegate and one of the main architects of the Constitution, defends the slave trade clause as the best compromise that could be obtained, and predicts the gradual elimination of slavery in the United States.

From *Debates of the Convention, of the State of Pennsylvania on the Constitution, Proposed for the Government of the United States*, Thomas Lloyd, ed. Philadelphia, 1788.

With respect to the clause, restricting congress from prohibiting the migration or importation of such persons, as any of the states now existing, shall think proper to admit, prior to the year 1808. The honorable gentleman [William Findley] says, that this clause is not only dark, but intended to grant to congress, for that time, the power to admit the importation of slaves. No such thing was intended; but I will tell you what was done, and it give me high pleasure, that so much was done. Under the present confederation, the states may admit the importation of slaves as long as they please; but by this article after the year 1808, the congress will have power to prohibit such importation, notwithstanding the disposition of any state to the contrary. I consider this as laying the foundation for banishing slavery out of this country; and though the period is more distant than I could wish, yet it will produce the same kind, gradual change, which was pursued in Pennsylvania. It is with much satisfaction I view this power in the general government, whereby they may lay an interdiction on this reproachful trade; but an immediate advantage is also obtained, for a tax or duty may be imposed on such importation,

Preserving the Union

James Madison, an owner of slaves, spoke against the slave trade at the Constitutional Convention, but he accepted its compromises on the issue as a necessary price to assure the support of all the states for the Constitution. In this passage from a June 17, 1788, speech at the Virginia ratifying convention, Madison responds to George Mason's criticisms of the slave trade provisions in the Constitution.

I should conceive this clause to be impolitic, if it were one of those things which could be excluded without encountering greater evils.—The Southern States would not have entered into the Union of America, without the temporary permission of that trade. And if they were excluded from the Union, the consequences might be dreadful to them and to us. We are not in a worse situation than before. That traffic is prohibited by our laws, and we may continue the prohibition. The Union in general is not in a worse situation. Under the articles of Confederation, it might be continued forever: But by this clause an end may be put to it after twenty years. There is therefore an amelioration of our circumstances. . . . Great as the evil is, a dismemberment of the Union would be worse. If those States should disunite from the other States, for not indulging them in the temporary continuance of this traffic, they might solicit and obtain aid from foreign powers.

not exceeding ten dollars for each person; and, this sir, operates as a partial prohibition; it was all that could be obtained, I am sorry it was no more; but from this I think there is reason to hope, that yet a few years, and it will be prohibited altogether; and in the mean time, the new states which are to be formed, will be under the control of congress in this particular; and slaves will never be introduced amongst them.

The gentleman says, that it is unfortunate in another point of view; it means to prohibit the introduction of white people from Europe, as this tax may deter them from coming amongst us; a little impartiality and attention will discover the care that the convention took in selecting their language. The words are, the *migration or* IMPORTATION of such persons, &c. shall not be prohibited by congress prior to the year 1808, but a tax or duty may be imposed on such IMPORTATION; it is observable here, that the term migration is dropped, when a tax or duty is mentioned; so that congress have power to impose the tax, only on those imported.

CHAPTER 4

Creating the Office of President

Chapter Preface

The creation of the presidency was the focus of much debate and contention, both within the Constitutional Convention and during the subsequent ratification debates. The creators of the Constitution sought to create an executive strong enough to execute the laws and unite the nation, yet not so strong as to become an elected monarch.

Among the proposals discussed and rejected at the Constitutional Convention were making the executive a committee of three people, not paying the president a salary, ruling the president ineligible for reelection, and making the president answerable to a constitutionally established "privy council" of advisers. James Wilson, a Pennsylvania delegate who served on the Convention's Committee of Detail, was instrumental in creating the office of a single executive with a legislative veto and responsibility for foreign affairs. In spite of his arguments that the president should be elected directly by the people, the Convention, after much debate, settled on the method of choosing the president by "electors" selected by the states.

Supporters of the Constitution had to overcome fears that the president would turn into a despot or a king—an argument frequently found in anti-federalist literature. Perhaps the most important person in the debates over the executive was one who spoke and wrote little: George Washington. The Virginia planter who had been commander in chief of the American armed forces during the Revolutionary War was viewed by many as the obvious choice to be the first president. His repeated statements in support of republicanism and his previous retirement from public life following the Revolutionary War reassured many Americans, including the writers of the Constitution, that America's first president, at least, would not turn king.

VIEWPOINT 1

"Decision, activity, secrecy, and dispatch will generally characterise the proceedings of one man . . . [more] than the proceedings of any greater number."

The Executive Should Be One Person

Alexander Hamilton (1755-1804)

Alexander Hamilton, a military aide to George Washington during the Revolutionary War and later secretary of the treasury during Washington's presidency, was one of the main advocates for a stronger national government to replace the Articles of Confederation. A New York delegate to the Constitutional Convention in Philadelphia, Hamilton's role and influence were limited, in part because he was continually outvoted by other members of his own New York delegation. However, he did play a major role in getting the Constitution ratified in New York in 1788.

As part of the ratification effort Hamilton organized and wrote, along with James Madison and John Jay, a series of newspaper articles explaining and supporting the different parts of the new Constitution. The essays, written under the pseudonym of "Publius," were later published in book form as *The Federalist*. The following is taken from *Federalist* No. 70, in which Hamilton defends the office of the president as created by the Constitution. He argues that the need for an "energetic" executive is best served when the executive is a single person, and opposes proposals for a plural executive or for the constitutional creation of an executive council that would oversee and share powers with the president.

From "Publius," open letter "To the People of the State of New York" (*Federalist* no. 70), New York *Independent Journal*, May 1788.

There is an idea, which is not without its advocates, that a vigorous executive is inconsistent with the genius of republican government. The enlightened well wishers to this species of government must at least hope that the supposition is destitute of foundation; since they can never admit its truth, without at the same time admitting the condemnation of their own principles. Energy in the executive is a leading character in the definition of good government. It is essential to the protection of the community against foreign attacks: It is not less essential to the steady administration of the laws, to the protection of property against those irregular and high handed combinations, which sometimes interrupt the ordinary course of justice, to the security of liberty against the enterprises and assaults of ambition, of faction and of anarchy. Every man the least conversant in Roman story knows how often that republic was obliged to take refuge in the absolute power of a single man, under the formidable title of dictator, as well against the intrigues of ambitious individuals, who aspired to the tyranny, and the seditions of whole classes of the community, whose conduct threatened the existence of all government, as against the invasions of external enemies, who menaced the conquest and destruction of Rome.

There can be no need however to multiply arguments or examples on this head. A feeble executive implies a feeble execution of the government. A feeble execution is but another phrase for a bad execution: And a government ill executed, whatever it may be in theory, must be in practice a bad government.

Taking it for granted, therefore, that all men of sense will agree in the necessity of an energetic executive; it will only remain to inquire, what are the ingredients which constitute this energy— how far can they be combined with those other ingredients which constitute safety in the republican sense? And how far does this combination characterise the plan, which has been reported by the convention?

The ingredients, which constitute energy in the executive, are first unity, secondly duration, thirdly an adequate provision for its support, fourthly competent powers.

The circumstances which constitute safety in the republican sense are, Ist. a due dependence on the people, secondly a due responsibility.

Those politicians and statesmen, who have been the most celebrated for the soundness of their principles, and for the justness of their views, have declared in favor of a single executive and a numerous legislature. They have with great propriety considered energy as the most necessary qualification of the former, and have regarded this as most applicable to power in a single hand; while they have with equal propriety considered the latter as best adapted to deliberation and wisdom, and best calculated to conciliate the confidence of the people and to secure their privileges and interests.

That unity is conducive to energy will not be disputed. Decision, activity, secrecy, and dispatch will generally characterise the proceedings of one man, in a much more eminent degree, than the proceedings of any greater number; and in proportion as the number is increased, these qualities will be diminished.

The expectation that George Washington would be the nation's first president greatly influenced the Constitutional Convention's shaping of that office. Washington was able to find time in July 1787, while the Convention was in session, to sit for this portrait by Charles Willson Peale.

This unity may be destroyed in two ways; either by vesting the power in two or more magistrates of equal dignity and authority; or by vesting it ostensibly in one man, subject in whole or in part to the controul and co-operation of others, in the capacity of counsellors to him. Of the first the two consuls of Rome may serve as an example; of the last we shall find examples in the constitutions of several of the states. New-York and New-Jersey, if I recollect right, are the only states, which have entrusted the executive authority wholly to single men. Both these methods of destroying the unity of the executive have their partisans; but the votaries of an executive council are the most numerous. They are both liable, if not to equal, to similar objections; and may in most lights be examined in conjunction.

The experience of other nations will afford little instruction on this head. As far however as it teaches any thing, it teaches us not to be inamoured of plurality in the executive. We have seen that the Achæans on an experiment of two Prætors, were induced to abolish one. The Roman history records many instances of mischiefs to the republic from the dissentions between the consuls, and between the military tribunes, who were at times substituted to the consuls. But it gives us no specimens of any peculiar advantages derived to the state, from the circumstance of the plurality of those magistrates. . . .

But quitting the dim light of historical research, and attaching ourselves purely to the dictates of reason and good sense, we shall discover much greater cause to reject than to approve the idea of plurality in the executive, under any modification whatever.

Unnecessary Divisions

Wherever two or more persons are engaged in any common enterprize or pursuit, there is always danger of difference of opinion. If it be a public trust or office in which they are cloathed with equal dignity and authority, there is peculiar danger of personal emulation and even animosity. From either and especially from all these causes, the most bitter dissentions are apt to spring. Whenever these happen, they lessen the respectability, weaken the authority, and distract the plans and operations of those whom they divide. If they should unfortunately assail the supreme executive magistracy of a country, consisting of a plurality of persons, they might impede or frustrate the most important measures of the government, in the most critical emergencies of the state. And what is still worse, they might split the community into the most violent and irreconcilable factions adhering differently to the different individuals who composed the magistracy. . . .

Upon the principles of a free government, inconveniencies from the source just mentioned must necessarily be submitted to in the formation of the legislature; but it is unnecessary and therefore unwise to introduce them into the constitution of the executive. It is here too that they may be most pernicious. In the legislature, promptitude of decision is oftener an evil than a benefit. The differences of opinion, and the jarrings of parties in that department of the government, though they may sometimes obstruct salutary plans, yet often promote deliberation and circumspection; and serve to check excesses in the majority. When a resolution too is once taken, the opposition must be at an end. That resolution is a law, and resistance to it punishable. But no favourable circumstances palliate or atone for the disadvantages of dissention in the executive department. Here they are pure and unmixed. There is no point at which they cease to operate. They serve to embarrass and weaken the execution of the plan or measure, to which they relate, from the first step to the final conclusion of it. They constantly counteract those qualities in the executive, which are the most necessary ingredients in its composition, vigour and expedition, and this without any counterballancing good. In the conduct of war, in which the energy of the executive is the bulwark of the national security, every thing would be to be apprehended from its plurality.

It must be confessed that these observations apply with principal weight to the first case supposed, that is to a plurality of magistrates of equal dignity and authority; a scheme the advocates for which are not likely to form a numerous sect: But they apply, though not with equal, yet with considerable weight, to the project of a council, whose concurrence is made constitutionally necessary to the operations of the ostensible executive. An artful cabal in that council would be able to distract and to enervate the whole system of administration. If no such cabal should exist, the mere diversity of views and opinions would alone be sufficient to tincture the exercise of the executive authority with a spirit of habitual feebleness and dilatoriness.

But one of the weightiest objections to a plurality in the executive, and which lies as much against the last as the first plan, is that it tends to conceal faults, and destroy responsibility. Responsibility is of two kinds, to censure and to punishment. The first is the most important of the two; especially in an elective office. Man, in public trust, will much oftener act in such a manner as to render him unworthy of being any longer trusted, than in such a manner as to make him obnoxious to legal punishment. But the multiplication of the executive adds to the difficulty of detection in either case. It often becomes impossible, amidst mutual accusations, to determine on whom the blame or the punishment of a pernicious measure, or series of pernicious measures ought really to fall. It is shifted from one to another with so much dexterity, and under such plausible appearances, that the public opinion is left in suspense about the real author. The circumstances which may have led to any national miscarriage or misfortune are sometimes so complicated, that where there are a number of actors who may have had different degrees and kinds of agency, though we may clearly see upon the whole that there has been mismanagement, yet it may be impracticable to pronounce to whose account the evil which may have been incurred is truly chargeable.

"I was overruled by my council. The council were so divided in their opinions, that it was impossible to obtain any better resolution on the point." These and similar pretexts are constantly at hand, whether true or false. And who is there that will either take

167

the trouble or incur the odium of a strict scrutiny into the secret springs of the transaction? Should there be found a citizen zealous enough to undertake the unpromising task, if there happen to be a collusion between the parties concerned, how easy is it to cloath the circumstances with so much ambiguity, as to render it uncertain what was the precise conduct of any of those parties? . . .

It is evident from these considerations, that the plurality of the executive tends to deprive the people of the two greatest securities they can have for the faithful exercise of any delegated power; first, the restraints of public opinion, which lose their efficacy as well on account of the division of the censure attendant on bad measures among a number, as on account of the uncertainty on whom it ought to fall; and secondly, the opportunity of discovering with facility and clearness the misconduct of the persons they trust, in order either to their removal from office, or to their actual punishment, in cases which admit of it.

In England the king is a perpetual magistrate; and it is a maxim, which has obtained for the sake of the public peace, that he is unaccountable for his administration, and his person sacred. Nothing therefore can be wiser in that kingdom than to annex to the king a constitutional council, who may be responsible to the nation for the advice they give. Without this there would be no responsibility whatever in the executive department; an idea inadmissible in a free government. But even there the king is not bound by the resolutions of his council, though they are answerable for the advice they give. He is the absolute master of his own conduct, in the exercise of his office; and may observe or disregard the council given to him at his sole discretion.

Against a Council to the Executive

But in a republic, where every magistrate ought to be personally responsible for his behaviour in office, the reason which in the British constitution dictates the propriety of a council not only ceases to apply, but turns against the institution. In the monarchy of Great-Britain, it furnishes a substitute for the prohibited responsibility of the chief magistrate; which serves in some degree as a hostage to the national justice for his good behaviour. In the American republic it would serve to destroy, or would greatly diminish the intended and necessary responsibility of the chief magistrate himself.

The idea of a council to the executive, which has so generally obtained in the state constitutions, has been derived from that maxim of republican jealousy, which considers power as safer in the hands of a number of men than of a single man. If the maxim should be admitted to be applicable to the case, I should contend that the advantage on that side would not counterballance the numerous disadvantages on the opposite side. But I do not think the rule at all applicable to the executive power. I clearly concur in opinion in this particular with a writer whom the celebrated Junius pronounces to be "deep, solid and ingenious," that, "the executive power is more easily confined when it is one": That it is far more safe there should be a single object for the jealousy and watchfulness of the people; and in a word that all multiplication of the executive is rather dangerous than friendly to liberty.

A little consideration will satisfy us, that the species of security sought for in the multiplication of the executive is unattainable. Numbers must be so great as to render combination difficult; or they are rather a source of danger than of security. The united credit and influence of several individuals must be more formidable to liberty than the credit and influence of either of them separately. When power therefore is placed in the hands of so small a number of men, as to admit of their interests and views being easily combined in a common enterprise, by an artful leader, it becomes more liable to abuse and more dangerous when abused, than if it be lodged in the hands of one man; who from the very circumstance of his being alone will be more narrowly watched and more readily suspected, and who cannot unite so great a mass of influence as when he is associated with others. The Decemvirs of Rome, whose name denotes their number [ten], were more to be dreaded in their usurpation than any ONE of them would have been. No person would think of proposing an executive much more numerous than that body, from six to a dozen have been suggested for the number of the council. The extreme of these numbers is not too great for an easy combination; and from such a combination America would have more to fear, than from the ambition of any single individual. A council to a magistrate, who is himself responsible for what he does, are generally nothing better than a clog upon his good intentions; are often the instruments and accomplices of his bad, and are almost always a cloak to his faults.

I forbear to dwell upon the subject of expence; though it be evident that if the council should be numerous enough to answer the principal end, aimed at by the institution, the salaries of the members, who must be drawn from their homes to reside at the seat of government, would form an item in the catalogue of public expenditures, too serious to be incurred for an object of equivocal utility.

I will only add, that prior to the appearance of the constitution, I rarely met with an intelligent man from any of the states, who did not admit as the result of experience, that the UNITY of the Executive of this state was one of the best of the distinguishing features of our constitution.

VIEWPOINT 2

"If the Executive is vested in three Persons. . . . will it not contribute to quiet the Minds of the People?"

The Executive Should Be a Committee

George Mason (1725-1792)

Virginia planter and political leader George Mason was one of the more active delegates at the Constitutional Convention, where he drew on his experience of helping to write Virginia's 1776 state constitution. However, when the Constitution was finished on September 17, 1787, Mason was one of three delegates who refused to sign it, in part because it lacked a bill of rights similar to the one Mason had written for Virginia's constitution.

The following is taken from a speech Mason made on June 4, 1787, when the Convention was debating how the executive should be set up in the proposed new government. Mason was generally supportive of James Madison's wishes for a stronger national government with a strong executive, but he feared the potential dangers of creating a new tyrant. In his speech, Mason proposes to prevent such a development by making the executive a committee of three people.

Reprinted from *The Papers of George Mason, 1725–1792*, edited by Robert A. Rutland. Copyright (1970) by The University of North Carolina Press. Used by permission.

The chief advantages which have been urged in favour of Unity in the Executive, are the Secrecy, the Dispatch, the Vigour and Energy which the Government will derive from it; especially in time of War. That these are great Advantages, I shall most readily allow. They have been strongly insisted on by all monarchical Writers—they have been acknowledged by the ablest and most candid Defenders of Republican Government; and it can not be denied that a Monarchy possesses them in a much greater Degree than a Republic. Yet perhaps a little Reflection may incline us to doubt whether these advantages are not greater in Theory than in Practice—or lead us to enquire whether there is not some prevailing Principle in Republican Government, which sets at Naught, and tramples upon this boasted Superiority—as hath been experienced, to their cost by most Monarchys, which have been imprudent enough to invade or attack their republican Neighbors. This invincible Principle is to be found in the Love the Affection the Attachment of the Citizens to their Laws, to their Freedom, and to their Country. Every Husbandman will be quickly converted into a Soldier, when he knows and feels that he is to fight not in defence of the Rights of a particular Family, or a Prince; but for his own. This is the true Construction of that pro Aris and focis [for altars and firesides] which has, in all Ages, perform'd such Wonders. It was this which, in ancient times, enabled the little Cluster of Grecian Republics to resist and almost constantly to defeat the Persian Monarch. It was this which supported the States of Holland against a Body of veteran Troops through a Thirty Years War with Spain, then the greatest Monarchy in Europe and finally rendered them victorious. It is this which preserves the Freedom and Independence of the Swiss Cantons, in the midst of the most powerful Nations. And who that reflects seriously upon the Situation of America, in the Beginning of the late War—without Arms—without Soldiers—without Trade, Money, or Credit—in a Manner destitute of all Resources, but must ascribe our Success to this pervading all-powerful Principle?

An Executive of Three Persons

We have not yet been able to define the Powers of the Executive; and however moderately some Gentlemen may talk or think upon the Subject, I believe there is a general Tendency to a strong Executive and I am inclined to think a strong Executive necessary. If strong and extensive Powers are vested in the Executive, and that Executive consists only of one Person, the Government will of course degenerate, (for I will call it degeneracy) into a Monarchy—A Government so contrary to the Genius of the People, that

George Mason argued consistently for safeguards against the abuse of government power. "At the core of George Mason's personality," wrote Christopher Collier and James Lincoln Collier, "was a deep-seated mistrust of other people."

they will reject even the Appearance of it. I consider the federal Government as in some Measure dissolved by the Meeting of this Convention. Are there no Dangers to be apprehended from procrastinating the time between the breaking up of this Assembly and the adoption of a new System of Government. I dread the Interval. If it should not be brought to an Issue in the Course of the first Year, the Consequences may be fatal. Has not the different Parts of this extensive Government, the several States of which it is composed a Right to expect an equal Participation in the Executive, as the best Means of securing an equal Attention to their Interests. Should an Insurrection, a Rebellion or Invasion happen in New Hampshire when the single supreme Magistrate is a Citizen of Georgia, would not the people of New Hampshire naturally ascribe any Delay in defending them to such a Circumstance and so vice versa. If the Executive is vested in three Persons, one chosen from the northern, one from the middle, and one from the Southern States, will it not contribute to quiet the Minds of the People, & convince them that there will be proper attention paid to their respective Concerns? Will not three Men so chosen bring with them, into Office, a more perfect and extensive Knowledge of the real Interests of this great Union? Will not such a Model of Appointment be the most effectual means of preventing Cabals and Intrigues between the Legislature and the Candidates for this

Office, especially with those Candidates who from their local Situation, near the seat of the federal Government, will have the greatest Temptations and the greatest Opportunities. Will it not be the most effectual Means of checking and counteracting the aspiring Views of dangerous and ambitious Men, and consequently the best Security for the Stability and Duration of our Government upon the invaluable Principles of Liberty? These Sir, are some of my Motives for preferring an Executive consisting of three Persons rather than of one.

Viewpoint 3

"When a man is at the head of an elective government invested with great powers ... an imperfect aristocracy bordering on monarchy may be established."

The Constitution May Create a Monarchy

"Cato"

Debate over the office of president of the United States did not end with the completion of the Constitution on September 17, 1787. The fear that the proposed chief executive would become a tyrannical monarch was a prominent theme of anti-federalist literature. One noteworthy example of such an argument is by "Cato," whose seven "Letters" or papers first published in the *New York Journal* received widespread attention and prompted numerous printed rebuttals during that state's vigorous debate over ratification. Some believe "Cato" was New York governor George Clinton, one of America's most prominent opponents of the Constitution, but the evidence for such identification is uncertain.

In the fourth of his seven "Letters," "Cato" argues that the executive created by Article II of the Constitution would hold too many powers and would soon resemble a king. He argues that the Constitution does not specifically provide for presidential elections every four years, raising the possibility of an executive-for-life. Another monarchical imitation, he asserts, would be the creation of a "court" at the nation's new capital full of the president's flatterers and favorites. Like many writers of his time, "Cato" cites famous political thinkers of Europe to support his arguments. In this excerpt he quotes Charles-Louis de Montesquieu, a French political philosopher whose 1748 work *The Spirit of the Laws* was widely read in America.

From "Cato," open letter "To the Citizens of the State of New York" (no. 4), *New York Journal*, November 8, 1787.

I shall begin with observations on the executive branch of this new system; and though it is not the first in order, as arranged therein, yet being the *chief*, is perhaps entitled by the rules of rank to the first consideration. The executive power as described in the 2d article, consists of a president and vice-president, who are to hold their offices during the term of four years; the same article has marked the manner and time of their election, and established the qualifications of the president; it also provides against the removal, death, or inability of the president and vice-president—regulates the salary of the president, delineates his duties and powers; and, lastly, declares the causes for which the president and vice-president shall be removed from office.

Notwithstanding the great learning and abilities of the gentlemen who composed the convention, it may be here remarked with deference, that the construction of the first paragraph of the first section of the second article is vague and inexplicit, and leaves the mind in doubt as to the election of a president and vice-president, after the expiration of the election for the first term of four years; in every other case, the election of these great officers is expressly provided for; but there is no explicit provision for their election in case of expiration of their offices, subsequent to the election which is to set this political machine in motion; no certain and express terms as in your state constitution, that *statedly* once in every four years, and as often as these offices shall become vacant, by expiration or otherwise, as is therein expressed, an election shall be held as follows, &c., this inexplicitness perhaps may lead to an establishment for life.

Dangerous Power

It is remarked by Montesquieu, in treating of republics, that *in all magistracies, the greatness of the power must be compensated by the brevity of the duration, and that a longer time than a year would be dangerous.* It is, therefore, obvious to the least intelligent mind to account why great power in the hands of a magistrate, and that power connected with considerable duration, may be dangerous to the liberties of a republic, the deposit of vast trusts in the hands of a single magistrate, enables him in their exercise to create a numerous train of dependents; this tempts his *ambition*, which in a republican magistrate is also remarked, *to be pernicious*, and the duration of his office for any considerable time favors his views, gives him the means and time to perfect and execute his designs, *he therefore fancies that he may be great and glorious by oppressing his fellow-citizens, and raising himself to permanent grandeur on the ruins of his country.* And here it may be necessary to compare the vast and important powers of the president, together with his continuance in office, with the foregoing doctrine—his eminent magisterial situation will attach many adherents to him, and he will be surrounded by expectants and courtiers, his power of nomination and influence on all appointments, the strong posts in each state comprised within his superintendence, and garrisoned by troops under his direction, his control over the army, militia, and navy, the unrestrained power of granting pardons for treason, which may be used to screen from punishment those whom he had secretly instigated to commit the crime, and thereby prevent a discovery of his own guilt, his duration in office of four years: these, and various other principles evidently prove the truth of the position, that if the president is possessed of ambition, he has power and time sufficient to ruin his country.

Though the president, during the sitting of the legislature, is assisted by the senate, yet he is without a constitutional council in their recess; he will therefore be unsupported by proper information and advice, and will generally be directed by minions and favorites, or a council of state will grow out of the principal officers of the great departments, the most dangerous council in a free country.

The President's Court

The ten miles square, which is to become the seat of government [see Article I, Section 8, of the Constitution], will of course be the place of residence for the president and the great officers of state; the same observations of a great man will apply to the court of a president possessing the powers of a monarch, that is observed of that of a monarch—*ambition with idleness—baseness with pride—the thirst of riches without labor—aversion to truth—flattery—treason—perfidy—violation of engagements—contempt of civil duties—hope from the magistrate's weakness; but above all, the perpetual ridicule of virtue*—these, he remarks, are the characteristics by which the courts in all ages have been distinguished.

The language and the manners of this court will be what distinguishes them from the rest of the community, not what assimilates them to it; and in being remarked for a behavior that shows they are not *meanly born*, and in adulation to people of fortune and power.

The establishment of a vice-president is as unnecessary as it is dangerous. This officer, for want of other employment, is made president of the senate, thereby blending the executive and legislative powers, besides always giving to some one state, from which he is to come, an unjust pre-eminence.

It is a maxim in republics that the representative of the people should be of their immediate choice; but by the manner in which the president is chosen, he arrives to this office at the fourth or fifth hand, nor does the highest vote, in the way he is elected, determine the choice, for it is only necessary that he should be taken from the highest of five, who may have a plurality of votes.

The Powers of the President

Compare your past opinions and sentiments with the present proposed establishment, and you will find, that if you adopt it, that it will lead you into a system which you heretofore reprobated as odious. Every American Whig, not long since, bore his emphatic testimony against a monarchical government, though limited, because of the dangerous inequality that it created

The President Can Easily Become King

One of the most dramatic expressions of fear of the presidency comes from noted orator and Constitution opponent Patrick Henry, taken from his long June 5, 1788, speech at the Virginia ratifying convention.

If your American chief, be a man of ambition, and abilities, how easy is it for him to render himself absolute: The army is in his hands, and, if he be a man of address, it will be attached to him; and it will be the subject of long mediation with him to seize the first auspicious moment to accomplish his design; and, Sir, will the American spirit solely relieve you when this happens? I would rather infinitely, and I am sure most of this Convention are of the same opinion, have a King, Lords, and Commons, than a Government so replete with such insupportable evils. If we make a King, we may prescribe the rules by which he shall rule his people, and interpose such checks as shall prevent him from infringing them: But the President, in the field, at the head of his army, can prescribe the terms on which he shall reign master, so far that it will puzzle any American ever to get his neck from under the galling yoke. I cannot with patience, think of this idea. If ever he violates the laws, one of the two things will happen: He shall come to the head of his army to carry every thing before him; or, will he give bail, or do what Mr. Chief Justice will order him. If he be guilty, will not the recollection of his crimes teach him to make one bold push for the American throne? Will not the immense difference between being master of every thing, and being ignominiously tried and punished, powerfully excite him to make this bold push? But, Sir, where is the existing force to punish him? Can he not at the head of his army beat down every opposition? Away with your President, we shall have a King: The army will salute him Monarch; your militia will leave you and assist in making him King, and fight against you: And what have you to oppose this force? What will then become of you and your rights? Will not absolute despotism ensue?

among citizens as relative to their rights and property; and wherein does this president, invested with his powers and prerogatives, essentially differ from the king of Great Britain (save as to the name, the creation of nobility, and some immaterial incidents, the offspring of absurdity and locality). The direct prerogatives of the president, as springing from his political character, are among the following: It is necessary, in order to distinguish him from the rest of the community, and enable him to keep, and maintain his court, that the compensation for his services, or in other words, his revenue, should be such as to enable him to appear with the splendor of a prince; he has the power of receiving ambassadors from, and a great influence on their appointments to foreign courts; as also to make treaties, leagues, and alliances with foreign states, assisted by the Senate, which when made become the supreme law of land: he is a constituent part of the legislative power, for every bill which shall pass the House of Representatives and Senate is to be presented for him for approbation; if he approves of it he is to sign it, if he disapproves he is to return it with objections, which in many cases will amount to a complete negative; and in this view he will have a great share in the power of making peace, coining money, etc., and all the various objects of legislation, expressed or implied in this Constitution: for though it may be asserted that the king of Great Britain has the express power of making peace or war, yet he never thinks it prudent to do so without the advice of his Parliament, from whom he is to derive his support, and therefore these powers, in both president and king, are substantially the same: he is the generalissimo of the nation, and of course has the command and control of the army, navy and militia; he is the general conservator of the peace of the union— he may pardon all offences, except in cases of impeachment, and the principal fountain of all offices and employments. Will not the exercise of these powers therefore tend either to the establishment of a vile and arbitrary aristocracy or monarchy? The safety of the people in a republic depends on the share or proportion they have in the government; but experience ought to teach you, that when a man is at the head of an elective government invested with great powers, and interested in his re-election, in what circle appointments will be made; by which means an *imperfect aristocracy* bordering on monarchy may be established.

No Resemblance to the Government of New York

You must, however, my countrymen, beware that the advocates of this new system do not deceive you by a fallacious resemblance between it and your own state [New York] government which you so much prize; and, if you examine, you will perceive that the chief magistrate of this state is your immediate choice, controlled and checked by a just and full representation of the people, divested of the prerogative of influencing war and peace, making treaties, receiving and sending embassies, and commanding standing armies and navies, which belong to the power of the confederation, and will be convinced that this government is no more like a true picture of your own than an Angel of Darkness resembles an Angel of Light.

CATO

VIEWPOINT 4

"In Britain their king is for life—In America our president will always be one of the people at the end of four years."

The Constitution Does Not Create a Monarchy

Tenche Coxe (1755-1824)

Tenche Coxe was a Philadelphia merchant who wrote many pamphlets in support of the Constitution in 1787 and 1788. A supporter of the development of manufacturing in America, he became assistant secretary of the treasury under President George Washington, and held several other federal posts under Presidents John Adams, Thomas Jefferson, and James Madison.

Among his writings were four federalist essays written under the pseudonym "An American Citizen." These were first published in Philadelphia in September and October of 1787, and were widely reprinted elsewhere. In this excerpt from the first of these papers, Coxe compares the powers of the president as created by the new Constitution with those of the king of England. He argues that the president holds much less power and is more closely connected with the people, refuting anti-federalist arguments to the contrary.

In the first place let us look at the nature and powers of the head of that country, and those of the ostensible head of ours.

The British King is the great Bishop or Supreme Head of an established church, with an immense patronage annexed. In this ca-

From "An American Citizen," essay (no. 1) in the Philadelphia *Independent Gazetteer*, September 26, 1787.

pacity he commands a number of votes in the House of Lords, by creating Bishops, who, besides their great incomes, have votes in that assembly, and are judges in the last resort. They have also many honorable and lucrative places to bestow, and thus from their wealth, learning, dignities, powers and patronage give a great lustre and an enormous influence to the crown.

Powers Retained by the People

In America our President will not only be *without* these influencing advantages, *but they will be in the possession of the people at large, to strengthen their hands in the event of a contest with him.* All religious funds, honors and powers, are in the gift of numberless, unconnected, disunited, and contending corporations, wherein the principle of perfect equality universally prevails. In short, danger from ecclesiastical tyranny, that long standing and still remaining curse of the people—that sacrilegious engine of royal power in some countries, can be feared by no man in the United States. In Britain their king is for life—In America our president will always be *one of the people* at the end of four years. In that country the king is hereditary and may be an idiot, a knave, or a tyrant by nature, or ignorant from neglect of his education, yet cannot be removed, for *"he can do no wrong."* In America, as the president is to be one of the people at the end of his short term, so will he and his fellow citizens remember, *that he was originally one of the people; and that he is created by their breath*—Further, he cannot be an idiot, probably not a knave or a tyrant, for those whom nature makes so, discover it before the age of thirty-five, until which period he cannot be elected. It appears we have not admitted that he can do no wrong, but have rather pre-supposed he may and will sometimes do wrong, by providing for *his impeachment, his trial, and his peaceable and complete removal.*

In England the king has a power to create members of the upper house, who are judges in the highest court, as well as legislators. Our president not only cannot make members of the upper house, but their creation, like his own, is by *the people* through their representatives, and a member of assembly may and will be as certainly dismissed at the end of his year for electing a weak or wicked senator, as for any other blunder or misconduct.

The king of England has legislative power, while our president can only use it when the other servants of the people are divided. But in all great cases affecting the national interests or safety, his modified and restrained power must give way to the sense of two-thirds of the legislature. In fact it amounts to no more, than a serious duty imposed upon him to request both houses to reconsider any matter on which he entertains doubts or feels apprehensions; and here the people have a strong hold upon him *from his sole and personal responsibility.*

The president of the upper house (or the chancellor) in England is appointed by the king, while our vice-president, who is chosen *by the people* through the electors and the senate, *is not at all dependant on the president*, but may exercise equal powers on some occasions. In all royal governments an helpless infant or an unexperienced youth, may wear the crown. *Our president must be matured by the experience of years*, and being born among us, his character at thirty-five must be fully understood. Wisdom, virtue, and active qualities of mind and body can alone make him the first servant of a free and enlightened people.

Our president will fall very far short indeed of any prince in his

Opponents Distort the Constitution

Alexander Hamilton defended the presidency as created by the Constitution in several essays in The Federalist, *the collection of articles he, along with James Madison and John Jay, wrote to explain and support the Constitution. The following is taken from* The Federalist *No. 67, in which he ridicules arguments made by opponents of the presidency.*

The writers against the Constitution seem to have taken pains to signalize their talent of misrepresentation, calculating upon the aversion of the people to monarchy, they have endeavoured to inlist all their jealousies and apprehensions in opposition to the intended President of the United States; not merely as the embryo but as the full grown progeny of that detested parent. To establish the pretended affinity they have not scrupled to draw resources even from the regions of fiction. The authorities of a magistrate, in few instances greater, and in some instances less, than those of a Governor of New-York, have been magnified into more than royal prerogatives. He has been decorated with attributes superior in dignity and splendor to those of a King of Great-Britain. He has been shown to us with the diadem sparkling on his brow, and the imperial purple flowing in his train. He has been seated on a throne surrounded with minions and mistresses; giving audience to the envoys of foreign potentates, in all the supercilious pomp of majesty. The images of Asiatic despotism and voluptuousness have scarcely been wanting to crown the exaggerated scene. We have been almost taught to tremble at the terrific visages of murdering janizaries; and to blush at the unveiled mysteries of a future seraglio.

Attempts so extravagant as these to disfigure, or it might rather be said, to metamorphose the object, render it necessary to take an accurate view of its real nature and form; in order as well to ascertain its true aspect and genuine appearance, as to unmask the disingenuity and expose the fallacy of the counterfeit resemblances which have been so insidiously as well as industriously propagated.

annual income, which will not be hereditary, but *the absolute allowance of the people passing through the hands of their other servants from year to year as it becomes necessary*. There will be no burdens on the nation to provide for his heir or other branches of his family. 'Tis probable, from the state of property in America and other circumstances, that many citizens will *exceed* him in shew and expence, those dazzling trappings of kingly rank and power. He will have no authority to make a treaty without *two-thirds of the senate*, nor can he appoint ambassadors or other great officers *without their approbation*, which will remove the idea of *patronage and influence*, and of personal obligation and dependance. The appointment of even the inferior officers may be taken out of his hands by an act of Congress at any time; he can create no nobility or titles of honor, nor take away offices during good behaviour. *His person is not so much protected as that of a member of the house of representatives; for he may be proceeded against like any other man in the ordinary course of law.* He appoints no officer of the separate states. He will have no influence *from placement* [government officials] *in the legislature*, nor can he prorogue or dissolve it. He will have no power *over the treasures of the state*; and lastly, as he is *created* through the electors by the people at large, *he must ever look up to the support of his creators.* From such a servant with powers so limited and transitory, there can be no danger, especially when we consider the solid foundations on which our national liberties are immovably fixed by the other provisions of this excellent constitution. Whatever of dignity or authority he possesses, *is a delegated part of their Majesty and their political omnipotence, transiently vested in him by the people themselves for their own happiness.*

CHAPTER 5

The Debate over Ratification

Chapter Preface

The process the Constitutional Convention settled on to ratify the Constitution was itself controversial. Article VII of the Constitution stipulated that "the ratification of the conventions of nine states shall be sufficient for the establishment of this Constitution." This departed from the procedures found in the Articles of Confederation in two important ways. First, only nine states instead of all thirteen were required for ratification. Second, the decision was to be made by special ratifying conventions, rather than the state legislatures as called for in the Articles.

Immediately after the Constitution was finished and signed on September 17, 1787, copies were sent to New York to be submitted to the Continental Congress, the national legislature under the Articles of Confederation, which would be made defunct by the Constitution. Some members of the Congress questioned the scope of the Constitution, and Richard Henry Lee of Virginia offered amendments adding a bill of rights. But supporters of the Constitution in Congress (some of whom had just returned from participating in the Constitutional Convention) persuaded the body to send the Constitution on to the states. Although Congress did so without endorsing the Constitution, the step kept the ratification process in motion.

Every state except Rhode Island elected delegates to a state ratifying convention. Over the next months the state conventions met, argued, and voted whether to ratify the Constitution. Debates took place not just within the conventions themselves, but also in the press. Hundreds of newspaper articles and pamphlets were published featuring arguments on ratification. These essays were often signed with pseudonyms, among which were "Centinel," "Cato," and "Brutus" attacking the Constitution and "Publius," "Americanus," and "A Patriotic Citizen" defending it. Historians have ascertained the identities of only some of the writers.

The viewpoints in this chapter are taken both from the speeches at the ratification conventions and from the newspaper and pamphlet debates. They demonstrate that the creation of the Constitution did not end with the adjournment of the Constitutional Convention in September 1787. The people involved in ratifying the Constitution share credit for its creation. And although the anti-federalists failed in blocking ratification of the Constitution, historians give them an important role. As Richard B. Bernstein writes in *Are We to Be a Nation?*:

> Although the Anti-Federalists failed, they are entitled to their just share of credit in the making of the Constitution. The adoption of the Constitution provoked, indeed required, a searching dialogue about the basic principles of the American polity—about the task of framing an instrument of government for a nation any one of whose states was larger and more diverse than any European nation, about traditional and new conceptions of government and governmental institutions, about the new and untried system of dual federalism, and about the place of individual rights in constitutional government. The Anti-Federalists forced the Constitution's supporters to engage in this dialogue and to explain and justify the new charter clause by clause. In resisting the Constitution, they compelled the American people to think more deeply than any other people, before or since, about what the basic principles of government should be and how they should be put into effect.

VIEWPOINT 1

"I consent, Sir, to this Constitution.... The Opinions I have had of its Errors, I sacrifice to the Public Good."

The Constitution Should Be Accepted in a Spirit of Compromise

Benjamin Franklin (1706-1790)

Publisher, scientist, politician, philanthropist, and diplomat, the many-faceted Franklin was, along with George Washington, one of early America's respected public figures. At 81 he was the oldest delegate at the 1787 Constitutional Convention. While age and failing health limited somewhat his participation in the debates, his influence on the Convention has been widely acknowledged. Historian Ralph Ketcham writes:

> Too weak to stand in debate and no match for [James] Madison, James Wilson, and other young members in creating new institutions, Franklin helped importantly to give the convention much needed confidence in itself and, through good humor and a gift for compromise, to prevent its acrimonious disruption.

An important example of Franklin's spirit of compromise comes from a speech he presented at the close of the Convention. In the address, which was read to the Convention by fellow Pennsylvania delegate James Wilson, Franklin urged all the delegates to sign the Constitution even if they disagreed with parts of it. Franklin himself saw many of his ideas, including a single-house legislature and a plural executive, rejected by the Conven-

Benjamin Franklin, address to the Constitutional Convention, September 17, 1787.

tion, but he nonetheless was willing to sign the document and give it his unqualified support because, in his words, "I expect no better, and because I am not sure it is not the best."

Franklin's attempts for a show of unity failed in that three of the forty-one delegates in attendance that day—Edmund Randolph, George Mason, and Elbridge Gerry—refused to sign. However, Franklin's speech was reprinted in newspapers at least fifty times in the following year, and was widely used by federalist supporters of the Constitution in support of ratification.

I confess that I do not entirely approve of this Constitution at present, but Sir, I am not sure I shall never approve it: For having lived long, I have experienced many Instances of being oblig'd, by better Information or fuller Consideration, to change Opinions even on important Subjects, which I once thought right, but found to be otherwise. It is therefore that the older I grow the more apt I am to doubt my own Judgment, and to pay more Respect to the Judgment of others. Most Men indeed as well as most Sects in Religion, think themselves in Possession of all Truth, and that wherever others differ from them it is so far Error. Steele, a Protestant in a Dedication tells the Pope, that the only Difference between our two Churches in their Opinions of the Certainty of their Doctrine, is, the Romish Church is infallible, and the Church of England is never in the Wrong. But tho' many private Persons think almost as highly of their own Infallibility, as of that of their Sect, few express it so naturally as a certain French Lady, who in a little Dispute with her Sister, said, I don't know how it happens, Sister, but I meet with no body but myself that's *always* in the right. *Il n'y a que moi qui a toujours raison.*

A Plea to Support the Constitution

In these Sentiments, Sir, I agree to this Constitution, with all its Faults, if they are such; because I think a General Government necessary for us, and there is no *Form* of Government but what may be a Blessing to the People if well administred; and I believe farther that this is likely to be well administred for a Course of Years, and can only end in Despotism as other Forms have done before it, when the People shall become so corrupted as to need Despotic Government, being incapable of any other. I doubt too whether any other Convention we can obtain, may be able to make a better Constitution: For when you assemble a Number of Men to have the Advantage of their joint Wisdom, you inevitably

Joseph Duplessis painted this portrait of Benjamin Franklin, who in his eighties had become the respected elder statesman of American politics.

assemble with those Men all their Prejudices, their Passions, their Errors of Opinion, their local Interests, and their selfish Views. From such an Assembly can a perfect Production be expected? It therefore astonishes me, Sir, to find this System approaching so near to Perfection as it does; and I think it will astonish our Enemies, who are waiting with Confidence to hear that our Councils are confounded, like those of the Builders of Babel, and that our States are on the Point of Separation, only to meet hereafter for the Purpose of cutting one anothers Throats. Thus I consent, Sir, to this Constitution because I expect no better, and because I am not sure that it is not the best. The Opinions I have had of its Errors, I sacrifice to the Public Good. I have never whisper'd a Syllable of them abroad. Within these Walls they were born, and here they shall die. If every one of us in returning to our Constituents were to report the Objections he has had to it, and use his Influence to gain Partizans in support of them, we might prevent its being generally received, and thereby lose all the salutary Effects and great Advantages resulting naturally in our favour among foreign Nations, as well as among ourselves, from our real or apparent Unanimity. Much of the Strength and Efficiency of any Government, in procuring and securing Happiness to the People depends on Opinion, on the general Opinion of the Goodness of that Government as well as of the Wisdom and Integrity of its Governors. I hope therefore that for our own Sakes, as a Part of the People, and for the sake of our Posterity, we shall act heartily and unanimously in recommending this Constitution, wherever our Influence may extend, and turn our future Thoughts and Endeavours to the Means of having it well administred.

On the whole, Sir, I cannot help expressing a Wish, that every Member of the Convention, who may still have Objections to it, would with me on this Occasion doubt a little of his own Infallibility, and to make *manifest* our *Unanimity*, put his Name to this instrument.

VIEWPOINT 2

"Are we to accept a form of government which we do not entirely approve of, merely in hopes that it will be administered well?"

Principles of Liberty Should Not Be Compromised by Accepting the Constitution

"Z"

In the newspaper debates over whether to ratify the Constitution, one of the most influential articles on the federalist side was Benjamin Franklin's speech to the Constitutional Convention on September 17, 1787. Franklin's speech, reprinted in the *Boston Gazette* of December 3, 1787, and subsequently in many other newspapers, included pleas for support of the Constitution as the best compromise solution to the problems facing America. Franklin's speech and person were both harshly attacked by anti-federalist opponents of the Constitution. An anonymous writer in the *Massachusetts Gazette* for December 14, 1787, called Franklin an "enfeebled sage" and argued that the "puerile speech" should not have been printed, but left "concealed beneath the roof where the liberties of America have been relinquished."

A somewhat less caustic response appeared in the December 6, 1787, edition of the *Independent Chronicle* of Boston under the pseudonym of "Z." The author focuses on Franklin's expressions of disagreement with and misgiving about the Constitution, and questions how Franklin could then support the document. Included in the essay is a call for the Constitution to include "an express reservation of certain inherent unalienable rights" of the people that the government could not invade.

"Z," Boston *Independent Chronicle*, December 6, 1787.

When I read Dr. FRANKLIN's address to the President of the late Convention, in the last Monday's Gazette, I was at a loss to judge, till I was informed by mere accident, from which of the contending parties it went to the press. "I confess," says the Doctor, (and observe the Printers tell us it was *immediately* before his signing) "I confess that I do not entirely approve of this Constitution at present." Surely, I thought, no zealous fœderalist, in his right mind, would have exposed his cause so much as to publish to the world that this great philosopher *did not* entirely approve the Constitution at the very moment when his "hand marked" his approbation of it; especially after the fœderalists themselves had so often and so loudly proclaimed, that he had *fully* and *decidedly* adopted it. The Doctor adds, "I am not sure I shall never approve it." This then is the only remaining hope of the fœderalists, so far as the Doctor's judgment is or may be of any service to their cause, that one time or another he *may* approve the new Constitution.

Power Is Dangerous

Again, says the Doctor, "In these sentiments I agree to this Constitution, with all its faults, if they are such; because I think a general government necessary for us, and there is no FORM of government but what may be a blessing to the people, if well administered. But are we to accept a form of government which we do not entirely approve of merely in hopes that it *will* be administered well? Does not every man know, that nothing is more liable to be abused than power. Power, without a check, in *any* hands, is tyranny; and such powers, in the hands of even *good men*, so infatuating is the nature of it, will probably be wantonly, if not tyrannically exercised. The world has had experience enough of this, in every stage of it. Those among us who cannot entirely approve the *new* Constitution as it is called, are of opinion, in order that any form may be well administered, and thus be made a blessing to the people, that there ought to be at least, an express reservation of certain inherent unalienable rights, which it would be equally sacrilegious for the people to *give away* as for the government to *invade*. If the rights of conscience, for instance, are not sacredly reserved to the people, what security will there be, in case the government should have in their heads a predilection for any *one* sect in religion? what will hinder the civil power from erecting a national system of religion, and committing the law to a set of lordly priests, reaching, as the great Dr. [Jonathan] *Mayhew* expressed it, from the desk to the skies? An *Hierarchy* which has ever been the grand engine in the hand of civil tyranny; and tyrants in return will afford them opportunity enough to vent their rage on *stubborn hereticks*, by *wholesome severities*, as they were called by national religionists, in a country which has long boasted its freedom. It was doubtless for the peace of *that* nation, that there should be an *uniformity* in religion, and for the same *wise* and *good* reason, the act of uniformity remains *in force* to these enlightened times. [Editor's note: "Z" is criticizing England and its 1662 Act of Uniformity, which required all clergy to subscribe to the precepts of the Church of England.]

Betraying the Revolution

A common theme of anti-federalist writing was that the Constitution betrayed the ideals of the American Revolution. One example comes from an article by "Philadelphiensis," which appeared in the Philadelphia Freeman's Journal *on December 5, 1787. "Philadelphiensis," who wrote twelve articles in all, is believed by some historians to have been Benjamin Workman, an Irish immigrant who taught mathematics at the University of Pennsylvania.*

The independence of America, with great propriety, was thought, during our late glorious struggle, an object of such immense value, that we could scarce pay too high a price for it; an object that even dignified human nature; and that thousands of our countrymen magnanimously and cheerfully paid their blood for its purchase. But, great as this was, I say that the adoption of the new constitution is an object of much greater concern. The parents of a child may rejoice at his birth, as a happy circumstance, but his character and conduct in manhood only can give real and permanent pleasure; if these be bad, their pain is increased by disappointment; the recollection of their former joyous hopes, now augments their misery; yea, the misconduct of a son has frequently compelled his parents to curse the very day of his nativity. In this relation, the independence of America, and the new constitution exactly coincide. For if we adopt this plan of government in its present form; I say that we shall have reason to curse the day that America became independent. Horrid thought! that the greatest blessing God ever bestowed on a nation, should terminate in its misery and disgrace. Strange reverse this! that the freemen of America, *the favored of heaven*, should submit to a government so arbitrary in its embryo, that even *a bill of rights* cannot be obtained, to secure to the people their unalienable privileges.

The Doctor says, he is "*not* sure that this is *not* the best Constitution that we may expect." Nor can he be sure that it might not have been made *better* than it now is, if the Convention had adjourned to a distant day, that they might have availed themselves of the sentiments of the people at large. It would have been no great condescension, even in that *august* Body, to have shown so *small* a testimony of regard to the judgment of their constituents. Would it not be acting more like men who wish for a *safe* as well as a *stable* government, to propose such amendments as would meliorate the form, than to approve it, as the Dr. would have us, "with all its faults, if they are such." *Thus* the Doctor consents, and hopes the Convention will "act *heartily* and *unanimously* in recommending the Constitution, wherever their influence may extend, and turn their future thoughts and endeavors to the means of having it well administered." Even a bad form of government may, in the Doctor's opinion, be well administered—for, says he, there is *no* form of government, but what may be made a blessing to the people, *if* well administered. He evidently, I think, builds his hopes, that the Constitution proposed, will be a blessing to the people,—not on the *principles* of the government itself, but on the *possibility*, that, with *all its faults*, it *may* be well administered;—and concludes, with wishing, that others, *who had objections* to it, would yet, like him, doubt of their own infallibility, and put their names to the instrument, to make an *Unanimity* MANIFEST! No wonder he *shed a tear*, as it is said he did, when he gave *his* sanction to the *New* Constitution.

Viewpoint 3

"These, my countrymen, are the objections that have been made to the new proposed system of government; ... you will find them all to be founded in truth."

A List of Objections to the Constitution

"An Officer of the Late Continental Army"

On September 29, 1787, less than two weeks after the end of the Constitutional Convention, the state legislature of Pennsylvania was one of the first to authorize a ratifying convention, setting a date for delegate elections of November 6. The tactics of the Constitution's supporters in getting this early vote (which included forcibly dragging two anti-federalist legislators to the statehouse to attain a necessary quorum), helped intensify the press debate over ratification. The debate was further intensified by sectional and class divisions within the state, with eastern merchants supporting the Constitution and western farmers opposing it.

Among the newspaper essays attacking the Constitution during this time was one signed by "An Officer of the Late Continental Army." Some historians have suggested the author was William Findley (1741-1821), a state representative from western Pennsylvania and one of the leading opponents of ratification at the Pennsylvania ratifying convention. The article, published in the November 6 edition of the Philadelphia newspaper *Independent Gazetteer* and later reprinted as a pamphlet, was one of many press responses to a speech made by Constitutional Convention delegate James Wilson on October 6 and reprinted numerous

An Officer of the Late Continental Army, a letter "To the Citizens of Philadelphia," Philadelphia *Independent Gazetteer*, November 6, 1787.

195

times in Pennsylvania and other states. Wilson's subsequent prominence made him a target for personal criticism by critics of the Constitution, who accused him of, among other things, a past lack of patriotism during the American Revolution and a haughty and imperious manner.

The following viewpoint, in its attacks on James Wilson and other Constitutional Convention delegates, provides some idea of the intensity and nature of the debates over ratification. It also furnishes a useful summary of the objections the anti-federalists had about the Constitution and what they believed to be its threats to liberty. It concludes that the proposed Constitution is far inferior to the existing Pennsylvania state constitution (which was more democratic than those of many other states), and urges rejecting the Constitution to preserve America's freedoms.

Mr. OSWALD,

By inserting the following in your impartial paper, you will oblige yours, &c.

To the Citizens of Philadelphia.

Friends, Countrymen, Brethren and Fellow Citizens,

The important day is drawing near when you are to elect delegates to represent you in a Convention, on the result of whose deliberations will depend, in a great measure, your future happiness.

This convention is to determine whether or not the commonwealth of Pennsylvania shall adopt the plan of government proposed by the late convention of delegates from the different states, which sat in this city.

With a heart full of anxiety for the preservation of your dearest rights, I presume to address you on this important occasion—In the name of sacred liberty, dearer to us than our property and our lives, I request your most earnest attention.

The proposed plan of continental government is now fully known to you. You have read it I trust with the attention it deserves—You have heard the objections that have been made to it—You have heard the answers to these objections.

If you have attended to the whole with candor and unbiassed minds, as becomes men that are possessed and deserving of freedom, you must have been alarmed at the result of your observations. Notwithstanding the splendor of names which has attended the publication of the new constitution, notwithstanding the sophistry and vain reasonings that have been urged to support its principles; alas! you must at least have concluded that great men are not always infallible, and that patriotism itself may be led into essential errors.

Objections to the Constitution

The objections that have been made to the new constitution, are these:

1. It is not merely (as it ought to be) a CONFEDERATION of STATES, but a GOVERNMENT of INDIVIDUALS.

2. The powers of Congress extend to the *lives*, the *liberties* and the *property* of every citizen.

3. The *sovereignty* of the different states is *ipso facto* destroyed in its most essential parts.

4. What remains of it will only tend to create violent dissentions between the state governments and the Congress, and terminate

---

Deformities of the Constitution

Patrick Henry, the leading figure in Virginia state politics and one of the early outspoken supporters of American independence from Great Britain, led the fight against ratification in Virginia. Many of the most impassioned arguments made against the Constitution can be found in the speeches Henry gave before the Virginia state ratifying convention. The following is taken from an address made on June 7, 1788, and provides a good example of Henry's style of argument.

This Constitution is said to have beautiful features; but when I come to examine these features, sir, they appear to me horribly frightful. Among other deformities, it has an awful squinting; it squints towards monarchy; and does not this raise indignation in the breast of every true American?

Your President may easily become king. Your Senate is so imperfectly constructed that your dearest rights may be sacrificed by what may be a small minority; and a very small minority may continue forever unchangeably this government, although horridly defective. Where are your checks in this government? Your strongholds will be in the hands of your enemies. It is on a supposition that your American governors shall be honest, that all the good qualities of this government are founded, but its defective and imperfect construction puts it in their power to perpetrate the worst of mischiefs, should they be bad men; and, sir, would not all the world, from the eastern to the western hemisphere, blame our distracted folly in resting our rights upon the contingency of our rulers being good or bad? Show me that age and country where the rights and liberties of the people were placed on the sole chance of their rulers being good men, without a consequent loss of liberty! I say that the loss of that dearest privilege has ever followed, with absolute certainty, every such mad attempt.

---

in the ruin of the one or the other.

5. The consequence must therefore be, either that the *union* of the states will be destroyed by a violent struggle, or that their sovereignty will be swallowed up by silent encroachments into a universal aristocracy; because it is clear, that if two different *sovereign powers* have a co-equal command over the *purses* of the citizens, they will struggle for the spoils, and the weakest will be in the end obliged to yield to the efforts of the strongest.

6. Congress being possessed of these immense powers, the liberties of the states and of the people are not secured by a bill or DECLARATION OF RIGHTS.

7. The *sovereignty* of the states is not expressly reserved, the *form* only, and not the SUBSTANCE of their government, is guaranteed to them by express words.

8. TRIAL BY JURY, that sacred bulwark of liberty, is ABOLISHED IN CIVIL CASES, and Mr. W— (James Wilson), one of the convention, has told you, that not being able to agree as to the FORM of establishing this point, they have left you deprived of the SUBSTANCE. Here are his own words—*The subject was involved in difficulties. The convention found the task* TOO DIFFICULT *for them, and left the business as it stands.*

9. THE LIBERTY OF THE PRESS is not secured, and the powers of congress are fully adequate to its destruction, as they are to have the trial of *libels*, or *pretended libels* against the United States, and may by a cursed abominable STAMP ACT (as the *Bowdoin administration* has done in Massachusetts) preclude you effectually from all means of information. *Mr. W— has given you no answer to these arguments.*

10. Congress have the power of keeping up a STANDING ARMY in time of peace, and Mr. W— has told you THAT IT WAS NECESSARY.

11. The LEGISLATIVE and EXECUTIVE powers are not kept separate as every one of the American constitutions declares they ought to be; but they are mixed in a manner entirely novel and unknown, even to the constitution of Great Britain; because,

12. In England the king only, has a *nominal negative* over the proceedings of the legislature, which he has NEVER DARED TO EXERCISE since the days of *King William*, whereas by the new constitution, both the *president general* and the *senate* TWO EXECUTIVE BRANCHES OF GOVERNMENT, have that negative, and are intended to *support each other in the exercise of it.*

Problems with Congress

13. The representation of the lower house is too small, consisting only of 65 members.

14. That of the *senate* is so small that it renders its extensive powers extremely dangerous: it is to consist only of 26 members,

two-thirds of whom must concur to conclude any *treaty or alliance* with foreign powers: Now we will suppose that five of them are absent, sick, dead, or unable to attend, *twenty-one* will remain, and eight of these (*one-third*, and *one* over) may prevent the conclusion of any treaty, even the most favorable to America. Here will be a fine field for the intrigues and even the *bribery* and *corruption* of European powers.

15. The most important branches of the EXECUTIVE DEPARTMENT are to be put into the hands of a *single magistrate*, who will be in fact an ELECTIVE KING. The MILITARY, the land and naval forces are to be entirely at his disposal, and therefore:

16. Should the *senate*, by the intrigues of foreign powers, become devoted to foreign influence, as was the case of late in *Sweden*, the people will be obliged, as the *Swedes* have been, to seek their refuge in the arms of the *monarch* or PRESIDENT GENERAL.

17. ROTATION, that noble prerogative of liberty, is entirely excluded from the new system of government, and great men may and probably will be continued in office during their lives.

18. ANNUAL ELECTIONS are abolished, and the people are not to re-assume their rights until the expiration of *two, four* and *six* years.

19. Congress are to have the power of fixing the *time, place* and *manner* of holding elections, so as to keep them forever subjected to their influence.

20. The importation of slaves is not to be prohibited until the year 1808, and SLAVERY will probably resume its empire in Pennsylvania.

21. The MILITIA is to be under the immediate command of congress, and men *conscientiously scrupulous of bearing arms*, may be compelled to perform military duty.

22. The new government will be EXPENSIVE beyond any we have ever experienced, the *judicial* department alone, with its concomitant train of *judges, justices, chancellors, clerks, sheriffs, coroners, escheators, state attornies and solicitors, constables, &c.* in every state and in every county in each state, will be a burden beyond the utmost abilities of the people to bear, and upon the whole:

23. A government partaking of MONARCHY and aristocracy will be fully and firmly established, and liberty will be but a name to adorn the *short* historic page of the halcyon days of America.

These, my countrymen, are the objections that have been made to the new proposed system of government; and if you read the system itself with attention, you will find them all to be founded in truth. But what have you been told in answer?

Mr. Wilson's Lack of Patriotism

I pass over the sophistry of Mr. W—, in his equivocal speech at the state house. His pretended arguments have been echoed and re-echoed by every retailer of politics, and *victoriously* refuted by

Defending Those Who Oppose the Constitution

"Centinel" was one of many writers who responded to the arguments made in an October 6, 1787, speech by James Wilson. In the passage excerpted here, he argues that opposition to the proposed Constitution is widespread, and includes the majority of members of the Continental Congress. "Centinel" is believed by historians to have been Samuel Bryan, a former clerk of the Pennsylvania state assembly.

The opposition is not so partial and interested as Mr. *Wilson* asserts. It consists of a respectable yeomanry throughout the union, of characters far removed above the reach of his unsupported assertions. It comprises many worthy members of the late convention, and a majority of the present Congress, for a motion made in that honorable body, for their *approbation* and *recommendation* of the new plan, was after two days animated discussion, prudently withdrawn by its advocates, and a simple *transmission* of the plan to the several states could only be obtained; yet this has been palmed upon the people as the approbation of Congress; and to strengthen the deception, the bells of the city of Philadelphia were rung for a whole day.

Are Mr. *Wilson*, and many of his coadjutors in the late Convention, the disinterested patriots they would have us believe? Is their conduct any recommendation of their plan of government? View them the foremost and loudest on the floor of Congress, in our Assembly, at town meetings, in sounding its eulogiums:—View them preventing investigation and discussion, and in the most despotic manner endeavouring to compel its adoption by the people, with such precipitancy as to preclude the possibility of a due consideration, and then say whether the motives of these men can be pure.

My fellow citizens, such false detestable *patriots* in every nation, have led their blind confiding country, shouting their applauses, into the jaws of *despotism* and *ruin*. May the wisdom and virtue of the people of America, save them from the usual fate of nations.

several patriotic pens. Indeed if you read this famous speech in a cool dispassionate moment, you will find it to contain no more than a train of pitiful sophistry and evasions, unworthy of the man who spoke them. I have taken notice of some of them in stating the objections, and they must, I am sure, have excited your *pity* and *indignation*. Mr. W— is a man of sense, learning and extensive information, unfortunately for him he has never sought the more solid fame of *patriotism*. During the late war he narrowly escaped the effects of popular rage, and the people seldom arm themselves against a citizen in vain. The whole tenor of his political conduct has always been strongly tainted with the spirit of *high aristocracy*, he has never been known to join in a truly popular measure, and his talents have ever been devoted to the patrician interest. His lofty carriage indicates the lofty mind that animates him, a mind able to conceive and perform great things, but which unfortunately can see nothing great out of the pale of power and worldly grandeur; despising what he calls the inferior order of the people, popular liberty and popular assemblies offer to his exalted imagination an idea of meanness and contemptibility which he hardly seeks to conceal—He sees at a distance the pomp and pageantry of courts, he sighs after those stately palaces and that apparatus of human greatness which his vivid fancy has taught him to consider as the supreme good. Men of sublime minds, he conceives, were born a different race from the rest of the sons of men, to them, and them only, he imagines, high heaven intended to commit the reins of earthly government, the remaining part of mankind he sees below at an immense distance, they, he thinks were born to serve, to administer food to the ambition of their superiors, and become the footstool of their power—Such is Mr. W—, and fraught with these high ideas, it is no wonder that he should exert all his talents to support a form of government so admirably contrived to carry them into execution—But when the people, who possess collectively a mass of knowledge superior to his own, inquire into the principles of that government on the establishment or rejection of which depend their dearest concerns, when he is called upon by the voice of thousands to come and explain that favorite system which he holds forth as an object of their admiration, he comes—he attempts to support by reasoning what reason never dictated, and finding the attempt vain, his great mind, made for nobler purposes, is obliged to stoop to mean evasions and pitiful sophistry; himself not deceived, he strives to deceive the people, and the treasonable attempt delineates his true character. . . .

And yet that speech, weak and insidious as it is, is the only attempt that has been made to support by argument that political monster THE PROPOSED CONSTITUTION. I have sought in vain amidst the immense heap of trash that has been published on the subject, an argument worthy of refutation, and I have not been able to find it. If you can bear the disgust which the reading of those pieces must naturally occasion, and which I have felt in the highest degree, read them, my fellow citizens, and say whether they contain the least shadow of logical reasoning, say (laying your hands upon your hearts) whether there is any thing in them that can impress unfeigned conviction upon your unprejudiced minds.

One of them only I shall take notice of, in which I find that argument is weakly attempted. This piece is signed "AN AMERICAN CITIZEN" and has appeared with great pomp in four succeeding numbers in several of our newspapers. But if you read it attentively, you will find that it does not tell us what the new constitution IS, but what it IS NOT, and extolls it on the sole ground that it does not contain ALL the principles of tyranny with which the European governments are disgraced.

Washington and Franklin

But where argument entirely failed, nothing remained for the supporters of the new constitution but to endeavor to inflame your passions—The attempt has been made and I am sorry to find not entirely without effect. The great names of WASHINGTON and FRANKLIN, have been taken in vain and shockingly prostituted to effect the most infamous purposes. What! because our august chieftain has subscribed his name in his capacity of president of the convention to the plan offered by them to the states, and because the venerable sage of Pennsylvania, has *testified* by his signature that *the majority of the delegates of this state* assented to the same plan, will any one infer from this that it has met with their entire approbation, and that they consider it as the master piece of human wisdom? I am apt to think the contrary, and I have good reasons to ground my opinion on.

In the first place we have found by the publication of *Charles Cotesworth Pinckney*, Esquire, one of the *signing* members of the convention, who has expressed the most pointed disapprobation of many important parts of the new plan of government, that all the members whose names appear at the bottom of this instrument of tyranny have not concurred in its adoption. Many of them might conceive themselves bound by the opinion of the majority of their state, and leaving the people to their own judgment upon the form of government offered to them, might have conceived it impolitic by refusing to sign their names, to offer to the world the lamentable spectacle of the disunion of a body on the decisions of whom the people had rested all their hopes. We KNOW, and the long sitting of the convention tells us, that, (as it is endeavoured to persuade us) concord and unanimity did not reign exclusively among them. The thick veil of secrecy with which their proceedings have been covered, has left us entirely in the dark, as to the *debates* that took place, and the unaccountable SUPPRESSION OF THEIR JOURNALS, the highest insult that could be offered to the majesty of the people, shews clearly that the whole of the new plan was entirely the work of an *aristocratic majority*.

But let us suppose for a moment that the proposed government was the unanimous result of the deliberations of the convention—must it on that account preclude an investigation of its merits? Are the people to be dictated to without appeal by any set of men, however great, however dignified? Freedom spurns at the idea and rejects it with disdain—We appeal to the collective wisdom of a great nation, we appeal to their general sense which is easily to be obtained through the channel of a multitude of free presses, from the opinions of *thirty-nine* men, who secluded from the rest of the world, without the possibility of conferring with the rest of their fellow-citizens, have had no opportunity of rectifying the errors into which they may have been led by the *most designing* among them. We have seen names not less illustrious than those of the members of the late convention, subscribed to the present *reprobated* articles of confederation, and if those patriots have erred, there is no reason to suppose that a succeeding set should be more free from error. Nay the very men, who advocate so strongly the new plan of government, and support it with the infallibility of Doctor Franklin, affect to despise the present constitution of Pennsylvania, which was dictated and avowed by that venerable patriot—They are conscious that he does not entirely approve of the new plan, whose principles are so different from those he has established in our ever-glorious constitution, and there is no doubt that it is the reason that has induced them to leave his respected name out of the *ticket* for the approaching election.

Now then my fellow-citizens, my brethren, my friends; if the sacred flame of liberty be not extinguished in your breasts, if you have any regard for the happiness of yourselves, and your posterity, let me entreat you, earnestly entreat you by all that is dear and sacred to freemen, to consider well before you take an awful step which may involve in its consequences the ruin of millions yet unborn—You are on the brink of a dreadful precipice;—in the name therefore of holy liberty, for which I have fought and for which we have all suffered, I call upon you to make a solemn pause before you proceed. One step more, and perhaps the scene of freedom is closed forever in America. Let not a set of aspiring despots, *who make us* SLAVES *and tell us 'tis our* CHARTER, wrest from you those invaluable blessings, for which the most illustrious sons of America have bled and died—but exert yourselves, like men, like freemen and like Americans, to transmit unimpaired to your latest posterity those rights, those liberties, which have ever been so dear to you, and which it is yet in your power to preserve.

VIEWPOINT 4

"I have answered all the objections, and supported my answers by fair quotations from the new constitution."

A Rebuttal to the Objections to the Constitution

"Plain Truth"

Back-and-forth press debates in which people directly addressed arguments presented earlier were common during the months the nation debated whether to ratify the Constitution. A good example comes from the pseudonymous "Plain Truth" in a November 10, 1787, article in the Philadelphia *Independent Gazetteer*. The article is a direct reply to one published four days earlier by "An Officer of the Late Continental Army," which was itself an attack on a speech by federalist leader James Wilson. The author mostly ignores the personal attacks on James Wilson published in the earlier article, choosing instead to refute the twenty-three objections summarized in the earlier tract point by point, supporting his arguments with quotations and references to parts of the Constitution.

FRIEND OSWALD,

Seeing in thy paper of yesterday, twenty-three objections to the new plan of federal government, I am induced to trouble the public once more; and shall endeavour to answer them distinctly, and concisely. That this may be done with candour, as well as per-

"Plain Truth," Philadelphia *Independent Gazetteer*, November 10, 1787.

spicuity, I request thee to reprint them as they are stated by *"an officer of the late continental army,"* and to place my answers in the same order.

I shall pass over every thing that is not in point, and leave the strictures on friend W—[James Wilson] to those who are acquainted with him: I will only observe that "his lofty carriage," is very likely to be the effect of habit; for I know by experience that a man who wears spectacles, must keep his head erect to see through them with ease, and to prevent them from falling off his nose.

Now for the Objections.

"1. It is not merely (as it ought to be) a CONFEDERATION of STATES, but a GOVERNMENT of INDIVIDUALS."

Answer 1. It is more a government *of the people*, than the present Congress ever was, because, the members of Congress have been hitherto chosen by the legislatures of the several states. The proposed representatives are to be chosen "BY THE PEOPLE." If therefore it be not a confederation of *the states*, it is a popular compact, something more in favour of liberty. Art. 1. Sect. 2.

"2. The powers of Congress extend to the *lives*, the *liberties* and the *property* of every citizen."

2. Is there a government on earth, where the life, liberty and property of a citizen, may not be forfeited by a violation of the laws of God and man? It is only when justified by such crimes, that the new government has such power; and all crimes (except in cases of impeachment) are expressly to be TRIED BY JURY, *in the state where they may be committed.* Art. 3. Sect. 2.

The Constitution and the States

"3. The *sovereignty* of the different states, is *ipso facto* destroyed in its most essential parts."

3. Can the sovereignty of each state in all its parts exist, if there be a sovereignty over the whole. Is it not nonsense in terms, to suppose an united government *of any kind*, over 13 co-existent sovereignties? "It is obviously impracticable in the federal government of these states, to secure all the rights of independent sovereignty to each, and yet provide for the interest and safety of all." *President's letter.* [George Washington's letter transmitting the Constitution to the Continental Congress]

"4. What remains of it, will only tend to create violent dissentions between the state governments and the Congress, and terminate in the ruin of the one or the other."

4. No such dissention can happen, unless some state oppose the interests of the whole collectively; and it is to overcome such opposition by a majority of 12 to 1, "to ensure domestic tranquility, to provide for the common defence, promote the general welfare, and secure the blessings of liberty," that the union is now, and has

ever been thought indispensable. (*Introduction to the new plan.*)

"5. The consequence must therefore be, either that the *union* of the states will be destroyed by a violent struggle, or that their sovereignty will be swallowed up by silent encroachments into a universal aristocracy; because it is clear, that if two different *sovereign powers* have a co-equal command over the *purses* of the citizens, they will struggle, for the spoils, and the weakest will be in the end obliged to yield to the efforts of the strongest."

5. The preceding petition being eradicated, this *consequence* falls to the ground. It may be observed however, that the revenue to be raised by Congress, is not likely to interfere with the taxes of any state. Commerce is the source to which they will naturally apply, because that is one great and uniform object, and they cannot attend to detail: The burden too, will in this way be scarcely felt by the people. All foreigners who may sell merchandise at a loss (and that often has been, and often will be the case in an extensive degree) will pay the impost in addition to that loss, and the duties on all that may be sold at a profit, will be eventually paid by the consumers: Thus the taxes will be insensibly included in the price, and every man will have the power of refusal, by not consuming the taxed luxuries.

No Bill of Rights

"6. Congress being possessed of these immense powers, the liberties of the states and of the people, are not secured by a bill or DECLARATION of RIGHTS."

6. Notwithstanding all that has been written against it, I must recur to friend W—'s definition on this subject. A state government is designed for ALL CASES WHATSOEVER, consequently what is not reserved, is tacitly given. A federal government is expressly only for FEDERAL PURPOSES, and its power is consequently bounded by the terms of the compact. In the first case a Bill of Rights is indispensable, in the second it would be at best useless, and if one right were to be omitted, it might injuriously grant by implication, what was intended to be reserved.

"7. The *sovereignty* of the states is not expressly reserved, the *form* only, and not the SUBSTANCE of their government, is guaranteed to them by express words."

7. When man emerged from a state of nature, he surely did not reserve the natural right of being the judge of his wrongs, and the executioner of the punishments he might think they deserved. A renunciation of such rights, is the price he paid for the blessings of good government; and for the same reason, state sovereignty (as I have before observed) is as incompatible with the federal union, as the natural rights of human vengeance is, with the peace of society.

The Best Form of Government Ever Offered

James Wilson, a Pennsylvania delegate to the Constitutional Convention, made a speech on October 6, 1787, at the Pennsylvania State House Yard explaining and defending the proposed Constitution. The speech was printed dozens of times in newspapers across the country. At the conclusion of his speech, Wilson argues that opponents of the Constitution are motivated by self-interest to preserve their privileged positions in the existing political structure.

After all, my fellow citizens, it is neither extraordinary or unexpected, that the constitution offered to your consideration, should meet with opposition. It is the nature of man to pursue his own interest, in preference to the public good; and I do not mean to make any personal reflection, when I add, that it is the interest of a very numerous, powerful, and respectable body to counteract and destroy the excellent work produced by the late convention. All the offices of government, and all the appointments for the administration of justice and the collection of the public revenue, which are transferred from the individual to the aggregate sovereignty of the states, will necessarily turn the stream of influence and emolument into a new channel. Every person therefore, who either enjoys, or expects to enjoy, a place of profit under the present establishment, will object to the proposed innovation; not, in truth, because it is injurious to the liberties of his country, but because it affects his schemes of wealth and consequence. I will confess indeed, that I am not a blind admirer of this plan of government, and that there are some parts of it, which if my wish had prevailed, would certainly have been altered. But, when I reflect how widely men differ in their opinions, and that every man (and the observation applies likewise to every state) has an equal pretension to assert his own, I am satisfied that any thing nearer to perfection could not have been accomplished. If there are errors, it should be remembered, that the seeds of reformation are sown in the work itself, and the concurrence of two thirds of the congress may at any time introduce alterations and amendments. Regarding it then, in every point of view, with a candid and disinterested mind, I am bold to assert, that it is the best form of government which has ever been offered to the world.

"The United States shall guarantee to every state, a republican form of government." That is, they shall guarantee it against monarchical or aristocratical encroachments; Congress can go no further, for the states would justly think themselves insulted, if they should presume to interfere in other alterations which may be individually thought more consistent with the good of the people. Art. 4. Sect. 4.

"8. TRIAL BY JURY, that sacred bulwark of liberty, is ABOLISHED IN CIVIL CASES, and Mr. W—, one of the convention, has told you, that not being able to agree as to the FORM of establishing this point, they have left you deprived of the SUBSTANCE. Here is his own words—*The subject was involved in difficulties. The convention found the task* TOO DIFFICULT *for them, and left the business as it stands."*

8. Trial by jury has been seen to be expressly preserved in criminal cases. In civil cases, the federal court is like a court of chancery, except that it has original jurisdiction only in state affairs; in all other matters it has "appellate jurisdiction both as to law and fact, *with such exceptions and under such regulations as congress shall make." Art. 3. sect. 2.* Nobody every complained that trials in chancery were not by jury. A court of chancery "may issue injunctions in various stages of a cause, saith Blackstone, and stay oppressive judgement." Yet courts of chancery are every where extolled as the most equitable; the federal court has not such an extent of power, and what it has is to be always under the *exceptions and regulations of the United states in Congress.*

Friend W—has well observed that it was impossible to make one imitation of thirteen different models, and the matter seems now to stand, as well as human wisdom can permit.

Freedom of the Press

"9. THE LIBERTY OF THE PRESS is not secured, and the powers of congress are fully adequate to its destruction, as they are to have the trial of *libels,* or *pretended libels* against the United States, and may by a cursed abominable STAMP ACT (as the *Bowdoin administration* has done in Massachusetts) preclude you effectually from all means of information. *Mr. W—has given you no answer to these arguments."*

9. The liberty of the press in each state, can only be in danger from the laws of that state, and it is every where well secured. Besides, as the new congress can only have the defined powers given, it was needless to say any thing about liberty of the press, liberty of conscience, or any other liberty that a freeman ought never to be deprived of. It is remarkable in this instance, that among all the cases to which the federal jurisdiction is to extend (*art.* 3) not a word is said of "*libels or pretended libels.*" Indeed in this extensive continent, and among this enlightened people, no government whatever *could* controul the press: For after all that is said about "balance of power," there is one power which no tyranny on earth could subdue if once roused by this great and general grievance, that is THE PEOPLE. This respectable power has preserved the press in Great Britain in spite of government; and none but a madman could ever think of controuling it in America.

"10. Congress have the power of keeping up a STANDING ARMY in time of peace, and Mr. W— has told you THAT IT IS NECESSARY."

10. The power here referred to is this, "to raise and support

armies, *but no appropriation of money to that use shall be for a longer term than two years.*"—*Art.* 1, *sect.* 8. Thus the representatives of the people have it in their power to disband this army every two years, by refusing supplies. Does not every American feel that no standing army in the power of congress to raise, could support despotism over this immense continent, where almost every citizen is a soldier? If such an apprehension came, in my opinion, within the bounds of possibility, it would not indeed become my principles to oppose this objection.

The Legislative and Executive Branches

"11. The LEGISLATIVE and EXECUTIVE powers are not kept separate as every one of the American constitutions declares they ought to be; but they are mixed in a manner entirely novel and unknown, even to the constitution of Great Britain."

11. The first article of the constitution defines the legislative, the second, the executive, and the third the judicial powers; this does not seem like *mixing* them. It would be strange indeed if a professed democratist should object, that the president's power is made subject to "the advice and consent of two-thirds of the senate." *Art.* 2. *sect.* 2.

"12. In England, the king only has a *nominal negative* over the proceedings of the legislature, which he has NEVER DARED TO EXERCISE since the days of *King William*, whereas by the new constitution, both the *president general* and the *senate*, TWO EXECUTIVE BRANCHES OF GOVERNMENT, have that negative, and are intended to *support each other in the exercise of it.*"

12. Whoever will read the 7th section of the 4th article, will feel that the president has only a *conditional* negative, which is effectual or not as two-thirds of the senate and two-thirds of the representatives may on reconsideration determine. If the *"two executive branches"* (as they are here called) should agree in the negative, it would not be novel, as to the power of the senate; for I believe every senate on the continent, and every upper house in the world, may refuse concurrence and quash a bill before it arrives at the executive department: The king of England has an *unconditional* negative, and has often exercised it in his former colonies.

"13. The representation of the lower house is too small, consisting only of 65 members."

13. The congress on the old plan had but 13 voices, and of these, some were frequently lost by equal divisions. If 65 voices be yet too few, it must follow that the new plan has made some progress towards perfection.

"14. That of the *senate* is so small that it renders its extensive powers extremely dangerous: it is to consist only of 26 members, two-thirds of whom must concur to conclude any *treaty or alliance* with foreign powers: Now we will suppose that five of them are absent, sick, dead, or unable to attend, *twenty one* will remain, and eight of these (*one-third*, and *one* over) may prevent the conclusion of any treaty, even the most favorable to America. Here will be a fine field for the intrigues and even the *bribery* and *corruption* of European powers."

An Admirable System of Government

George Washington's generally favorable opinions on the Constitution are found mainly in private letters to friends and associates. This passage is taken from a February 7, 1788, letter to the Marquis de Lafayette.

It appears to me . . . little short of a miracle, that the Delegates from so many different States (which States you know are also different from each other in their manners, circumstances and prejudices) should unite in forming a system of national Government, so little liable to well founded objections. Nor am I yet such an enthusiastic, partial or undiscriminating admirer of it, as not to perceive it is tinctured with some real (though not radical) defects. The limits of a letter would not suffer me to go fully into an examination of them; nor would the discussion be entertaining or profitable, I therefore forbear to touch upon it. With regard to the two great points (the pivots on which the whole machine must move) my Creed is simply:—

1st.—That the general Government is not invested with more Powers than are indispensably necessary to perform the functions of a good Government; and, consequently, that no objection ought to be made against the quantity of Power delegated to it:

2ly.—That these Powers (as the appointment of all Rulers will forever arise from, and, at short stated intervals, recur to the free suffrage of the People) are so distributed among the Legislative, Executive, and Judicial Branches, into which the general Government is arranged, that it can never be in danger of degenerating into a monarchy, an Oligarchy, an Aristocracy, or any other despotic or oppressive form; so long as there shall remain any virtue in the body of the People.

14. This like the former objection is mere matter of opinion. The instance as to supposed vacancies does not apply, for "if vacancies happen by resignation *or otherwise* during the recess of the legislature of any state, the executive thereof may make temporary appointments until the meeting of the legislature which shall then fill such vacancies." *Art.* 1 *sec.* 3. This provision expressly implies that accidental vacancies shall be *immediately* filled.

"15. The most important branches of the EXECUTIVE DEPARTMENT are to be put into the hands of a *single magistrate*, who will be in fact an ELECTIVE KING. The MILITARY, the land and naval forces are to be entirely at his disposal."

15. It was mentioned as a grievance in the 12th objection that this supposed "elective king," had his powers clogged by the conjunction of another branch; here he is called a "*single magistrate*." Yet the new constitution provides that he shall act "by and with the advice and consent of the senate." *Art*. 2. *sec*. 2, and can in no instance act alone, except in the cause of humanity by granting reprieves or pardons.

"16. Should the *senate*, by the intrigues of foreign powers, become devoted to foreign influence, as was the case of late in *Sweden*, the people will be obliged, as the *Swedes* have been, to seek their refuge in the arms of the *monarch* or PRESIDENT GENERAL."

16. The comparison of a little kingdom to a great republic, cannot be just. The revolution in Sweden, was the affair of a day, and the success of it was owing to its confined bounds. To suppose a similar event in this extensive country, 3000 miles distant from European intrigues, is, in the nature of things, a gross absurdity.

"17. ROTATION, that noble prerogative of liberty, is entirely excluded from the new system of government, and great men may and probably will be continued in office during their lives."

17. How can this be the case, when at stated periods the government reverts to the people, and to the representatives of the people, for a new choice in every part of it.

"18. ANNUAL ELECTIONS are abolished, and the people are not to re-assume their rights until the expiration of *two, four* and *six* years."

18. Annual changes in a federal government would beget confusion; it requires years to learn a trade, and men in this age are not legislators by inspiration: One third of the senate as well as all the representatives are to be elected every *two* years. *Art*. 1. *sec*. 3.

"19. Congress are to have the power of fixing the *time, place* and *manner* of holding elections, so as to keep them forever subjected to their influence."

19. Congress are not to have power to fix the place of choosing senators; and the time place and manner of electing representatives are to be fixed by each state itself. Congress indeed are to have controul to prevent undue influence in elections, which we all know but too often happens through party zeal. *Art*. 1. *sec*. 4.

Further Objections Answered

"20. The importation of slaves is not to be prohibited until the year 1808, and SLAVERY will probably resume its empire in Pennsylvania."

20. . . . . Congress will have no power to meddle in the business 'til 1808. All that can be said against this offending clause is, that we

may have no alteration in this respect for 21 years to come, but 21 years is fixed as a period when we may be better, and in the mean time we cannot be worse than we are now. *Article* 1. *section* 9.

"21. The MILITIA is to be under the immediate command of Congress, and men *conscienciously scrupulous of bearing arms*, may be compelled to perform military duty."

21. Congress may "provide for *calling forth* the militia," "and may provide for organizing, arming and disciplining it."—But the states respectively can only *raise it*, and they expressly reserve the right of "appointment of officers and of training it."—Now we know that men conscienciously scrupulous by sect or profession are not *forced* to bear arms in any of the states, a pecuniary compensation being accepted in lieu of it.—Whatever may be my sentiments on the present state of this matter is foreign to the point: But it is certain that whatever redress may be wished for, or expected, can only come from *the state Legislature*, where, and where only, the dispensing power, or enforcing power, is *in the first instance* placed. *Article* 1. *section* 8.

"22. The new government will be EXPENSIVE beyond any we have ever experienced, the *judicial* department alone, with its concomitant train of *judges, justices, chancellors, clerks, sheriffs, coroners, escheators, state attornies and solicitors, constables, &c.* in every state and in every county in each state, will be a burden beyond the utmost abilities of the people to bear."

22. This mighty expence would be paid by about one shilling a man throughout the states. The other part of this objection is not intelligible, nothing is said in the new constitution of a judicial department in *"states* and *counties,"* other than what is already established.

"23. A government partaking of MONARCHY and aristocracy will be fully and firmly established, and liberty will be but a name to adorn the *short* historic page of the halcyon days of America."

23. The 5th article expressly provides against every danger, by pointing out a mode of amendment when necessary. And liberty will thus be a name to adorn the *long* historic page of American virtue and happiness.

Quoting George Washington

Thus I have answered all the objections, and supported my answers by fair quotations from the new constitution; and I particularly desire my readers to examine all the references with accurate attention. If I have mistaken any part, it will, I trust, be found to be an error of judgment, not of will, and I shall thankfully receive any candid instruction on the subject.—One quotation more and I have done.—"In all our deliberations on this subject (saith GEORGE WASHINGTON) we kept steadily in our view, that which appears to us the greatest interest of every true American, the consolidation of our union, in which is involved our prosperity, felicity, safety, perhaps our national existence. This important consideration, seriously and deeply impressed on our minds, led each state in the Convention to be less rigid on points of inferior magnitude, than might have been otherwise expected; and thus the constitution which we now present, is the result of a spirit of amity, and of that mutual deference and concession which the peculiarity of our political situation rendered indispensable."

VIEWPOINT 5

"These ... moneyed men ... expect to get into Congress themselves; ... and get all the power and all the money into their own hands."

The Constitution Benefits the Elite

Amos Singletary (1742-1812)

A common criticism of the Constitution, both during the ratification debates and continuing to the present day, is that it created a government for the benefit of social and economic elites at the expense of average Americans. One expression of this argument comes from Amos Singletary, a delegate to the Massachusetts ratifying convention, which convened in January 1788. A mill operator and local justice of the peace, Singletary represented the central Massachusetts town of Sutton in the Massachusetts legislature during colonial times (when it was called the General Court) and following independence.

On January 25, 1788, Fisher Ames, a thirty-two-year-old ratification delegate, asked veterans of the 1775 revolutionary struggles against Great Britain to unite in support of the Constitution. Singletary responded with this speech addressed to the president and other members of the ratifying convention. He argues that powers given by the Constitution to the national government are similar to the taxing powers of Great Britain that precipitated the drive for independence. He contends that the new Congress will be dominated by the wealthy who will unfairly exploit and tax the common people. Although Singletary's views were shared by many, Massachusetts voted to ratify the Constitution by a narrow margin.

From *The Debates in the Several State Conventions on the Adoption of the Federal Constitution, etc., etc.* 2nd ed. Jonathan Elliot, ed. New York, 1888.

The following passage is taken from the account of Singletary's speech as first published in the *Massachusetts Centinel* on February 13, 1788. It begins by describing Fisher Ames's call for unity and then goes on to record Singletary's response.

Mr. [Fisher] AMES, in a short discourse, called on those who stood forth in 1775 to stand forth now; to throw aside all interested and party views; to have one purse and one heart for the whole; and to consider that, as it was necessary then, so was it necessary now, to unite,—or die we must.

Hon. Mr. SINGLETARY. Mr. President, I should not have troubled the Convention again, if some gentlemen had not called on them that were on the stage in the beginning of our troubles, in the year 1775. I was one of them. I have had the honor to be a member of the court [Massachusetts General Court, the colonial legislature] all the time, Mr. President, and I say that, if any body had proposed such a constitution as this in that day, it would have been thrown away at once. It would not have been looked at. We contended with Great Britain, some said for a threepenny duty on tea; but it was not that; it was because they claimed a right to tax us and bind us in all cases whatever. And does not this Constitution do the same? Does it not take away all we have—all our property? Does it not lay *all* taxes, duties, imposts, and excises? And what more have we to give? They tell us Congress won't lay dry taxes [property taxes] upon us, but collect all the money they want by impost [import duties]. I say, there has always been a difficulty about impost. Whenever the General Court was going to lay an impost, they would tell us it was more than trade could bear, that it hurt the fair trader, and encouraged smuggling; and there will always be the same objection: they won't be able to raise money enough by impost, and then they will lay it on the land, and take all we have got. These lawyers, and men of learning, and moneyed men, that talk so finely, and gloss over matters so smoothly, to make us poor illiterate people swallow down the pill, expect to get into Congress themselves; they expect to be the managers of this Constitution, and get all the power and all the money into their own hands, and then they will swallow up all us little folks, like the great *Leviathan*, Mr. President; yes, just as the whale swallowed up *Jonah*. This is what I am afraid of; but I won't say any more at present, but reserve the rest to another opportunity.

VIEWPOINT 6

"I don't think the worse of the Constitution because lawyers, and men of learning, and moneyed men, are fond of it."

The Constitution Will Benefit All the People

Jonathan Smith (c.1740-1802)

The state of Massachusetts posed the first major test for supporters of the ratification of the Constitution. Wealthy members of the commercial and legal establishment of the larger towns of the eastern part of the state were in favor of it. But a large number of delegates, especially from the poorer agrarian middle and western parts of the state, were firmly opposed to the establishment of a new national government with the power to tax. A common argument heard was that such a powerful and remote government was precisely what people had fought against in the American Revolution.

Jonathan Smith was one of the few ratification convention delegates with a western, agrarian background to speak for the Constitution. A farmer who held important offices in the western Massachusetts town of Lanesborough, he was also a colonel in the Massachusetts militia and a delegate to Massachusetts's 1780 state constitutional convention. Speaking at the Massachusetts state ratifying convention on January 25, 1788, and directly responding to the arguments of fellow delegate Amos Singletary, Smith defends the Constitution. He recalls the previous year's crisis caused by Shays's Rebellion (the "black cloud that rose in the east"), an insurrection of Massachusetts farmers protesting

From *The Debates in the Several State Conventions on the Adoption of the Federal Constitution, etc., etc.* 2nd ed. Jonathan Elliot, ed. New York, 1888.

state tax policy. Smith argues that the rebellion revealed the threat of anarchy, and that the Constitution would forestall such dangers. He disputes the argument that the Constitution should be opposed because rich and elite men support it and that such people can be assumed to always abuse their power. An account of the exchange between Smith and Singletary was printed in the *Massachusetts Centinel* on February 13, and later reprinted sixteen times in newspapers around the country. The following is taken from the *Centinel* account, and includes descriptions of interruptions of Smith's speech by other convention delegates.

Hon. Mr. SMITH. Mr. President, I am a plain man, and get my living by the plough. I am not used to speak in public, but I beg your leave to say a few words to my brother ploughjoggers in this house. I have lived in a part of the country where I have known the worth of good government by the want of it. There was a black cloud that rose in the east last winter, and spread over the west. (*Here Mr. William Widgery interrupted. Mr. President, I wish to know what the gentleman means by the east.*) I mean, sir, the county of Bristol; the cloud rose there, and burst upon us, and produced a dreadful effect. It brought on a state of anarchy, and that led to tyranny. I say, it brought anarchy. People that used to live peaceably, and were before good neighbors, got distracted, and took up arms against government. (*Here Mr. Kingsley called to order, and asked, what had the history of last winter to do with the Constitution. Several gentlemen, and among the rest the Hon. Mr. Samuel Adams, said the gentleman was in order—let him go on in his own way.*) I am going, Mr. President, to show you, my brother farmers, what were the effects of anarchy, that you may see the reasons why I wish for good government. People I say took up arms; and then, if you went to speak to them, you had the musket of death presented to your breast. They would rob you of your property; threaten to burn your houses; oblige you to be on your guard night and day; alarms spread from town to town; families were broken up; the tender mother would cry, "O, my son is among them! What shall I do for my child!" Some were taken captive, children taken out of their schools, and carried away. Then we should hear of an action, and the poor prisoners were set in the front, to be killed by their own friends. How dreadful, how distressing was this! Our distress was so great that we should have been glad to snatch at any thing that looked like a government. Had any person, that was able to protect us, come and set up his standard, we should all have flocked to it, even if it had been a monarch; and that monarch might have proved a tyrant;—so that you see that anarchy leads to tyranny, and better have one tyrant than so many at once.

A Cure for Disorder

Now, Mr. President, when I saw this Constitution, I found that it was a cure for these disorders. It was just such a thing as we wanted. I got a copy of it, and read it over and over. I had been a member of the Convention to form our own state constitution, and had learnt something of the checks and balances of power, and I found them all here. I did not go to any lawyer, to ask his opinion; we have no lawyer in our town, and we do well enough without. I formed my own opinion, and was pleased with this Constitution. My honorable old daddy there (*pointing to Mr. Singletary*) won't think that I expect to be a Congress-man, and swallow up the liberties of the people. I never had any post, nor do I want one. But I don't think the worse of the Constitution because lawyers, and men of learning, and moneyed men, are fond of it. I don't suspect that they want to get into Congress and abuse their power. I am not of such a jealous make. They that are honest men themselves are not apt to suspect other people. I don't know why our constituents have not a good right to be as jealous of us as we seem to be of the Congress; and I think those gentlemen, who are so very suspicious that as soon as a man gets into power he turns rogue, had better look at home.

We are, by this Constitution, allowed to send ten members to Congress. Have we not more than that number fit to go? I dare say, if we pick out ten, we shall have another ten left, and I hope ten times ten; and will not these be a check upon those that go? Will they go to Congress, and abuse their power, and do mischief, when they know they must return and look the other ten in the face, and be called to account for their conduct? Some gentlemen think that our liberty and property are not safe in the hands of moneyed men, and men of learning. I am not of that mind.

A Time to Reap

Brother farmers, let us suppose a case, now: Suppose you had a farm of 50 acres, and your title was disputed, and there was a farm of 5000 acres joined to you, that belonged to a man of learning, and his title was involved in the same difficulty; would you not be glad to have him for your friend, rather than to stand alone in the dispute? Well, the case is the same. These lawyers, these moneyed men, these men of learning, are all embarked in the same cause with us, and we must all swim or sink together; and shall we throw the Constitution overboard because it does not please us alike? Suppose two or three of you had been at the pains to break up a piece of rough land, and sow it with wheat; would you let it lie waste because you could not agree what sort of a fence to make? Would it not be better to put up a fence that did not please every one's fancy, rather than not fence it at all, or keep disputing about it until the wild beasts came in and devoured it? Some gentlemen say, Don't be in a hurry; take time to consider, and don't take a leap in the dark. I say, Take things in time; gather fruit when it is ripe. There is a time to sow and a time to reap; we sowed our seed when we sent men to the federal Convention; now is the harvest, now is the time to reap the fruit of our labor; and if we won't do it now, I am afraid we never shall have another opportunity.

VIEWPOINT 7

"It is the opinion of this convention, that certain amendments ... in the said constitution, would remove the fears ... of many of the good people of this commonwealth."

The Constitution Should Be Ratified with Suggested Future Amendments

Samuel Adams and the Massachusetts Ratifying Convention

The Massachusetts ratifying convention was a crucial turning point in the national debate over ratifying the Constitution. When it convened on January 9, 1788, five states had already voted to ratify; only four more were needed. But of the five states, most were small, with little organized opposition. The one large state to ratify, Pennsylvania, did so in a manner that left widespread opposition and bitterness in its wake—bitterness that led to riots and other violence. Anti-federalist sentiment was mounting in Virginia, New York, and other key states that had yet to vote.

Massachusetts was the first state in which federalist supporters of the Constitution faced serious anti-federalist opposition and in which the majority of its ratification delegates were presumed to be against the document. Many delegates insisted the Constitution needed amendments before they could ratify it. Federalists argued that the Constitution had to be accepted or rejected as it stood. In Massachusetts both sides made a key compromise. The convention proposed that, instead of *conditional* amendments as demanded by the anti-federalists, the convention would instead pro-

Samuel Adams, from *Debates, Resolutions and Other Proceedings of the Convention of the Commonwealth of Massachusetts . . .*, Benjamin Russell, ed. Boston, 1788. "The Form of the Ratification of Massachusetts" as it appeared in the *Massachusetts Gazette*, February 8, 1788.

vide a list of *recommended* amendments that would be pursued by Congress after the Constitution went into effect, using the amendment mechanism found in Article V of the Constitution.

The compromise helped convince two influential veterans of the American Revolution to support ratification. John Hancock, then governor of Massachusetts and president of the convention, introduced the proposed compromise on January 31. Samuel Adams, the revolutionary leader whose activities included the 1773 Boston Tea Party, made a speech the same day, which is reprinted in Part I of this viewpoint. He argues that the compromise will influence other states to ratify the Constitution in a similar fashion with their own recommended amendments, thus ensuring both that the Constitution would soon take effect and that desired changes would be made. Part II of this viewpoint is taken from the official February 6 ratification by the Massachusetts convention, including its recommended amendments. Historian Richard B. Bernstein writes in *Are We to Be a Nation?*:

> This formula was the salvation of the Constitution, swaying undecided votes in many states and reconciling moderate Anti-Federalists to ratification, especially when Federalist leaders pledged to support amendments when the new national legislature should convene. Just as important was the Anti-Federal delegates' reaction to the close vote in the Massachusetts convention—187-168 for ratification. The defeated delegates' gracious pledges to accept the decision of the convention and to work for peaceful implementation of the Constitution and its subsequent amendment eliminated concerns that the divisions spawned by the ratification controversy were irreparable.

I

Hon. Mr. ADAMS. Mr. President—I feel myself happy in contemplating the idea, that many benefits will result from your Excellency's [John Hancock] conciliatory proposition, to this commonwealth and to the United States; and I think it ought to precede the motion made by the gentleman from Newbury-Port [Theophilus Parsons]; and to be at this time considered by the Convention. I have said, that I have had my doubts of this Constitution—I could not digest every part of it, as readily as some gentlemen; but this, sir, is my misfortune, not my fault. Other gentlemen have had their doubts, but, in my opinion the proposition submitted, will have a tendency to remove such doubts, and to conciliate the minds of the convention, and the people without doors. This subject, sir, is of the greatest magnitude, and has employed the attention of every rational man in the United States: but the minds of the people are not so well agreed on it as all of us could wish. A proposal, of this sort, coming from Massachusetts, from her importance, will have its weight. Four or five states have considered and ratified the constitution as it stands; but we know there is a diversity of opinion even in these states, and one of them is greatly agitated. If this Convention should particularize the amendments necessary to be proposed, it appears to me it must have weight in other States where Conventions have not yet met. I have observed the sentiments of gentlemen on the subject, as far as Virginia; and I have found that the objections were similar, in the news papers, and in some of the Conventions.—Considering these circumstances, it appears to me that such a measure will have the most salutary effect throughout the union.—It is of the greatest importance, that *America* should still be united in sentiment. I think I have not been heretofore unmindful of the advantage of such an union. It is essential that the people should be united in the federal government, to withstand the common enemy, and to preserve their valuable rights and liberties. We find in the great State of Pennsylvania, one third of the Convention are opposed to it: should there then be large minorities in the several states, I should fear the consequences of such disunion.

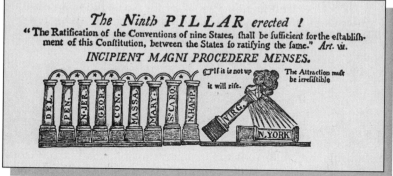

From January to August 1788, the Massachusetts Centinel, *a pro-Constitution newspaper, published a running allegorical cartoon on the states' ratification of the Constitution. Each ratifying state was symbolized by a pillar supporting the arches of government.*

Sir, there are many parts of it I esteem as highly valuable, particularly the article which empowers Congress to regulate commerce, to form treaties &c. [Article I, Sec. 8]. For want of this power in our national head, our friends are grieved, and our enemies insult us. Our ambassadour at the court of London [John

Adams] is considered as a mere cypher, instead of the representative of the United States.—Therefore it appears to me, that a power to remedy this evil should be given to Congress, and the remedy applied as soon as possible.

Future Amendments

The only difficulty on gentlemen's minds is, whether it is best to accept this Constitution on conditional amendments, or to rely on amendments in future, as the Constitution provides. When I look over the article which provides for a revision [Article V], I have my doubts. Suppose, sir, nine states accept the Constitution without any conditions at all; and the four states should wish to have amendments, where will you find nine States to propose, and the legislatures of nine States to agree, to the introduction of amendments—Therefore it seems to me, that the expectation of amendments taking place at some future time, will be frustrated. This method [Hancock's proposal], if we take it, will be the most likely to bring about the amendments, as the Conventions of New-Hampshire, Rhode-Island, New-York, Maryland, Virginia, and South-Carolina, have not yet met. I apprehend, sir, that these States will be influenced by the proposition which your Excellency has submitted, as the resolutions of Massachusetts have ever had their influence. If this should be the case, the necessary amendments would be introduced more early, and more safely. From these considerations, as your Excellency did not think it proper to make a motion, with submission, I move, that the paper read by your Excellency, be now taken under consideration, by the Convention.

II

COMMONWEALTH of MASSACHUSETTS.
In convention of the delegates of the people of the commonwealth of Massachusetts, Feb. 6, 1788.

The convention having impartially discussed, and fully considered, the constitution for the United States of America, reported to Congress, by the convention of delegates from the United States, of America, and submitted to us, by a resolution of the General Court of the said commonwealth, passed the twenty fifth day of October last past; and acknowledging with grateful hearts the goodness of the Supreme Ruler of the universe, in affording the people of the United States, in the course of his Providence, an opportunity, deliberately and peaceably, without fraud or surprise, of entering into an explicit and solemn compact with each other, by assenting to and ratifying a new constitution, in order to form a more perfect union, establish justice, insure domestick tranquillity, provide for the common defence, promote the general welfare, and secure the blessings of liberty to themselves, and their posterity—DO, in the name and in behalf of the people of the commonwealth of Massachusetts, ASSENT to and RATIFY the said *constitution, for the United States of America.*

Recommended Amendments

And as it is the opinion of this convention, that certain amendments and alterations in the said constitution, would remove the fears, and quiet the apprehensions of many of the good people of this commonwealth, and more effectually guard against an undue administration of the federal government, the convention do therefore recommend, that the following alterations and provisions be introduced into the said constitution:

First. That it be explicitly declared, that all powers, not expressly delegated by the aforesaid constitution, are reserved to the several states, to be by them exercised.

Secondly. That there shall be one representative to every thirty thousand persons, according to the census mentioned in the constitution, until the whole number of the representatives amounts to two hundred.

Thirdly. That Congress do not exercise the powers vested in them by the 4th sect. of the Ist art. [the power to change state legislature laws governing congressional elections] but [except] in cases when a state neglect or refuse to make regulations therein mentioned, or shall make regulations subversive of the rights of the people, to a free and equal representation in Congress, agreeably to the constitution.

Fourthly. That Congress do not lay direct taxes, but when the monies arising from the impost and excise are insufficient for the publick exigencies; nor then, until Congress shall have first made a requisition upon the states, to assess, levy and pay their respective proportions of such requisition, agreeably to the census fixed in the said constitution, in such way and manner as the legislature of the state shall think best,—and in such case, if any state shall neglect or refuse to pay its proportion, pursuant to such requisition, then Congress may assess and levy such states proportion, together with interest thereon, at the rate of six per cent. per annum, from the time of payment prescribed in such requisition.

Fifthly. That Congress erect no company of merchants with exclusive advantages of commerce.

Sixthly. That no person shall be tried for any crime by which he may incur an infamous punishment, or loss of life, until he be first indicted by a grand jury, except in such cases as may arise in the government and regulation of the land and naval forces.

Seventhly. The supreme judicial federal court shall have no jurisdiction of causes between citizens of different states, unless the matter in dispute . . . be of the value of three thousand dollars, at the least: Nor shall the federal judicial powers extend to any actions between citizens of different states where the matter in dispute, whether it concerns the reality or personality, is not of the value of fifteen hundred dollars, at the least.

A Plea for Unity

In a speech to the state ratifying convention on February 6, 1788, Massachusetts governor John Hancock endorsed the plan to ratify the Constitution with a recommendation for future amendments and called for national unity amidst a "spirit of conciliation."

I give my assent to the Constitution in full confidence that the amendments proposed will soon become a part of the system—these amendments being in no wise local, but calculated to give security and ease alike to all the States, I think that all will agree to them.

Suffer me to add, that let the question be decided as it may, there can be no triumph on the one side, or chagrin on the other—Should there be a great division, every good man, every one who loves his country, will be so far from exhibiting extraordinary marks of joy, that he will sincerely lament the want of unanimity, and strenuously endeavour to cultivate a spirit of conciliation, both in Convention, and at home. The people of this Commonwealth, are a people of great light—of great intelligence in publick business—They know that we have none of us an interest separate from theirs—that it must be our happiness to conduce to theirs—and that we must all rise or fall together—They will never, therefore, forsake the first principle of society, that of being governed by the voice of the majority; and should it be that the proposed form of government should be rejected, they will zealously attempt another. Should it by the vote now to be taken be ratified, they will quietly acquiesce, and where they see a want of perfection in it, endeavour in a constitutional way to have it amended.

The question now before you is such as no nation on earth, without the limits of America, have ever had the privilege of deciding upon. As the Supreme Ruler of the Universe has seen fit to bestow upon us this glorious opportunity, let us decide upon it—appealing to him for the rectitude of our intentions—and in humble confidence that he will yet continue to bless and save our country.

Eighthly. In civil actions, between citizens of different states, every issue of fact, arising in actions at common law, shall be tried by a jury, if the parties, or either of them, request it.

Ninthly. Congress shall, at no time, consent, that any person, holding an office of trust or profit, under the United States, shall accept of a title of nobility, or any other title or office, from any king, prince, or foreign state.

And the Convention do, in the name and in behalf of the people of this commonwealth, enjoin it upon their representatives in Congress, at all times, until the alterations and provisions aforesaid have been considered, agreeably to the fifth article of the said constitution, to exert all their influence, and use all reasonable and legal methods to obtain a ratification of the said alterations and provisions in such manner as is provided in the said article.

And that the United States in Congress assembled may have due notice of the assent and ratification of the said constitution by this Convention—It is

RESOLVED, That the assent and ratification aforesaid be engrossed on parchment, together with the recommendation and injunction aforesaid, and with this resolution; and that his excellency JOHN HANCOCK, esquire, president, and the honourable WILLIAM CUSHING, esquire, vice-president, of this Convention, transmit the same, countersigned by the secretary of the Convention, under their hands and seals, to the United States in Congress assembled.

> (Signed) JOHN HANCOCK, President,
> WILLIAM CUSHING, Vice-President.

(Countersigned)
GEORGE RICHARDS MINOT, Sec'y.

VIEWPOINT 8

"The very suggestion, that we ought to trust to the precarious hope of amendments ... after we have voluntarily fixed the shackles on our own necks should have awakened to a double degree of caution."

The Proposed Constitution Should Not Be Ratified

Mercy Otis Warren (1728-1814)

On February 6, 1788, the Massachusetts ratifying convention voted 187-168 to ratify the Constitution while at the same time proposing a list of amendments to be added to it after ratification. Later that month a pamphlet by "A Columbian Patriot" was printed in Boston. The essay, sharply critical of the Constitution and the Massachusetts compromise of proposed future amendments, was believed by some to have been written by Elbridge Gerry, the Massachusetts delegate to the Constitutional Convention who had refused to sign the final document. However, in 1930 noted historian Charles Warren discovered family papers that revealed the author to be Mercy Otis Warren.

Warren was an accomplished essayist, playwright, historian, and poet. Her works include *The History of the Rise, Progress, and Termination of the American Revolution*, published in 1805. She was a close associate of many important figures of the American Revolution, including her brother, James Otis, and husband, James Warren. In her essay attacking the Massachusetts ratification decision, excerpts of which are reprinted here, she argues that the new Constitution, in creating a powerful federal government while failing to provide for people's rights, betrays the ideals of the Revolution.

From *Observations on the New Constitution, and on the Federal and State Conventions* by "A Columbian Patriot," Boston, 1788.

All writers on government agree, and the feelings of the human mind witness the truth of these political axioms, that man is born free and possessed of certain unalienable rights—that government is instituted for the protection, safety, and happiness of the people, and not for the profit, honour, or private interest of any man, family, or class of men—That the origin of all power is in the people, and that they have an incontestible right to check the creatures of their own creation, vested with certain powers to guard the life, liberty and property of the community: And if certain selected bodies of men, deputed on these principles, determine contrary to the wishes and expectations of their constituents, the people have an undoubted right to reject their decisions, to call for a revision of their conduct, to depute others in their room, or if they think proper, to demand further time for deliberation on matters of the greatest moment: it therefore is an unwarrantable stretch of authority or influence, if any methods are taken to preclude this reasonable, and peaceful mode of enquiry and decision. And it is with inexpressible anxiety, that many of the best friends to the Union of the States—to the peaceable and equal participation of the rights of nature, and to the glory and dignity of this country, behold the insiduous arts, and the strenuous efforts of the partisans of arbitrary power, by their vague definitions of the best established truths, endeavoring to envelope the mind in darkness the concomitant of slavery, and to lock the strong chains of domestic despotism on a country, which by the most glorious and successful struggles is but newly emancipated from the sceptre of foreign dominion.—But there are certain seasons in the course of human affairs, when Genius, Virtue, and Patriotism, seems to nod over the vices of the times, and perhaps never more remarkably, than at the present period; or we should not see such a passive disposition prevail in some, who we must candidly suppose, have liberal and enlarged sentiments; while a supple multitude are paying a blind and idolatrous homage to the opinions of those who by the most precipitate steps are treading down their dear bought privileges; and who are endeavouring by all the arts of insinuation, and influence, to betray the people of the United States, into an acceptance of a most complicated system of government; marked on the one side with the *dark, secret* and *profound intrigues,* of the statesman, long practised in the purlieus of despotism; and on the other, with the ideal projects of *young ambition,* with its wings just expanded to soar to a summit, which imagination has painted in such gawdy colours as to intoxicate the *inexperienced votary,* and send *him* rambling from State to State, to collect materials to construct the ladder of preferment.

OBSERVATIONS

ON THE

New CONSTITUTION,

AND ON THE

FŒDERAL AND STATE

CONVENTIONS.

BY A COLUMBIAN PATRIOT.

SIC TRANSIT GLORIA AMERICANA.

BOSTON PRINTED, NEW YORK RE-PRINTED,
M, DCC, LXXX, VIII.

Mercy Otis Warren's pamphlet, Observations on the Constitution, *originally printed in Boston, was reprinted in New York and widely distributed by anti-federalists there in April 1788, shortly before the election of delegates to the New York state ratifying convention.*

1. But as a variety of objections to the *heterogeneous phantom*, have been repeatedly laid before the public, by men of the best abilities and intentions; I will not expatiate long on a Republican *form* of government, founded on the principles of monarchy—a democratick branch with the *features* of aristocracy. . . . But I leave the field of general censure on the secrecy of its birth, the rapidity of its growth, and the fatal consequences of suffering it to live to the age of maturity, and will particularize some of the most weighty objections to its passing through this continent in a gigantic size. . . .

2. There is no security in the profered system, either for the rights of conscience, or the liberty of the Press: Despotism usually while it is gaining ground, will suffer men to think, say, or write what they please; but when once established, if it is thought necessary to subserve the purposes of arbitrary power, the most unjust restrictions may take place in the first instance, and an *imprimator*

on the Press in the next, may silence the complaints, and forbid the most decent remonstrances of an injured and oppressed people.

3. There are no well defined limits of the Judiciary Powers, they seem to be left as a boundless ocean, that has broken over the chart of the Supreme Lawgiver "*thus far shalt thou go and no further*," and as they cannot be comprehended by the clearest capacity, or the most sagacious mind, it would be an Herculean labour to attempt to describe the dangers with which they are replete.

4. The Executive and the Legislative are so dangerously blended as to give just cause of alarm, and every thing relative thereto, is couched in such ambiguous terms—in such vague and indifinite expression, as is a sufficient ground without any other objection, for the reprobation of a system, that the authors dare not hazard to a clear investigation.

5. The abolition of trial by jury in civil causes.—This mode of trial the learned Judge [William] Blackstone [author of *Commentaries on the Laws of England*] observes, "has been coeval with the first rudiments of civil government, that property, liberty and life, depend on maintaining in its legal force the constitutional trial by jury.". . .

Additional Objections

10. The inhabitants of the United States, are liable to be draged from the vicinity of their own county, or state, to answer to the litigious or unjust suit of an adversary, on the most distant borders of the Continent: in short the appelate jurisdiction of the Supreme Federal Court, includes an unwarrantable stretch of power over the liberty, life, and property of the subject, through the wide Continent of America.

11. One Representative to thirty thousand inhabitants is a very inadequate representation; and every man who is not lost to all sense of freedom to his country, must reprobate the idea of Congress altering by law, or on any pretence whatever, interfering with any regulations for the time, places, and manner of choosing our own Representatives. . . .

14. There is no provision by a bill of rights to guard against the dangerous encroachments of power in too many instances to be named. . . . We are told by a gentleman of too much virtue and real probity to suspect he has a design to deceive [Massachusetts governor James Bowdoin, speaking at the Massachusetts ratifying convention, January 23, 1788]—"that the whole constitution is a declaration of rights"—but mankind must think for themselves, and to many very judicious and discerning characters, the whole constitution with very few exceptions appears a perversion of the rights of particular states, and of private citizens.—But the gentleman goes on to tell us, "that the primary object is the general government, and that the rights of individuals are only incidentally

mentioned, and that there was a clear impropriety in being very particular about them." But, asking pardon for dissenting from such respectable authority, who has been led into several mistakes, more from his prediliction in favour of certain modes of government, than from a want of understanding or veracity. The rights of individuals ought to be the primary object of all government, and cannot be too securely guarded by the most explicit declarations in their favor. . . .

17. The first appearance of the article which declares the ratification of nine states sufficient for the establishment of the new system, wears the face of dissention, is a subversion of the union of the Confederated States, and tends to the introduction of anarchy and civil convulsions, and may be a means of involving the whole country in blood.

18. The mode in which this constitution is recommended to the people to judge without either the advice of Congress, or the legislatures of the several states, is very reprehensible—it is an attempt to force it upon them before it could be thoroughly understood, and may leave us in that situation, that in the first moments of slavery the minds of the people agitated by the remembrance of their lost liberties, will be like the sea in a tempest, that sweeps down every mound of security.

Recommending Future Amendments an Absurd Idea

But it is needless to enumerate other instances, in which the proposed constitution appears contradictory to the first principles which ought to govern mankind; and it is equally so to enquire into the motives that induced to so bold a step as the annihilation of the independence and sovereignty of the thirteen distinct states.—They are but too obvious through the whole progress of the business, from the first shutting up the doors of the federal convention and resolving that no member should correspond with gentlemen in the different states on the subject under discussion; till the trivial proposition of *recommending* a few amendments was artfully ushered into the convention of the Massachusetts. The questions that were then before that honorable assembly were profound and important, they were of such magnitude and extent, that the consequences may run parallel with the existence of the country; and to see them waived and hastily terminated by a measure too absurd to require a serious refutation, raises the honest indignation of every true lover of his country. Nor are they less grieved that the ill policy and arbitrary disposition of some of the sons of America has thus precipitated to the contemplation and discussion of questions that no one could rationally suppose would have been agitated among us, till time had blotted out the principles on which the late revolution was grounded; or till the last traits of the many political tracts, which defended the seperation from Britain, and the rights of men were consigned to everlasting oblivion. After the severe conflicts this country has suffered, it is presumed that they are disposed to make every reasonable sacrifice before the altar of peace.—But when we contemplate the nature of men and consider them originally on an equal footing, subject to the same feelings, stimulated by the same passions, and recollecting the struggles they have recently made, for the security of their civil rights; it cannot be expected that the inhabitants of the Massachusetts, can be easily lulled into a fatal security, by the declamatory effusions of gentlemen, who, contrary to the experience of all ages would perswade them there is no danger to be apprehended, from vesting discretionary powers in the hands of man, which he may, or may not abuse. The very suggestion, that we ought to trust to the precarious hope of amendments and redress, after we have voluntarily fixed the shackles on our own necks should have awakened to a double degree of caution.—This people have not forgotten the artful insinuations of a former Governor [Thomas Hutchinson, colonial governor of Massachusetts from 1771-1774], when pleading the unlimited authority of [the British] parliament before the legislature of the Massachusetts. . . .

Submitting to Be Slaves

"Cato" was among several anti-federalist writers who ridiculed the idea of ratifying the Constitution in the hopes that future amendments would be enacted, as he writes in this excerpt from the sixth of his seven essays, first published December 16, 1787, in the New York Journal.

But you are told to adopt this government first, and you will always be able to alter it afterwards; this would first be submitting to be slaves and then taking care of your liberty; and when your chains are on, then to act like freemen.

We were then told by him, in all the soft language of insinuation, that no form of government of human construction can be perfect—that we had nothing to fear—that we had no reason to complain—that we had only to acquiesce in their illegal claims, and to submit to the requisitions of parliament, and doubtless the lenient hand of government would redress all grievances, and remove the oppressions of the people:—Yet we soon saw armies of mercenaries encamped on our plains—our commerce ruined—our harbours blockaded—and our cities burnt. It may be replied, that this was in consequence of an obstinate defense of our privileges; this may be true; and when the *"ultima ratio"* is called to aid, the weakest must fall. But let the best informed historian produce an instance when bodies of men were intrusted with power, and the proper checks relinquished, if they were ever found destitute of ingenuity sufficient to furnish pretences to abuse it. And the people at large are already sensible, that the liberties which America has claimed, which reason has justified, and which have been so gloriously defended by the sword of the brave; are not about to fall before the tyranny of foreign conquest: it is native usurpation that is shaking the foundations of peace, and spreading the sable curtain of despotism over the United States. The banners of freedom were erected in the wilds of America by our ancestors, while the wolf prowled for his prey on the one hand, and more savage man on the other; they have been since rescued from the invading hand of foreign power, by the valor and blood of their posterity; and there was reason to hope they would continue for ages to illumine a quarter of the globe, by nature kindly seperated from the proud monarchies of Europe, and the infernal darkness of Asiatic slavery.—And it is to be feared we shall soon see this country rushing into the extremes of confusion and violence, in consequence of the proceedings of a set of gentlemen, who disregarding the purposes of their appointment, have assumed powers unauthorised by any commission, have unnecessarily rejected the confederation of the United States, and annihilated the sovereignty and independence of the individual governments.—The causes which have inspired a few men assembled for very different purposes with such a degree of temerity as to break with a single stroke the union of America, and disseminate the seeds of discord through the land may be easily investigated, when we survey the partizans of monarchy in the state conventions, urging the adoption of a mode of government that militates with the former professions and exertions of this country, and with all ideas of republicanism, and the equal rights of men. . . .

A Second Convention Needed

It has been observed by a zealous advocate for the new system, that most governments are the result of fraud or violence, and this with design to recommend its acceptance—but has not almost every step towards its fabrication been fraudulent in the extreme? Did not the prohibition strictly enjoined by the general Convention, that no member should make any communication to his Constituents, or to gentlemen of consideration and abilities in the other States, bear evident marks of fraudulent designs?—This circumstance is regretted in strong terms by Mr. [Luther] Martin, a member from Maryland, who acknowledges "He had no idea that all the wisdom, integrity, and virtue of the States was contained in that Convention, and that he wished to have corresponded with gentlemen of eminent political characters abroad, and to give their sentiments due weight"—he adds, "so extremely solicitous were they, that their proceedings should not transpire, that the members were prohibited from taking copies of their resolutions, or extracts from the Journals, without express permission, by vote."— And the hurry with which it has been urged to the acceptance of the people, without giving time, by adjournments, for better information, and more unanimity has a deceptive appearance; and if finally driven to resistance, as the only alternative between that and servitude, till in the confusion of discord, the reins should be seized by the violence of some enterprizing genius, that may sweep down the last barrier of liberty, it must be added to the score of criminality with which the fraudulent usurpation at Philadelphia, may be chargeable.—Heaven avert such a tremendous scene! and let us still hope a more happy termination of the present ferment:—may the people be calm, and wait a legal redress; may the mad transport of some of our infatuated capitals subside; and every influential character through the States, make the most prudent exertions for a new general Convention, who may vest adequate powers in Congress, for all national purposes, without annihilating the individual governments, and drawing blood from every pore by taxes, impositions and illegal restrictions.—This step might again re-establish the Union, restore tranquility to the ruffled mind of the inhabitants, and save America from distresses, dreadful even in contemplation.

VIEWPOINT 9

*"My mind will not be quieted till I see something
substantial come forth in the shape of a Bill of Rights."*

A Bill of Rights Is
Necessary for Ratification

Patrick Henry (1736-1799)

A recurring criticism of the Constitution by the anti-federalists
was that it lacked a bill of rights—a list of fundamental freedoms
retained by the people that the government could not infringe.
Beginning with Virginia in 1776, the majority of the states had included a bill of rights in their state constitutions. However, the
Constitutional Convention, rejecting the wishes of some of its
members, did not include such a list. People fearful and critical of
creating a new and powerful national government considered
this omission as evidence that such a government could threaten
people's liberties.

An example of such an argument comes from Patrick Henry,
perhaps the most prominent and renowned of the anti-federalists.
Henry was a longtime Virginia political leader whose acclaimed
oratorical skills had helped to inspire the American Revolution.
As a multiple-term governor and leading member of Virginia's
House of Delegates, he dominated Virginia state politics in the
1770s and 1780s. Seldom out of Virginia, he strongly supported
state sovereignty. He was elected a delegate to the Constitutional
Convention, but "smelt a rat" and refused to attend. At the Virginia ratifying convention he led the forces opposing the Constitution, presenting numerous lengthy and eloquent speeches con-
demning the document. The following viewpoint is taken from
speeches made before the ratifying convention on June 16 and 17,

From *Debates and Other Proceedings of the Convention of Virginia*, David Robertson, ed.
Petersburg, VA, 1788.

1788. Henry argues that the new Constitution will supersede Virginia's constitution and its bill of rights, thus endangering American freedoms. The absence of a bill of rights, Henry asserts, demonstrates how far removed the Constitution is from the true American spirit of liberty.

---

16 June 1788

Mr. Chairman.—The necessity of a Bill of Rights appear to me to be greater in this Government, than ever it was in any Government before. . . .

All nations have adopted this construction—That all rights not expressly and unequivocally reserved to the people, are impliedly and incidentally relinquished to rulers; as necessarily inseparable from the delegated powers. It is so in Great-Britain: For every possible right which is not reserved to the people by some express provision or compact, is within the King's prerogative. It is so in that country which is said to be in such full possession of freedom. It is so in Spain, Germany, and other parts of the world.

Let us consider the sentiments which have been entertained by the people of America on this subject. At the revolution, it must be admitted, that it was their sense to put down those great rights which ought in all countries to be held inviolable and sacred. Virginia did so we all remember. She made a compact to reserve, expressly, certain rights. When fortified with full, adequate, and abundant representation, was she satisfied with that representation? No.—She most cautiously and guardedly reserved and secured those invaluable, inestimable rights and privileges, which no people, inspired with the least glow of the patriotic love of liberty, ever did, or ever can, abandon. She is called upon now to abandon them, and dissolve that compact which secured them to her. She is called upon to accede to another compact which most infallibly supercedes and annihilates her present one. Will she do it?—This is the question. If you intend to reserve your unalienable rights, you must have the most express stipulation. For if implication be allowed, you are ousted of those rights. If the people do not think it necessary to reserve them, they will be supposed to be given up. How were the Congressional rights defined when the people of America united by a confederacy to defend their liberties and rights against the tyrannical attempts of Great-Britain? The States were not then contented with implied reservation. No, Mr. Chairman. It was expressly declared in our Confederation that every right was retained by the States respectively,

236

which was not given up to the Government of the United States. But there is no such thing here. You therefore by a natural and unavoidable implication, give up your rights to the General Government. Your own example furnishes an argument against it. If you give up these powers, without a Bill of Rights, you will exhibit the most absurd thing to mankind that ever the world saw—A Government that has abandoned all its powers—The powers of direct taxation, the sword, and the purse. You have disposed of them to Congress, without a Bill of Rights—without check, limitation, or controul. And still you have checks and guards—still you keep barriers—pointed where? Pointed against your weakened, prostrated, enervated State Government! You have a Bill of Rights to defend you against the State Government, which is bereaved of all power; and yet you have none against Congress, though in full and exclusive possession of all power! You arm yourselves against the weak and defenceless, and expose yourselves naked to the armed and powerful. Is not this a conduct of unexampled absurdity? What barriers have you to oppose to this most strong energetic Government? To that Government you have nothing to oppose. All your defence is given up. This is a real actual defect.—It must strike the mind of every Gentleman. When our Government was first instituted in Virginia, we declared the common law of England to be in force.—That

Objections to the Constitution

George Mason, a Virginia delegate to the Constitutional Convention, was one of three delegates who refused to sign the finished document. He wrote down his reasons for not signing as the Convention was coming to a close in September 1787, and by October manuscript copies of his original objections were being privately circulated in several states. His reasons for rejecting the Constitution, primarily its lack of a bill of rights, were published in the Massachusetts Centinel *and the* Virginia Journal *in late November, and were subsequently republished many times.*

There is no Declaration of Rights; and the Laws of the general Government being paramount to the Laws and Constitutions of the several States, the Declaration of Rights in the separate States are no Security. Nor are the people secured even in the Enjoyment of the Benefits of the common-Law: which stands here upon no other Foundation than its having been adopted by the respective Acts forming the Constitutions of the several States. . . .

There is no Declaration of any kind for preserving the Liberty of the Press, the Tryal by Jury in civil Causes; nor against the Danger of standing Armys in time of Peace.

system of law which has been admired, and has protected us and our ancestors, is excluded by that system.—Added to this, we adopted a Bill of Rights. By this Constitution, some of the best barriers of human rights are thrown away. Is there not an additional reason to have a Bill of Rights? By the ancient common law, the trial of all facts is decided by a jury of impartial men from the immediate vicinage. This paper speaks of different juries from the common law, in criminal cases; and in civil controversies excludes trial by jury altogether. There is therefore more occasion for the supplementary check of a Bill of Rights now, than then. Congress from their general powers may fully go into the business of human legislation. They may legislate in criminal cases from treason to the lowest offence, petty larceny. They may define crimes and prescribe punishments. In the definition of crimes, I trust they will be directed by what wise Representatives ought to be governed by. But when we come to punishments, no latitude ought to be left, nor dependence put on the virtue of Representatives. What says our Bill of Rights? "That excessive bail ought not to be required, nor excessive fines imposed, nor cruel and unusual punishments inflicted." Are you not therefore now calling on those Gentlemen who are to compose Congress, to prescribe trials and define punishments without this controul? Will they find sentiments there similar to this Bill of Rights? You let them loose—you do more—you depart from the genius of your country. That paper tells you, that the trial of crimes shall be by jury, and held in the State where the crime shall have been committed.—Under this extensive provision, they may proceed in a manner extremely dangerous to liberty.—Persons accused may be carried from one extremity of the State to another, and be tried not by an impartial jury of the vicinage, acquainted with his character, and the circumstances of the fact; but by a jury unacquainted with both, and who may be biassed against him.—Is not this sufficient to alarm men?—How different is this from the immemorial practice of your British ancestors, and your own? I need not tell you, that by the [English] common law a number of hundredors [residents from the same group of one hundred] were required to be on a jury, and that afterwards it was sufficient if the jurors came from the same county. With less than this the people of England have never been satisfied. That paper ought to have declared the common law in force.

A Bill of Rights Wanted by the People

In this business of legislation, your Members of Congress will lose the restriction of not imposing excessive fines, demanding excessive bail, and inflicting cruel and unusual punishments.— These are prohibited by your Declaration of Rights. What has dis-

The People Are Entitled to a Bill of Rights

Thomas Jefferson, then American ambassador to France, participated in the debates over the Constitution through correspondence with friends in America. In a December 20, 1787, letter to James Madison, he praised the Constitution, but then described what he saw as its flaws, of which the most serious was the lack of a bill of rights.

I will now add what I do not like. First the omission of a bill of rights providing clearly and without the aid of sophisms for freedom of religion, freedom of the press, protection against standing armies, restriction against monopolies, the eternal and unremitting force of the habeas corpus laws, and trials by jury in all matters of fact triable by the laws of the land and not by the law of Nations. To say, as Mr. [James] Wilson does that a bill of rights was not necessary because all is reserved in the case of the general government which is not given, while in the particular ones all is given which is not reserved might do for the Audience to whom it was addressed, but is surely gratis dictim [a statement not supported by fact], opposed by strong inferences from the body of the instrument, as well as from the omission of the clause of our present confederation which had declared that in express terms. It was a hard conclusion to say because there has been no uniformity among the states as to the cases triable by jury, because some have been so incautious as to abandon this mode of trial, therefore the more prudent states shall be reduced to the same level of calamity. It would have been much more just and wise to have concluded the other way that as most of the states had judiciously preserved this palladium [safeguard], those who had wandered should be brought back to it, and to have established general right instead of general wrong. Let me add that a bill of rights is what the people are entitled to against every government on earth, general or particular, and what no just government should refuse, or rest on inference.

tinguished our ancestors?—That they would not admit of tortures, or cruel and barbarous punishments. But Congress may introduce the practice of the civil law, in preference to that of the common law.—They may introduce the practice of France, Spain, and Germany—Of torturing to extort a confession of the crime. They will say that they might as well draw examples from those countries as from Great-Britain; and they will tell you, that there is such a necessity of strengthening the arm of Government that they must have a criminal equity, and extort confession by torture, in order to punish with still more relentless severity. We are then lost and undone.—And can any man think it troublesome, when we can by a small interference prevent our rights from being lost?—If you will, like the Virginian Government, give them knowledge of the extent of the rights retained by the people, and the powers themselves, they will, if they be honest men, thank you for it.—Will they not wish to go on sure grounds?—But if you leave them otherwise, they will not know how to proceed; and being in a state of uncertainty, they will assume rather than give up powers by implication. A Bill of Rights may be summed up in a few words. What do they tell us?—That our rights are reserved.—Why not say so? Is it because it will consume too much paper? Gentlemen's reasonings against a Bill of Rights, do not satisfy me. Without saying which has the right side, it remains doubtful. A Bill of Rights is a favourite thing with the Virginians, and the people of the other States likewise. It may be their prejudice, but the Government ought to suit their geniuses, otherwise its operation will be unhappy. A Bill of Rights, even if its necessity be doubtful, will exclude the possibility of dispute, and with great submission, I think the best way is to have no dispute. In the present Constitution, they are restrained from issuing general warrants to search suspected places, or seize persons not named, without evidence of the commission of the fact, &c. There was certainly some celestial influence governing those who deliberated on that Constitution:—For they have with the most cautious and enlightened circumspection, guarded those indefeasible rights, which ought ever to be held sacred. The officers of Congress may come upon you, fortified with all the terrors of paramount federal authority.—Excisemen may come in multitudes:—For the limitation of their numbers no man knows.—They may, unless the General Government be restrained by a Bill of Rights, or some similar restriction, go into your cellars and rooms, and search, ransack and measure, every thing you eat, drink and wear. They ought to be restrained within proper bounds. With respect to the freedom of the press, I need say nothing; for it is hoped that the Gentlemen who shall compose Congress, will take care as little as possible, to infringe the rights of human nature.—This will result from their integrity. They should from prudence, abstain from violating the rights of their constituents. They are not however expressly restrained.—But whether they will intermeddle with that palladium of our liberties or not, I leave you to determine.

17 June 1788

[Editor's note: In the following argument Henry examines the ninth section of Article I of the Constitution (see appendix), and argues that it is a meager substitute for a substantive bill of rights.]

Mr. Chairman.—We have now come to the ninth section [of Article I], and I consider myself at liberty to take a short view of the whole. I wish to do it very briefly. Give me leave to remark, that there is a Bill of Rights in that Government [established by the

Constitution]. There are express restrictions which are in the shape of a Bill of Rights: But they bear the name of the ninth section. The design of the negative expressions in this section is to prescribe limits, beyond which the powers of Congress shall not go. These are the sole bounds intended by the American Government. Where abouts do we stand with respect to a Bill of Rights? Examine it, and compare it to the idea manifested by the Virginian Bill of Rights, or that of the other States. The restraints in this Congressional Bill of Rights, are so feeble and few, that it would have been infinitely better to have said nothing about it. The fair implication is, that they can do every thing they are not forbidden to do. What will be the result if Congress, in the course of their legislation, should do a thing not restrained by this ninth section? It will fall as an incidental power to Congress, not being prohibited expressly in the Constitution. The first prohibition is, that the privilege of the writ of *habeas corpus* shall not be suspended, but when in cases of rebellion, or invasion, the public safety may require it. It results clearly, that if it had not said so, they could suspend it in all cases whatsoever. It reverses the position of the friends of this Constitution, that every thing is retained which is not given up. For instead of this, every thing is given up, which is not expressly reserved. . . .

Limited Protections

You are told, that your rights are secured in this new Government. They are guarded in no other part but this ninth section. The few restrictions in that section are your only safeguards. They may controul your actions, and your very words, without being repugnant to that paper. The existence of your dearest privileges will depend on the consent of Congress: For these are not within the restrictions of the ninth section.

If Gentlemen think that securing the slave trade is a capital object; that the privilege of the *habeas corpus* is sufficiently secured; that the exclusion of *ex post facto* laws will produce no inconvenience; that the publication from time to time will secure their property; in one word, that this section alone will sufficiently secure their liberties, I have spoken in vain.—Every word of mine, and of my worthy coadjutor [George Mason], is lost. I trust that Gentlemen, on this occasion, will see the great objects of religion, liberty of the press, trial by jury, interdiction of cruel punishments, and every other sacred right secured, before they agree to that paper. These most important human rights are not protected by that section, which is the only safeguard in the Constitution.— My mind will not be quieted till I see something substantial come forth in the shape of a Bill of Rights.

"I conceive every fair reasoner will agree, that there is no just cause to suspect that they [rights] will be violated."

A Bill of Rights Is Not Necessary for Ratification

Edmund Randolph (1753-1813)

Edmund Randolph, the governor of Virginia from 1786 to 1788, was one of three delegates to the Constitutional Convention who refused to sign the Constitution. In a letter to the speaker of Virginia's House of Delegates that was widely reprinted in pamphlet form and in newspapers, Randolph provided some of his reasons for his decision not to sign the Constitution and endorsed the idea of a second constitutional convention. But at the Virginia ratifying convention he surprised anti-federalist opponents of the Constitution by promoting ratification with the prospect of subsequent amendments—the compromise that had originated in the Massachusetts ratifying convention.

At the Virginia ratifying convention Randolph spoke several times in support of the Constitution. The following is taken from his June 17 response to Patrick Henry's criticism of the Constitution's lack of a bill of rights. Randolph argues that the national government, with its defined and limited powers and its checks and balances among the three branches, will not threaten the civil liberties enjoyed by Americans. No passages in the Constitution authorize the violation of liberties, Randolph argues, and therefore a bill of rights is unnecessary. He concludes by arguing that Virginia should ratify the Constitution or risk dividing the country.

From *Debates and Other Proceedings of the Convention of Virginia*, David Robertson, ed. Petersburg, VA, 1788.

I declared some days ago that I would give my suffrage for this Constitution, not because I considered it without blemish, but because the critical situation of our country demanded it. I invite those who think with me to vote for the Constitution.—But where things occur in it which I disapprove of, I shall be candid in exposing my objections. . . .

On the subject of a Bill of Rights, the want of which has been complained of, I will observe that it has been sanctified by such reverend authority, that I feel some difficulty in going against it. I shall not, however, be deterred from giving my opinion on this occasion, let the consequence be what it may. At the beginning of the [Revolutionary] war we had no certain Bill of Rights: For our charter cannot be considered as a Bill of Rights. It is nothing more than an investiture in the hands of the Virginian citizens, of those rights which belonged to the British subjects. When the British thought proper to infringe our rights, was it not necessary to mention in our Constitution, those rights which ought to be paramount to the power of the Legislature? Why are the Bill of Rights distinct from the Constitution? I consider Bills of Rights in this view, that the Government should use them when there is a departure from its fundamental principles, in order to restore them. This is the true sense of a Bill of Rights. If it be consistent with the Constitution, or contains additional rights, why not put it in the Constitution? If it be repugnant to the Constitution, there will be a perpetual scene of warfare between them. The Honorable Gentleman [Patrick Henry] has praised the Bill of Rights of Virginia, and called it his guardian angel, and vilified this Constitution for not having it. Give me leave to make a distinction between the Representatives of the people of a particular country, who are appointed as the ordinary Legislature, having no limitation to their powers, and another body arising from a compact and certain delineated powers. Were a Bill of Rights necessary in the former, it would not in the latter; for the best security that can be in the latter is the express enumeration of its powers. But let me ask the Gentleman where his favourite rights are violated? They are not violated by the tenth section, which contains restrictions on the States. Are they violated by the enumerated powers? . . . —Is there not provision made in this Constitution for the trial by jury in criminal cases? Does not the third article provide, that the trial of all crimes shall be by jury, and held in the State where the said crimes shall have been committed? Does it not follow, that the cause and nature of the accusation must be produced, because otherwise they cannot proceed on the cause? Every one knows, that the witnesses must be brought before the jury, or else the prisoner will be discharged.

Calling for evidence in his favor is co-incident to his trial. There is no suspicion, that less than twelve jurors will be thought sufficient. The only defect is, that there is no speedy trial.—Consider how this could have been amended. We have heard complaints against it, because it is supposed the jury is to come from the State at large. It will be in their power to have juries from the vicinage. And would not the complaints have been louder, if they had appointed a Federal Court to be had in every county in the State? —Criminals are brought in this State from every part of the country to the General Court, and jurors from the vicinage are summoned to the trials. There can be no reason to prevent the General Government from adopting a similar regulation.

Criminal Justice Freedoms

As to the exclusion of excessive bail and fines, and cruel and unusual punishments, this would follow of itself without a Bill of Rights. Observations have been made about watchfulness over those in power, which deserve our attention. There must be a combination—We must presume corruption in the House of Representatives, Senate, and President, before we can suppose that excessive fines can be imposed, or cruel punishments inflicted. Their number is the highest security.—Numbers are the highest security in our own Constitution, which has attracted so many eulogiums from the Gentleman. Here we have launched into a sea of suspicions. How shall we check power?—By their numbers. Before these cruel punishments can be inflicted, laws must be passed, and Judges must judge contrary to justice. This would excite universal discontent, and detestation of the Members of the Government. They might involve their friends in the calamities resulting from it, and could be removed from office. I never desire a greater security than this, which I believe to be absolutely sufficient.

That general warrants are grievous and oppressive, and ought not to be granted, I fully admit. I heartily concur in expressing my detestation of them. But we have sufficient security here also. We do not rely on the integrity of any one particular person or body; but on the number and different orders of the Members of the Government: Some of them having necessarily the same feelings with ourselves. Can it be believed, that the Federal Judiciary would not be independent enough to prevent such oppressive practices? If they will not do justice to persons injured, may they not go to our own State Judiciaries and obtain it?

Gentlemen have been misled to a certain degree, by a general declaration, that the trial by jury was gone. We see that in the most valuable cases, it is reserved. Is it abolished in civil cases? Let him put his finger on the part where it is abolished. The Constitution is silent on it.—What expression would you wish the

The Folly of Parchment Barriers

James Madison did not support adding a bill of rights to the Constitution when it was first proposed in the Constitutional Convention. In an October 17, 1788, letter to his friend Thomas Jefferson (then serving as an American diplomat in France), Madison argues that a bill of rights is ineffective against majority opinion, which is where he believes the real power of government lies.

Experience proves the inefficacy of a bill of rights on those occasions when its controul is most needed. Repeated violations of these parchment barriers have been committed by overbearing majorities in every State. In Virginia I have seen the bill of rights violated in every instance where it has been opposed to a popular current. Notwithstanding the explicit provision contained in that instrument for the rights of Conscience, it is well known that a religious establishment would have taken place in that State, if the Legislative majority had found as they expected, a majority of the people in favor of the measure; and I am persuaded that if a majority of the people were now of one sect, the measure would still take place and on narrower ground than was then proposed, notwithstanding the additional obstacle which the law has since created.

Wherever the real power in a Government lies, there is the danger of oppression. In our Governments the real power lies in the majority of the Community, and the invasion of private rights is chiefly to be apprehended, not from acts of Government contrary to the sense of its constituents, but from acts in which the Government is the mere instrument of the major number of the Constituents. This is a truth of great importance, but not yet sufficiently attended to; and is probably more strongly impressed on my mind by facts, and reflections suggested by them, than on yours which has contemplated abuses of power issuing from a very different quarter.

Constitution to use, to establish it? Remember we were not making a Constitution for Virginia alone, or we might have taken Virginia for our directory. But we were forming a Constitution for thirteen States. The trial by jury is different in different States. In some States it is excluded in cases in which it is admitted in others. In Admiralty causes it is not used. Would you have a jury to determine the case of a capture? The Virginian Legislature thought proper to make an exception of that case. These depend on the law of nations, and no twelve men that could be picked up would be equal to the decision of such a matter.

Press and Religious Freedom

Then, Sir, the freedom of the press is said to be insecure. God forbid that I should give my voice against the freedom of the press. But I ask, (and with confidence that it cannot be answered) where is the page where it is restrained? If there had been any regulation about it, leaving it insecure, then there might have been reason for clamours. But this is not the case. If it be, I again ask for the particular clause which gives liberty to destroy the freedom of the press.

He has added religion to the objects endangered in his conception. Is there any power given over it? Let it be pointed out. Will he not be contented with the answer which has been frequently given to that objection? That variety of sects which abounds in the United States is the best security for the freedom of religion. No part of the Constitution, even if strictly construed, will justify a conclusion, that the General Government can take away, or impair the freedom of religion.

The Gentleman asks with triumph, shall we be deprived of these valuable rights? Had there been an exception, or express infringement of those rights, he might object.—But I conceive every fair reasoner will agree, that there is no just cause to suspect that they will be violated.

But he objects, that the common law is not established by the Constitution. The wisdom of the Convention is displayed by its omission; because the common law ought not to be immutably fixed. Is it established in our own Constitution, or the Bill of Rights which has been resounded through the House? It is established only by an act of the Legislature, and can therefore be changed as circumstances may require it. Let the Honorable Gentleman consider what would be the destructive consequences of its establishment in the Constitution. Even in England, where the firmest opposition has been made to encroachments upon it, it has been frequently changed. What would have been our dilemma if it had been established?—Virginia has declared, that children shall have equal portions of the real estates of their intestate parents, and it is consistent to the principles of a Republican Government.—The immutable establishment of the common law, would have been repugnant to that regulation. It would in many respects be destructive to republican principles, and productive of great inconveniences. I might indulge myself, by shewing many parts of the common law which would have this effect. I hope I shall not be thought to speak ludicrously, when I say, that the *writ* of *burning heretics*, would have been revived by it. It would tend to throw real property in few hands, and prevent the introduction of many salutary regulations. Thus, were the common law adopted in that system, it would destroy the principles of Republican Government. But it is not excluded. It may be established by an act of the Legislature. Its defective parts may be altered, and it may be changed and modified as the convenience

Binding Future Generations

Noah Webster, the author of the first American dictionary, was an avid federalist who wrote numerous articles under various pseudonyms supporting the Constitution. In an article written for his American Magazine *in December 1787, Webster argued that future generations should not be bound by the present generation's understandings of essential rights.*

I undertake to prove that a standing *Bill of Rights* is *absurd*, because no constitutions, in a free government, can be unalterable. The present generation have indeed a right to declare what *they* deem a *privilege*; but they have no right to say what the *next* generation shall deem a privilege. A State is a supreme corporation that never dies. Its powers, when it acts for itself, are at all times, equally extensive; and it has the same right to *repeal* a law this year, as it had to *make* it the last. If therefore our posterity are bound by our constitutions, and can neither amend nor annul them, they are to all intents and purposes our slaves.

But it will be enquired, have we then no right to say, that trial by jury, the liberty of the press, the habeas corpus writ and other invaluable privileges, shall never be infringed nor destroyed? By no means. We have the same right to say that lands shall descend in a particular mode to the heirs of the deceased proprietor, and that such a mode shall never be altered by future generations, as we have to pass a law that the trial by jury shall never be abridged. The right of Jury-trial, which we deem invaluable, may in future cease to be a privilege; or other modes of trial more satisfactory to the people, may be devised. Such an event is neither impossible nor improbable. Have we then a right to say that our posterity shall not be judges of their own circumstances? The very attempt to make *perpetual* constitutions, is the assumption of a right to control the opinions of future generations; and to legislate for those over whom we have as little authority as we have over a nation in Asia.

of the public may require it. . . .

I cast my eyes to the actual situation of America; I see the dreadful tempest, to which the present calm is a prelude, if disunion takes place. I see the anarchy which must happen if no energetic Government be established. In this situation, I would take the Constitution were it more objectionable than it is.—For if anarchy and confusion follow disunion, an enterprising man may enter into the American throne. I conceive there is no danger. The Representatives are chosen by and from among the people. They will have a fellow-feeling for the farmers and planters. The twenty-six Senators, Representatives of the States, will not be those desperadoes and horrid adventurers which they are represented to be. The State Legislatures, I trust, will not forget the duty they owe to their country so far, as to choose such men to manage their federal interests. I trust, that the Members of Congress themselves, will explain the ambiguous parts: And if not, the States can combine in order to insist on amending the ambiguities. I would depend on the present actual feelings of the people of America, to introduce any amendment which may be necessary. I repeat it again, though I do not reverence the Constitution, that its adoption is necessary to avoid the storm which is hanging over America, and that no greater curse can befal her, than the dissolution of the political connection between the States. Whether we shall propose previous or subsequent amendments, is now the only dispute. It is supererogation to repeat again the arguments in support of each.—But I ask Gentlemen, whether, as eight States have adopted it, it be not safer to adopt it, and rely on the probability of obtaining amendments, than by a rejection to hazard a breach of the Union?

CHAPTER 6

Historians Evaluate the Making of the Constitution

Chapter Preface

Although the process of ratification of the Constitution caused much debate and controversy, this divisiveness ceased remarkably quickly once the Constitution was ratified. Historian Richard D. Miles writes in *The Embattled Constitution:*

> The ratification of the U.S. Constitution was achieved by some of the most severely contested battles in American political history. Those who had drafted the Constitution . . . withstood a great deal of criticism and even vituperation. Once the procedure for establishing the new government got under way, however, the aspersions no longer flowed so freely. In fact, "all serious controversy over the Constitution ceased abruptly once it had been adopted," according to one authority. Within a year or two after Washington took office as President, little was heard about the deficiencies of the Convention and its work.

Since then Americans have generally looked on the Constitution and the people who created it with admiration, even reverence (Thomas Jefferson called the Constitutional Convention "an assembly of demigods"). The attitude of many was summed up by nineteenth-century British prime minister William Gladstone, when he called the U.S. Constitution the "most wonderful work ever struck off at a given time by the brain and purpose of man"—an attitude that largely characterized public perception of the Constitution during both its 1887 centennial and 1987 bicentennial.

This high esteem for the creators of the Constitution has been challenged on several grounds by twentieth-century historians. One of the first critiques, and perhaps the most notable, was in a 1913 book by Columbia University historian Charles A. Beard, *An Economic Interpretation of the Constitution.* Beard argued that the framers of the Constitution were not enlightened statesmen motivated by patriotism and a desire to help the nation, but rather were representatives of their economic class interests as merchants, owners of government bonds, slaveowners, and creditors. They created a national government in order to secure their property and interests, Beard wrote, much to the detriment of small farmers and debtors, who were not represented at the Constitutional Convention and who fought its ratification.

Beard's book created a storm of controversy when first published, but by the 1930s his interpretation had become the standard orthodoxy found in history textbooks and elsewhere. Since then, studies by Forrest McDonald, Robert E. Brown, and others have attacked Beard's work as being simplistic and a misuse of the economic data. Yet, although Beard's arguments are no longer so widely accepted as in the past, the questions he raised still concern historians today. As historian Leonard W. Levy writes in *Essays on the Making of the Constitution:*

> Since the *Economic Interpretation*, historians have engaged in a prolonged debate on questions raised by Beard either directly or indirectly. Were the framers enlightened, disinterested statesmen seeking to rescue—indeed to create—a nation then dangerously drifting toward anarchy? Were they conspiratorial representatives of a rising financial and industrial capitalism? . . . Was the Constitution mainly an economic or a political document? . . . In short, was the Constitution an undemocratic document framed and ratified by an undemocratic minority for an undemocratic society? Or, were the framers practical, though masterly, politicians keenly conscious of the need for popular approval if their work was to be accepted?

The two viewpoints by historians presented here address these questions from different perspectives. They focus especially on the relationship of the participants of the Constitutional Convention to "We the people of the United States."

VIEWPOINT 1

"The Framers continue to earn the acclaim of a grateful people . . . , not alone because they ordained and established an enduring constitution, but because they did it in such a resourceful way."

The Constitution Was Created by the Genius of the Framers

Clinton Rossiter (1917-1970)

Clinton Rossiter, who taught history and political science for many years at Cornell University in New York, was one of America's leading constitutional historians. His books include *Alexander Hamilton and the Constitution*, *The American Presidency*, and *1787: The Grand Convention*, from which the following is taken.

1787 is a popular history describing in detail the happenings of the Constitutional Convention, which Rossiter called one of the most important events in American (and world) history. Rossiter's stance toward the creation of the Constitution can be deduced from this passage in the book's opening chapter:

> 1787 is the year of the supreme event in the life of the American people: the Convention that sat in Philadelphia from May 25 to September 17 and hammered out the Constitution of the United States, the shrewd, resilient, enduring charter of government under which the first and only continental republic has risen from impotence and obscurity to power and glory. . . . There has been no greater happening in American history; there have not been many greater, certainly of a political nature, in the history of the world.

Reprinted from *1787: The Grand Convention* by Clinton Rossiter, with permission of W.W. Norton & Company, Inc. Copyright ©1966 by Clinton Rossiter.

In the following viewpoint, Rossiter gives an overall evaluation of the Constitutional Convention. He gives great credit to the participants of the Convention, praising their vision for America and their political abilities to compromise with each other in developing the Constitution. In his book he emphasizes that the Framers "were, indeed, a continental elite, the nearest thing to an 'establishment' that could exist in those days of poor communications, limited horizons, and divided loyalties." Their position as an elite, Rossiter argues, enabled them to envision and create a powerful and unifying national government—and then persuade an American populace wary of central governments to accept their creation. "In some things, they recognized, they would have to 'follow the people,'" Rossiter writes of the Framers, "but in others they guessed and gambled, the people would follow them"—a magnificent gamble that, he says, paid off better than anyone imagined. Rossiter concludes by listing and evaluating the Framers on how much each contributed to the creation of the Constitution.

As the delegates set out for home by stage, horseback, or packet (nine of them by way of Congress in New York), their heads were spinning with fatigue and confusion. They could recall where they had begun, and they could see where they had come out; but many must have wondered how they had ever managed to move from the good intentions of May 25 to the sensible conclusions of September 17. As fatigue gave way to composure and cheer, however, so did confusion to understanding, and some of them began to suspect that they had taken part in one of the most purposeful, skilled, and, they hoped, successful meetings of public men in the history of the Western World.

A Model Gathering

We of a later generation know what they could only suspect: that the Grand Convention was indeed a model gathering of statesmen-politicians, the archetype of the constituent assembly. The Framers continue to earn the acclaim of a grateful people, and also to deserve the attention of a curious world, not alone because they ordained and established an enduring constitution, but because they did it in such a resourceful way. The creation is exemplary; so, too, was the act of creation. Whatever one may think of the Constitution, it would not be easy to imagine a more effective process of constitution-making.

Many of the circumstances under which the Framers had gathered to transact their solemn business were, to be sure, extremely favorable. Their will to succeed was overpowering, nourished as it was by both a sense of the urgency of the hour and a spirit of mission for all mankind; their experience, much of which they had won in common, was exceptional, as was also their learning; their style of political life was self-disciplined, courteous, moderate, and healthily skeptical. They had a sense of the limits of their wisdom, a sense of the limits of the whole endeavor. And they represented, as we have seen, a consensus of principle and purpose that made it possible for them to keep talking across the barricades even in their most gladiatorial moments. Although the struggle for political power was sharp, it was never ferocious or malevolent. Since neither the existence of a religion nor the supremacy of a class nor the fortune of a party was at issue on the floor, the Framers could afford to set their sights on something less than total victory for the states, sections, and interests they represented. Since the process of selection had encouraged only a handful of committed anti-nationalists to appear in Philadelphia—all of whom bowed out before the end—they could abandon the sinking ship of the Confederation with few feelings of guilt or pity. And since the one great interest that lacked the nation-building instinct at this stage of American history—the small farmers of the back country—was only vaguely represented, the troubled leaders of the one great interest that had this instinct in abundance—the merchants and lawyers and planters in the more settled areas—could go about the task of laying a political foundation for the nation with some hope of adjusting their own differences and thus some hope of achieving success. I do not mean to draw too sharp a line between these two interests, in particular to suggest that all yeomen of the West were indifferent or hostile to the nationalist thrust and all gentlemen of the East caught up in it. Yet it must be understood that a majority of the continental elite was ready, for the sake of the Republic and also for the sake of its own power and prosperity, to move rapidly toward nationhood in the 1780's, while a majority of the yeomanry preferred, for the sake of "liberty" and also out of indifference or apathy or antipathy for the elite, to go on as before. If a dozen spokesmen of this interest had shown up in Philadelphia and then stuck to their guns, it is hard to see how James Madison and his friends could have pieced together a nationalist charter.

Favorable Circumstances

Once the Framers had gathered, they thereupon created for themselves, as we have also seen, the best possible circumstances under which to work. Their sessions were orderly but not stagy, decorous but not stilted, flexible but not flighty, secret but not conspiratorial. They worked hard, some almost too hard; and those who remained in Philadelphia attended faithfully. The standard of their debates was high—principally, one suspects, because they were talking only to each other and to posterity—and both long-windedness and irrelevance were at a discount except on a few painful days. The standard of leadership was equally high, and they seemed to know instinctively when to slog ahead blindly, to leave something to chance (which they never did on crucial matters), or to accept guidance from one of their more knowledgeable, committed, or commanding colleagues. Some of the best work of the Convention was done off the floor in private conversations, state caucuses, and informal conferences of like-minded, other-minded, or open-minded men. While the Indian Queen was the focus of this sort of activity, other scenes of discourse and persuasion were Mrs. House's public rooms, the City Tavern, Robert Morris's parlor, Dr. Benjamin Franklin's library, the yard of the State House, the well-paved streets of the city, and the trout stream at Valley Forge.

Perhaps the most impressive aspect of the Convention as a decision-making body was the confident, imaginative, and measured use of committees. At least four were as essential to the process of constitution-making as were the debates on the floor—the self-appointed Virginia caucus of May, the committee of detail, the committee on postponed matters, and the committee of style—and all were manned with delegates well qualified to act creatively for the whole Convention. Two others were essential to the resolution of harsh political problems—the compromising committees of eleven of July 2 and August 22—and they, too, were manned (in the first instance "loaded") to excellent purpose. While the Convention was quite willing to resort to this technique to help it over rough spots—five times in August alone—it did not work it to death, for plenty of "motions to commit" failed to win a majority. And while it gave each committee a confident mandate, it did not propose to swallow the medicine offered without a good look at the prescription. Every report of every committee received the compliment of unruffled scrutiny.

One can think, of course, of small improvements in timing and technique that would have made the Convention an even more effective body. A few less hours might have been spent on the problem of representation and a few more on the judiciary, which was, in a sense, the taken-for-granted stepchild of 1787. There ought, perhaps, to have been some arrangement under which the voluble Luther Martin could be cut off and the silent William Livingston, John Blair, and Robert Morris encouraged to speak. And it cannot be denied that this assembly, like all hard-working assemblies, rolled a little too fast as it neared the end. "It was not exempt," Madison acknowledged in later years, "from a degree of the hurrying influence introduced by fatigue and impatience in all such bodies," and as a result several critical questions went unanswered and several important arrangements unrefined. Yet these, surely, are minor blemishes on a splendid record of both performance and achievement. The political process of the liberal West, it bears repeating, had one of its finest moments in the intense, hard-headed session of give-and-take among independent gentlemen at Philadelphia in the summer of 1787. Imagined philosopher-kings might have done this work more efficiently than the Framers, but not real men with concrete interests—and with constituents waiting for them at home.

The Constitution and the American People

Those constituents—the legislators who had sent them, the voters who would elect (and presumably instruct) delegates to the ratifying conventions, the delegates themselves with their power to give or deny life to the Constitution—were much on the minds of the Framers, even in their most detached moments; and the longer the Convention ran, the more forcibly the thought of their constituents pressed upon them. That, of course, is exactly the way things should have been, for they had assembled to write rules not for Athens or Geneva or Utopia, but for the United States of America, an existing country made up of other real men with concrete interests. Since the men had principles as well as interests, and were indeed the most proudly self-governing in the world, the rules had to win the happy approval of the majority, the not unhappy sufferance of the minority, and the unforced obedience of all. At the same time, the Framers were members of an elite, gentlemen who had been taught to lead, although never to bully, and they had no intention of offering a constitution that was simply the lowest common denominator of the wishes, prejudices, and anxieties of the people. Moreover, they could sense that the only half-formed state of opinion in the country would never be more favorable to an imaginative exercise of the arts of political and intellectual leadership.

The search of the Convention, it seems in retrospect, was for solutions that would strike a subtle balance among four principal considerations that framers of constitutions must keep in mind, shifting them about on their personal scales in response to changing pressures of conviction and circumstance. The first is what their constituents have directed them to do, and the Framers were fortunate (or foresighted) enough to have imprecise directions that encouraged them to make the necessary gamble on an entirely new constitution. When William Paterson reminded his colleagues on June 16 that their "object" was "not such a government as may

The Writers of the Constitution

Christopher Collier, a professor of American history at the University of Connecticut at Storrs, and biographer and writer James Lincoln Collier were coauthors of Decision at Philadelphia, *an account of the Constitutional Convention. At the book's conclusion they provide their own assessment of individual Framers and the Convention as a whole.*

[There is] the question of whether or not the Constitution was just a happy accident. There are influential historians who think so—who believe that the delegates were mainly trying to devise a government that would allow them to line their own pockets, or that they were simply shrewd politicians who wanted a government that would keep the people in their place, but who had to compromise in order to sell the new government to their constituents.

We do not agree. This was, to begin with, an astonishing group of men. At least four of them were among the most remarkable men of modern times. There was Washington, who defeated the world's mightiest fighting force with his scrappy, ill-armed troops, and would go on to run a model presidency. There was James Madison, one of America's keenest political thinkers of any age. There was Alexander Hamilton, who would in large measure design the American economic system. There was Benjamin Franklin, old and infirm, but nonetheless considered by all one of the great men of his time.

Just a cut below them was a group of brilliant, clear-thinking, and farsighted men: Roger Sherman, Charles Pinckney, George Mason, James Wilson, Gouverneur Morris, and perhaps one or two others. And they were surrounded by another dozen or so men of high intelligence, who would have shone in any company but this one: William Paterson, John Dickinson, Robert Morris, C. C. Pinckney, John Rutledge, Oliver Ellsworth, William Samuel Johnson, Edmund Randolph, Elbridge Gerry, Rufus King, and more. There was among them at least one outright scoundrel, William Blount, and a few others of only moderate talent, like Gunning Bedford and John Francis Mercer. But at least twenty of these fifty-five men were remarkable people by any standard.

be best in itself, but such a one as our constituents have authorized us to prepare," James Wilson and Edmund Randolph were able to argue plausibly that the Convention, while it was "authorized to *conclude nothing*," was "at liberty to *propose anything*."

Anything, they meant to add, that the people would approve, for this is, of course, another principal consideration of would-be framers. The Framers of 1787 never forgot their constituents, "the people of America." "We must consult their rooted prejudices," Nathaniel Gorham advised his colleagues at one critical moment, "if we expect their concurrence in our propositions." "The plan must be accommodated to the public mind," Paterson warned them at another; it must "consult the genius, the temper, the habits, the prejudices of the people." "The genius of the people," George Mason, John Dickinson, and a half-dozen others echoed, commanded republicanism, forbade monarchy, expected bicameralism, and approved the separation of powers. "We must follow the example of Solon," Pierce Butler said in behalf of all his colleagues, "who gave the Athenians not the best government he could devise, but the best they would receive."

The best they would receive, however, was something different from the least they would expect. Throughout the Convention the delegates spoke admiringly of their constituents as men who were rightly tenacious about principles and sensibly flexible about details, and thus as men who were open to explanation and persuasion—especially, it would seem, in the critical area of nationalism. In some things, they recognized, they would have to "follow the people," but in others, they guessed and gambled, the people would follow them. Alexander Hamilton, in particular, was convinced that "the public mind," if properly instructed, would rouse to the challenge of nationhood and "adopt a solid plan."

However they may be instructed, and whatever they may hazard on the probabilities of public opinion, men who would write a long-lived constitution must also worry their heads over the practical question: will it work? Certainly the Framers kept this consideration firmly in mind. They sought not merely immediate approval but continuing viability for their charter, and they got it, one likes to think, because they understood—or came to understand in the course of the summer—what would and would not work in a country with the circumstances, traditions, prospects, and problems of the United States. While some of their attempts to be at all costs "practical" were destined to founder on the shoals of developments they could not anticipate—for example, their ingenious scheme for electing the President—most were to be successful beyond their fondest hopes.

Finally, would-be framers must occasionally raise their eyes above the real to contemplate the ideal, lest their style become that of narrow-minded cynics, and this the Framers of 1787 seemed able to do at the right times and in the right proportion. In a debate of June 22 over the question of how to pay legislators, Randolph sounded one of his truest notes of the summer.

> Mr. Randolph feared we were going too far, in consulting popular prejudices. Whatever respect might be due to them, in lesser matters, or in cases where they formed the permanent character of the people, he thought it neither incumbent on nor honorable for the Convention to sacrifice right and justice to that consideration.

The choicest story in this vein is one for whose veracity we must rely on the word of Gouverneur Morris. Since Morris told it in "an oration upon the death of General Washington," perhaps we can. Describing the discussions that took place just before the opening of the Convention, Morris saluted the shade of the great man—and drew a stern moral:

> Men of decided temper, who, devoted to the public, overlooked prudential considerations, thought a form of government should be framed entirely new. But cautious men, with whom popularity was an object, deemed it fit to consult and comply with the wishes of the people. AMERICANS!—let the opinion then delivered by the greatest and best of men, be ever present to your remembrance. He was collected within himself. His countenance had more than usual solemnity—His eye was fixed, and seemed to look into futurity. "It is (said he) too probable that no plan we propose will be adopted. Perhaps another dreadful conflict is to be sustained. If to please the people, we offer what we ourselves disapprove, how can we afterwards defend our work? Let us raise a standard to which the wise and the honest can repair. The event is in the hand of God."—this was the patriot voice of WASHINGTON; and this the constant tenor of his conduct.

The triumph of the Convention of 1787 is that in raising a standard to which the wise and honest could repair, it also raised one that met the threefold test of legitimacy, popularity, and viability.

One reason the Convention was able to strike the right balance between the urge to lead the people and the need to obey them, and between the urge to be noble and the need to be practical, was the disposition of most delegates to be "whole men" on stern principles and "half-way men" on negotiable details. Another was the way in which it worked with familiar materials—the state constitutions, the Articles of Confederation, the best of the colonial experiences—and thus presented the people with a constitution that surprised but did not shock. Rejoicing in philosophy but despising ideology, putting a high value on "reason" but an even higher one on "experience," interested in the institutions of other times and peoples but confident that their own were better, unafraid to contemplate the mysteries of the British Constitution but aware, in Wilson's words, that it "cannot be our own model," the Framers kept faith with the American past even as they prepared to make a break with it. Indeed, the excellence of their handiwork is as much a tribute to their sense of continuity as to their talent for creative statesmanship. The Constitution was an ingenious plan of government chiefly in the sense that its authors made a careful selection of familiar techniques and institutions, then fitted them together with an unerring eye for form. It had very little novelty in it, and that, we see with the aid of hindsight, was one of its strongest points.

A final reason—and also perhaps the most heartening lesson the Convention presents to supporters of constitutional democracy—was the process of give-and-take through which these masterful public men managed to create a constitution that could be carried home with some confidence to every part of a sprawling country. While the process may have often seemed unnecessarily erratic and time-wasting to those trapped in its midst, we can see that it was the only way in which self-respecting representatives of free men could have pieced together a set of operational rules of government and, at the same time, settled their outstanding political differences. In doing these things so well, and so acceptably to all but a handful of their colleagues, the men of 1787 met the supreme test of the democratic assembly: they proved beyond a doubt that the whole was wiser than the parts, that the collective was more creative than any individual in it. No single man, nor even the most artfully constructed team of four or five, could have provided so wisely for the constitutional needs of the American people as did "the cunning of reason" that operated through the whole Convention.

The Convention passed this test and became the archetype of the constituent assembly by acting both negatively and positively to demonstrate its collective wisdom. On one hand, it voted down a string of pet proposals that would have loaded the Constitution with weak, clumsy, or simply unacceptable techniques. Consider, for example, some of the serious suggestions made by serious men to improve the Presidency: Madison wanted to give the Supreme Court a share of the President's veto; Morris favored the Chief Justice as successor to the President; Mason proposed that "maladministration" be added to the list of impeachable offenses; Martin and Elbridge Gerry wanted to fix the size of the army in the Constitution itself; Charles Pinckney would have set a property qualification so high as to bar the Presidency to anyone not as rich as he; and Hugh Williamson agreed with Mason that three executives would be three times as good as one. Every one of these proposals, it should be noted, was thoroughly digested; every one was made, not in the early stages when men were lobbing ideas back and forth for practice, but in the late stages when they were passing on the final plan. Surely the Convention showed itself wiser than these men in rejecting such proposals.

On the other hand, and in a far more important demonstration of the power of collective wisdom, the Convention acted positively to produce those familiar compromises of July 16 and August 25 without which the Union would have collapsed, decayed, or been rent asunder. Especially in the matter of federalism—in drawing the line between nation and states and in adjusting the balance of large states and small—the whole body proved itself more astute than the men who were, in most things, its guiding spirits. If Wilson and Madison had had their way on the issues of representation, the powers of Congress, and the review of state legislation—and they did everything they could to have it—the Constitution could not possibly have won approval in more than a handful of states. By muddling through to "half-way" solutions, and by shaping the solutions to the "genius" of the country as it was interpreted through the prism of a collective mind, the Convention moved up step by step to the outer boundaries of the politically possible in a dozen critical areas, and then refused prudently to move one step beyond. All in all, it was a convincing demonstration of the truth that the highest political wisdom in a constitutional democracy lies in the assembly rather than in the individual lawmaker. The assembly must be of the right size and composition for its purpose, and it must be organized on sound principles and led in a skillful way; but if those conditions are met, as they were met with something to spare in 1787, it has a better chance to find the workable solution than any one man in it.

Ranking the Framers

This is not at all to disparage the importance of the individual, for the wisdom of the assembly is of necessity a projection, if not a simple sum, of the wisdom of those who sit in it. The collective triumph of 1787 was nourished on the experience, learning, dedication, and industry of remarkable individuals, and we might therefore end this review of the labors of the Convention by distributing our gratitude and admiration according to the several contributions of the delegates. Although "Ranking the Framers" will never be as popular an indoor sport as "Ranking the Presidents," a student of American history can always play it with pleasure. As I look back once more at all the Framers, limiting my gaze rigidly to their activities between May 14 and September 17, 1787, they seem to fall into eight fairly distinguishable groups, which might be labeled the Principals, the Influentials, the Very Usefuls, the Usefuls, the Visibles, the Ciphers, the Dropouts and Walkouts, and the Inexplicable Disappointments.

The Principals: James Madison. Although even Madison's admiring biographer reminds us that none of the men of 1787 would have dreamed of calling him (or anyone else) the "Father of the Constitution," he was, beyond a doubt, the leading spirit and, as Major Jackson could testify, "most efficient member" in this conclave. His foresight in drafting the Virginia Plan and making it the agenda of the Convention, his willingness to debate great issues and small with courteous and learned intensity, his dozens of suggestions of ways for his colleagues to extricate themselves from thickets, his membership on three of the four essential committees, even perhaps his doggedness in the major struggle for power—these are the solid credentials of the one Framer who stands, modestly and eternally, first among his splendid peers. And as if all these services were not enough, there remains the precious manuscript, written in blood as well as ink, that tells us most of what we know of the Great Happening.

James Wilson. Second only to Madison—and an honorable second—was the learned, inventive, painstaking lawyer from St. Andrews. As brother-in-arms to the Virginian in the cause of reform-minded nationalism, Wilson debated, drafted, bargained, and voted with unremitting zeal. He did most to give strength and independence to the executive, and to lay the foundations of the new government "broad and deep" upon the sovereign people of the United States.

George Washington. Washington's contribution was of a different kind from that of Madison and Wilson, but certainly we can imagine a far less pleasant outcome for a gathering that he had refused to grace or—this, admittedly, is hard to imagine—from which he had withdrawn in sorrow or fury. By lending a constant presence (he did not miss a single day), by presiding with dignity and understanding, by serving willy-nilly as the probable first President, and by giving the quiet support of his influence and vote to Madison, Washington helped mightily to make the Convention a success. Moreover, he did his uncomplaining duty as semi-official chief of state to the American people. He drank tea with the ladies of Philadelphia, dined with the Sons of St. Patrick, visited farms and museums and historic sites, sat through orations, reviewed troops ("at the importunity of General Mifflin"), received visiting dignitaries, and had his portrait painted by Charles Willson Peale. He even went, man of grace and tolerance that he was, "to the Romish Church to high mass."

Gouverneur Morris. The credentials of Gouverneur Morris as a giant of the Convention will always be slightly suspect to those who see him as a man too clever, too fickle, and too cynical "by half." Yet anyone who has traced and retraced his trail through the Convention—noting the frankness and superb timing of his important speeches, watching him shoulder most of the burden of committee work for his fellow Pennsylvanians, reading over his final draft of September 12—must recognize a magnificent contribution. Since the contribution was also quite unexpected, he stands out as the Framer whose reputation received the largest boost in this period. And if he had done nothing else, he would have earned our gratitude for making the Convention chuckle, and also think, with his pointed jokes about overhospitable Indians, hypocritical slavers (the South Carolinians thought, but did not chuckle) and restless Vice-Presidents.

The Influentials: John Rutledge, who spoke often and usefully, sat on five committees, guided the labors of the committee of detail, was the gadfly of the Convention in August and September, and served the cause of moderate nationalism with intelligence and devotion.

Benjamin Franklin, who poked fun along with Morris, spun out compromises and soothed hurt feelings along with the men of Connecticut, spoke up for the people even more confidently than Wilson and Madison, and joined Washington in fortifying both the prestige and the self-confidence of the Convention. (Franklin was one of the few delegates who were sorry to see it all come to an end. "Some tell me I look better," he wrote of his health to his sister, "and they suppose the daily exercise of going and returning from the State House has done me good.")

Roger Sherman, probably the most useful and certainly the most voluble delegate from Connecticut, who had a longer intellectual pilgrimage to make than any other man in the Convention, and who made it without surrendering a single one of his Yankee principles.

Charles Pinckney, who spoke often and earnestly, and who was at his best filling in the holes of the grand design that was taking shape on the floor.

Rufus King, who turned suddenly, perhaps under the influence of Hamilton, into an enthusiastic, sharp-witted, persuasive nationalist, and who was the champion committeeman of the summer.

Charles Cotesworth Pinckney, whose single-minded devotion to the interests of his class, state, section, and way of life did not prevent him from lending a powerful hand to the cause of a strong and stable government.

Oliver Ellsworth, the "half-way man" of the century, who may have done more in Philadelphia for the Union than Hamilton, Wilson, and the two Pinckneys together.

Nathaniel Gorham, who chaired the committee of the whole, sat on the committee of detail, and debated helpfully in the spirit of moderate nationalism.

George Mason, unhappily a non-signer, but always a faithful, industrious, honest exponent of old-fashioned republicanism.

Edmund Randolph, also a non-signer, whose performance was erratic, yet who gets considerable credit for the decision to enumerate the powers of Congress.

Elbridge Gerry, the non-signing "Grumbletonian," who never let the Convention forget that "the genius of the country" was indeed republican.

The Very Usefuls: John Dickinson, a victim of old age, poor health, and an unfortunate lack of perspective, whose overall performance, despite flashes of brilliance, failed to match his considerable reputation.

Hugh Williamson, the ablest and hardest-working of the North Carolinians, a member of five committees and a thoughtful participant in key debates.

William Samuel Johnson, the least talkative but by no means least persuasive member of the Connecticut delegation, who may have had more to do with the success of the committee of style than we think.

George Read, that admirable small-state man with prophetic big-nation ideas.

Pierce Butler, like General Pinckney a little too anxious to serve the interests of those who had sent him, yet also like Pinckney a man worth having in the ranks of the nationalist caucus.

William Paterson, the stubborn and successful advocate of state equality, whose departure in late July may have robbed him of a much higher ranking.

Luther Martin, garrulous, sour, and pigheaded, yet an influential pricker of egos and consciences.

The Usefuls: David Brearly, most faithful of the Jerseyites, supporter of Paterson, and chairman of the committee on postponed matters.

William Livingston, like Dickinson something of a disappointment, who did his best work on committees.

Richard Dobbs Spaight, who had several small triumphs as a plugger of holes.

Gunning Bedford, Jr., who proved explosively that the Framers were not really demigods, and who was an interesting example of the small-state nationalist.

Abraham Baldwin, far and away the best of the Georgians, an able committeeman and a force for intelligent compromise.

Daniel Carroll and John Langdon, each of whom spoke up on two dozen occasions for the cause of moderate nationalism.

William R. Davie, an agent if not an architect of the Great Compromise.

The Visibles: John Blair, who never spoke and never sat on a committee, but whose vote several times provided the margin of victory within the Virginia delegation for Madison and Washington against Mason and Randolph.

Daniel of St. Thomas Jenifer and William Few, who also made their presence felt by voting the right way at critical moments.

Jacob Broom, Caleb Strong, William Houstoun, George Clymer, Jonathan Dayton, and James McHenry, each of whom opened his mouth just often and sensibly enough to catch the ear of history.

James McClurg, who opened it three times, put his foot in twice, and went home to his patients.

The Ciphers: Richard Bassett, who somehow managed to sit

through the entire summer without making a speech, serving on a committee, or casting a decisive vote, and who did not make even a single convert to Methodism.

Thomas Mifflin, whose only recorded action was to second a motion of Charles Pinckney.

William Blount and Jared Ingersoll, who spoke up for the first time, and did it feebly, on the last day, and who served on no committees.

Thomas Fitzsimons, Nicholas Gilman, and Alexander Martin, none of whom made any recorded contribution to the proceedings.

The Dropouts and Walkouts: William Churchill Houston, William Pierce, and George Wythe, the last of whom might have been an Influential if fate had permitted him to remain in Philadelphia.

John Francis Mercer, the indignant blade, who could spare the Convention only two weeks and two score ill-tempered observations.

Robert Yates and John Lansing, Jr., the obstinate men from Albany, whose devotion to Governor Clinton forced them to withdraw huffily and rather ingloriously.

The Inexplicable Disappointments: Robert Morris. While in May no one expected the financier to be a Wilson or Madison, in October everyone must have wondered why he had made such a small splash in the proceedings. He had the political and forensic talents, as he had proved in the old days in Congress, to lend a powerful hand to the cause of nationalism, yet he spoke up only twice—to nominate Washington and to second a motion by Read to give Senators a life term—and served on no committee. One can think of many possible explanations for his cipherlike behavior—for example, the pressures of business, the eagerness of his junior colleagues Wilson and Gouverneur Morris, a realization that a new generation was taking over, a desire to mask his vast yet always suspect influence—yet none of them rings quite true. There must always be something a little pathetic in the contrast of the recorded activities of Robert and Gouverneur Morris. The former made no speeches, which puts him in a class with Blair, Few, Gilman, and Mifflin; the later made 173, which puts him in a class by himself.

Alexander Hamilton. Far and away the most disappointing man was the brilliant New Yorker who had done so much to bring the Convention to life. The wide gap between the possible and the actual in Hamilton's performance at Philadelphia comes as an unpleasant shock to the historian of the Convention, and leads him to wonder if there were not personal reasons for his lackluster showing that have never been revealed. Even when we take into account his eccentric hopes for a high-toned government and his anomalous position on the New York delegation,

265

we are left with the feeling that he could have been a Principal, or at worst an Influential, if he had simply behaved like the man he had been in 1783 or 1786 and was to be again in 1788 and 1790—and even was for a few exciting moments in June and September of 1787. He had so much to give, and he gave so little—that is the cheerless appraisal one is bound to make of Hamilton the Framer. . . .

A Collective Endeavor

It should be plain that some states had rather more to do than others with framing the Constitution of 1787. Every delegation had its moments of glory when it voted for liberty, justice, and union, but not every one played a steady and creative role. Indeed, if we are entirely honest, and prepared to endure the wrath of several state historical societies, we may well conclude that five states—Virginia, Pennsylvania (thanks to the dutiful zeal of three men), Connecticut, South Carolina, and Massachusetts, in that order—produced 95 per cent of the thoughts, decisions, and inventive moments that went into the document, and that the others were largely along for the ride. . . .

In the end, the two dozen truly eminent Framers and the five truly influential states merge into the larger reality of the Grand Convention as a collective, national endeavor. It was healthily collective, as we have seen, because self-propelling individuals gained new wisdom and strength from being thrown together, and went on to build an edifice that no one of them could have built alone. It was healthily national because self-interested states came sooner or later to see that their problems could best be solved, and their existence most effectively guaranteed, by placing the edifice in the keeping of the whole people. The "greatest single effort of national deliberation that the world has ever seen" had led to the discovery of a new kind of nation.

VIEWPOINT 2

"The Constitution was as democratic as it was because of the influence of popular movements that were a presence, even if not present."

The Constitution Was Created by the Genius of the American People

Alfred F. Young (1925-)

Alfred F. Young is a former professor of history at Northern Illinois University at De Kalb, Illinois. He has written and edited numerous books and articles on history, including *The American Revolution, The Debate over the Constitution,* and *Dissent; Explorations in the History of American Radicalism.* Much of his research and writing on American history has focused on social and political movements.

In the following viewpoint, taken from an article first published in *Radical History Review,* Young takes a look at the creation of the Constitution from a perspective that is less enamored of the participants of the 1787 Constitutional Convention than that found in the writings of Clinton Rossiter and other historians. He argues that in examining the creation of the Constitution, one must look beyond the Framers, who were members of a social elite, and recognize the importance of the rest of the American people. Young writes that the Framers of the Constitution who met in Philadelphia would have preferred a far less democratic document than

From Alfred F. Young, "The Framers of the Constitution and the 'Genius' of the People," *Radical History Review* 42 (Fall 1988). Reprinted with permission.

the one they created, but felt constrained by growing demands for liberty from the American people. The process of creating the Constitution was less a process of compromise between those who met in Philadelphia, Young argues, than it was a process of compromise between what the Framers wanted and what the American people would accept.

On June 18, 1787, about three weeks into the Constitutional Convention at Philadelphia, Alexander Hamilton delivered a six-hour address that was easily the longest and most conservative the Convention would hear. Gouverneur Morris, a delegate from Pennsylvania, thought it was "the most able and impressive he had ever heard."

Beginning with the premise that "all communities divide themselves into the few and the many," "the wealthy well born" and "the people," Hamilton added the corollary that the "people are turbulent and changing; they seldom judge or determine right." Moving through history, the delegate from New York developed his ideal for a national government that would protect the few from "the imprudence of democracy" and guarantee "stability and permanence": a president and senate indirectly elected for life ("to serve during good behavior") to balance a house directly elected by a popular vote every three years. This "elective monarch" would have an absolute veto over laws passed by Congress. And the national government would appoint the governors of the states, who in turn would have the power to veto any laws by the state legislatures.

If others quickly saw a resemblance in all of this to the King, House of Lords and House of Commons of Great Britain, with the states reduced to colonies ruled by royal governors, they were not mistaken. The British constitution, in Hamilton's view, remained "the best model the world has ever produced."

Three days later a delegate reported that Hamilton's proposals "had been praised by everybody," but "he has been supported by none." Acknowledging that his plan "went beyond the ideas of most members," Hamilton said he had brought it forward not "as a thing attainable by us, but as a model which we ought to approach as near as possible." When he signed the Constitution the framers finally agreed to on September 17, 1787, Hamilton could accurately say, "no plan was more remote from his own."

Why did the framers reject a plan so many admired? To ask this question is to go down a dark path into the heart of the Constitution few of its celebrants care to take. We have heard so much in our elementary and high school civics books about the "great compromises" within the Convention—between the large states and the small states, between the slaveholders and non-slaveholders, between North and South—that we have missed the much larger accommodation that was taking place between the delegates as a whole at the Convention and what they called "the people out of doors."

The Convention was unmistakably an elite body, . . . weighted with merchants, slaveholding planters and "monied men" who loaned money at interest. Among them were numerous lawyers and college graduates in a country where most men and only a few women had the rudiments of a formal education. They were far from a cross section of the four million or so Americans of that day, most of whom were farmers or artisans, fishermen or seamen, indentured servants or laborers, half of whom were women and about 600,000 of whom were African-American slaves.

The First Accommodation

Why did this elite reject Hamilton's plan that many of them praised? James Madison, the Constitution's chief architect, had the nub of the matter. The Constitution was "intended for the ages." To last it had to conform to the "genius" of the American people. "Genius" was a word eighteenth-century political thinkers used to mean spirit: we might say character or underlying values.

James Wilson, second only to Madison in his influence at Philadelphia, elaborated on the idea. "The British government cannot be our model. We have no materials for a similar one. Our manners, our law, the abolition of entail and primogeniture," which made for a more equal distribution of property among sons, "the whole genius of the people, are opposed to it."

This was long-range political philosophy. There was a short-range political problem that moved other realistic delegates in the same direction. Called together to revise the old Articles of Confederation, the delegates instead decided to scrap it and frame an entirely new constitution. It would have to be submitted to the people for ratification, most likely to conventions elected especially for the purpose. Repeatedly, conservatives recoiled from extreme proposals for which they knew they could not win popular support.

In response to a proposal to extend the federal judiciary into the states, Pierce Butler, a South Carolina planter, argued, "the people will not bear such innovations. The states will revolt at such encroachments." His assumption was "we must follow the example of Solon, who gave the Athenians not the best government he could devise but the best they would receive."

The suffrage debate epitomized this line of thinking. Gouverneur

Morris, Hamilton's admirer, proposed that the national government limit voting for the House to men who owned a freehold, i.e., a substantial farm, or its equivalent. "Give the vote to people who have no property and they will sell them to the rich who will be able to buy them," he said with some prescience. George Mason, author of Virginia's Bill of Rights, was aghast. "Eight or nine states have extended the right of suffrage beyond the freeholders. What will people there say if they should be disfranchised?"

An Elite Convention Creates an Elite Document

Political scientist and social commentator Michael Parenti, writing in his book Democracy for the Few, *argues that the Constitution was the product of an upper-class group of wealthy men who created an elitist document designed to protect the rights of property owners above all else. Its democratic features, he argues, arose only as concessions designed to forestall popular uprisings.*

The Constitution championed the rights of property over the rights and liberties of persons. For the founders, liberty meant something different from and antithetical to democracy. It meant liberty to invest, speculate, trade, and accumulate wealth and to secure its possession without encroachment by sovereign or populace. The civil liberties designed to give all individuals the right to engage in public affairs won little support from the delegates. When Colonel George Mason recommended that a committee be formed to draft "a Bill of Rights," a task he said could be accomplished "in a few hours," the other convention members offered little discussion on the motion and voted unanimously against it. . . .

Land seizures by the poor, food riots, and other violent disturbances occurred throughout the eighteenth century in just about every state and erstwhile colony. This popular ferment spurred the framers in their effort to erect a strong central government *but it also set a limit on what they could do.* The delegates "gave" nothing to popular interests; rather—as with the Bill of Rights—they reluctantly made concessions under the threat of democratic rebellion. They kept what they could and grudgingly relinquished what they felt they had to, driven not by a love of democracy but by a fear of it, not by a love of the people but by a prudent desire to avoid popular uprisings. The Constitution, then, was a product not only of class privilege but of class struggle—a struggle that continued and intensified as the corporate economy and the government grew.

Benjamin Franklin, the patriarch, speaking for one of the few times in the convention, paid tribute to "the lower class of freemen" who should not be disfranchised. James Wilson explained, "it would be very hard and disagreeable for the same person" who could vote for representatives for the state legislatures "to be excluded from a vote for this in the national legislature." Nathaniel Gorham, a Boston merchant, returned to the guiding principle: "the people will never allow" existing rights to suffrage to be abridged. "We must consult their rooted prejudices if we expect their concurrence in our propositions."

The result? Morris' proposal was defeated and the convention decided that whoever each state allowed to vote for its own assembly could vote for the House. It was a compromise that left the door open and in a matter of decades allowed states to introduce universal white male suffrage.

Ghosts of Years Past

Clearly there was a process of accommodation at work here. The popular movements of the Revolutionary Era were a presence at the Philadelphia Convention even if they were not present. The delegates, one might say, were haunted by ghosts, symbols of the broadly based movements elites had confronted in the making of the Revolution from 1765 to 1775, in waging the war from 1775 to 1781 and in the years since 1781 within their own states.

The first was the ghost of Thomas Paine, the most influential radical democrat of the Revolutionary Era. In 1776 Paine's pamphlet *Common Sense* (which sold at least 150,000 copies), in arguing for independence, rejected not only King George III but the principle of monarchy and the so-called checks and balances of the unwritten English constitution. In its place he offered a vision of a democratic government in which a single legislature would be supreme, the executive minimal, and representatives would be elected from small districts by a broad electorate for short terms so they could "return and mix again with the voters." John Adams considered *Common Sense* too "democratical," without even an attempt at "mixed government" that would balance "democracy" with "aristocracy."

The second ghost was that of Abraham Yates, a member of the state senate of New York typical of the new men who had risen to power in the 1780s in the state legislatures. We have forgotten him; Hamilton, who was very conscious of him, called him "an old Booby." He had begun as a shoemaker and was a self-taught lawyer and warm foe of the landlord aristocracy of the Hudson Valley which Hamilton had married into. As James Madison identified the "vices of the political system of the United States" in a memorandum in 1787, the Abraham Yateses were the number-one problem. The state legislatures had "an itch for paper money" laws, laws that prevented foreclosure on farm mortgages, and tax laws that soaked the rich. As Madison saw it, this meant that "debtors defrauded their creditors" and "the landed interest has borne hard on the mercantile interest." This, too, is what Hamilton had in mind when he spoke of the "depredations which the democratic spirit is apt to make on property" and what others meant by the "excess of democracy" in the states.

The third ghost was a very fresh one—Daniel Shays. In 1786 Shays, a captain in the Revolution, led a rebellion of debtor farmers in western Massachusetts which the state quelled with its own somewhat unreliable militia. There were "combustibles in every state," as George Washington put it, raising the specter of "Shaysism." This Madison enumerated among the "vices" of the system as "a want of guaranty to the states against internal violence." Worse still, Shaysites in many states were turning to the political system to elect their own kind. If they succeeded they would produce legal Shaysism, a danger for which the elites had no remedy.

The fourth ghost we can name was the ghost of Thomas Peters, although he had a thousand other names. In 1775, Peters, a Virginia slave, responded to a plea by the British to fight in their army and win their freedom. He served in an "Ethiopian Regiment," some of whose members bore the emblem "Liberty to Slaves" on their uniforms. After the war the British transported Peters and several thousand escaped slaves to Nova Scotia from whence Peters eventually led a group to return to Africa and the colony of Sierra Leone, a long odyssey to freedom. Eighteenth-century slaveholders, with no illusions about happy or contented slaves, were haunted by the specter of slaves in arms.

Elite Divisions

During the Revolutionary Era elites divided in response to these varied threats from below. One group, out of fear of "the mob" and then "the rabble in arms," embraced the British and became active Loyalists. After the war most of them went into exile. Another group who became patriots never lost their obsession with coercing popular movements. . . .

Far more important, however, were those patriot leaders who adopted a strategy of "swimming with a stream which it is impossible to stem." This was the metaphor of Robert R. Livingston, Jr., . . . a gentleman with a large tenanted estate in New York. Men of his class had to learn to "yield to the torrent if they hoped to direct its course."

Livingston and his group were able to shape New York's constitution, which some called a perfect blend of "aristocracy" and "democracy." John Hancock, the richest merchant in New England, had mastered this kind of politics and emerged as the most popular politician in Massachusetts. In Maryland Charles Carroll, a wealthy planter, instructed his anxious father about the need to "submit to partial losses" because "no great revolution can happen in a state without revolutions or mutations of private property. If we can save a third of our personal estate and all of our lands and Negroes, I shall think ourselves well off."

The major leaders at the Constitutional Convention in 1787 were heirs to both traditions: coercion and accommodation— Hamilton and Gouverneur Morris to the former, James Madison and James Wilson much more to the latter.

They all agreed on coercion to slay the ghosts of Daniel Shays and Thomas Peters. The Constitution gave the national government the power to "suppress insurrections" and protect the states from "domestic violence." There would be a national army under the command of the president, and authority to nationalize the state militias and suspend the right of habeas corpus in "cases of rebellion or invasion." In 1794 Hamilton, as secretary of the treasury, would exercise such powers fully (and needlessly) to suppress the Whiskey Rebellion in western Pennsylvania.

The Constitution's Forgotten People

Richard B. Morris, an author and former history professor at Columbia University in New York, states in a 1987 symposium presentation that the Constitution and the process that created it were notable for the American people left out.

The original Constitution, we now recognize, was basically a document of governance for free, white, propertied adult males, free from dependence upon others. Left out of its text, or dealt with ambiguously, were the forgotten people—those bound to servitude, white or black (slavery was implicitly, rather than overtly, recognized), debtors, paupers, Indians, and women—most of whom were not considered a part of the political constituency. True, the Founding Fathers held diverse views on the score of blacks, Indians, and women, but they managed to sidestep a direct confrontation on each of these . . . forgotten people—in numbers, a majority of the nation's inhabitants in 1787.

Southern slaveholders correctly interpreted the same powers as available to shackle the ghost of Thomas Peters. As it turned out, Virginia would not need a federal army to deal with Gabriel Prosser's insurrection in 1800 or Nat Turner's rebellion in 1830, but a federal army would capture John Brown after his raid at Harpers Ferry in 1859.

But how to deal with the ghosts of Thomas Paine and Abraham Yates? Here Madison and Wilson blended coercion with accommodation. They had three solutions to the threat of democratic majorities in the states.

Their first was clearly coercive. Like Hamilton, Madison wanted some kind of national veto over the state legislatures. He got several very specific curbs on the states written into fundamental law: no state could "emit" paper money or pass "laws impairing the obligation of contracts." Wilson was so overjoyed with these two clauses that he argued that if they alone "were inserted in the Constitution I think they would be worth our adoption."

But Madison considered the overall mechanism adopted to curb the states "short of the mark." The Constitution, laws and treaties were the "supreme law of the land" and ultimately a federal court could declare state laws unconstitutional. But this, Madison lamented, would only catch "mischiefs" after the fact. Thus they had clipped the wings of Abraham Yates but he could still fly.

The second solution to the problem of the states was decidedly democratic. They wanted to do an end-run around the state legislatures. The Articles of Confederation, said Madison, rested on "the pillars" of the state legislatures who elected delegates to Congress. The "great fabric to be raised would be more stable and durable if it should rest on the solid grounds of the people themselves"; hence, there would be popular elections to the House.

Wilson altered only the metaphor. He was for "raising the federal pyramid to a considerable altitude and for that reason wanted to give it as broad a base as possible." They would slay the ghost of Abraham Yates with the ghost of Thomas Paine.

This was risky business. They would reduce the risk by keeping the House of Representatives small. Under a ratio of one representative for every 30,000 people, the first house would have only 65 members; in 1776 Thomas Paine had suggested 390. But still, the House would be elected every two years, and with each state allowed to determine its own qualifications for voting, there was no telling who might end up in Congress.

There was also a risk in Madison's third solution to the problem of protecting propertied interests from democratic majorities: "extending the sphere" of government. Prevailing wisdom held that a republic could only succeed in a small geographic area; to rule an "extensive" country, some kind of despotism was considered inevitable.

Madison turned this idea on its head in his since famous *Federalist* essay No. 10. In a small republic, he argued, it was relatively easy for a majority to gang up on a particular "interest." "Extend the sphere," he wrote, and "you take in a greater variety of parties and interests." Then it would be more difficult for a majority "to discover their own strength and to act in unison with each other."

This was a prescription for a non-colonial empire that would expand across the continent, taking in new states as it dispossessed the Indians. The risk was there was no telling how far the "democratic" or "leveling" spirit might go in such likely would-be states as frontier Vermont, Kentucky and Tennessee.

Democratic Divisions

In the spectrum of state constitutions adopted in the Revolutionary Era, the federal Constitution of 1787 was, like New York's, somewhere between "aristocracy" and "democracy." It therefore should not surprise us—although it has eluded many modern critics of the Constitution—that in the contest over ratification in 1787-1788, the democratic minded were divided.

Among agrarian democrats there was a gut feeling that the Constitution was the work of an old class enemy. "These lawyers and men of learning and monied men," argued Amos Singletary, a working farmer at the Massachusetts ratifying convention, "expect to be managers of this Constitution and get all the power and all the money into their own hands and then will swallow up all of us little folks . . . just as the whale swallowed up Jonah."

Democratic leaders like Melancton Smith of New York focused on the small size of the proposed House. Arguing from Paine's premise that the members of the legislature should "resemble those they represent," Smith feared that "a substantial yeoman of sense and discernment will hardly ever be chosen" and the government "will fall into the hands of the few and the great." Urban democrats, on the other hand, including a majority of the mechanics and tradesmen of the major cities who in the Revolution had been a bulwark of Paineite radicalism, were generally enthusiastic about the Constitution. They were impelled by their urgent stake in a stronger national government that would advance ocean-going commerce and protect American manufacturers from competition. But they would not have been as ardent about the new frame of government without its saving graces. It clearly preserved their rights to suffrage. And the process of ratification, like the Constitution itself, guaranteed them a voice. As early as 1776 the New York Committee of Mechanics held it as "a right which God has given them in common with all men to judge whether it be consistent with their interest to accept or reject a constitution."

Mechanics turned out en masse in the parades celebrating ratification, marching trade by trade. The slogans and symbols they carried expressed their political ideals. In New York the upholsterers had a float with an elegant "Federal Chair of State" flanked by the symbols of Liberty and Justice that they identified with the Constitution. In Philadelphia the bricklayers put on their banner "Both buildings and rulers are the work of our hands."

Democrats who were skeptical found it easier to come over because of the Constitution's redeeming features. Thomas Paine, off in Paris, considered the Constitution "a copy, though not quite as base as the original, of the form of the British government." He had always opposed a single executive and he objected to the "long duration of the Senate." But he was so convinced of "the absolute necessity" of a stronger federal government that "I would have voted for it myself had I been in America or even for a worse, rather than have none." It was crucial to Paine that there was an amending process, the means of "remedying its defects by the same appeal to the people by which it was to be established."

The Second Accommodation

In drafting the Constitution in 1787 the framers, self-styled Federalists, made their first accommodation with the "genius" of the people. In campaigning for its ratification in 1788 they made their second. At the outset, the conventions in the key states—Massachusetts, New York and Virginia—either had an anti-Federalist majority or were closely divided. To swing over a small group of "antis" in each state, Federalists had to promise that they would consider amendments. This was enough to secure ratification by narrow margins in Massachusetts, 187 to 168; in New York, 30 to 27; and in Virginia, 89 to 79.

What the anti-Federalists wanted were dozens of changes in the structure of the government that would cut back national power over the states, curb the powers of the presidency as well as protect individual liberties. What they got was far less. But in the first Congress in 1789, James Madison, true to his pledge, considered all the amendments and shepherded 12 amendments through both houses. The first two of these failed in the states; one would have enlarged the House. The 10 that were ratified by December 1791 were what we have since called the Bill of Rights, protecting freedom of expression and the rights of the accused before the law. Abraham Yates considered them "trivial and unimportant." But other democrats looked on them much more favorably. In time the limited meaning of freedom of speech in the First Amendment was broadened far beyond the framers' original intent. Later popular movements thought of the Bill of Rights as an essential part of the "constitutional" and "republican" rights that belonged to the people.

The "Losers" Role

There is a cautionary tale here that surely goes beyond the process of framing and adopting the Constitution and Bill of Rights from 1787 to 1791. The Constitution was as democratic as it was because of the influence of popular movements that were a presence, even if not present. The losers helped shape the results. We owe the Bill of Rights to the opponents of the Constitution, as we do many other features in the Constitution put in to anticipate opposition.

In American history popular movements often shaped elites, especially in times of crisis when elites were concerned with the "system." Elites have often divided in response to such threats and according to their perception of the "genius" of the people. Some have turned to coercion, others to accommodation. We run serious risk if we ignore this distinction.

Appendices

The Articles of Confederation

To all to whom these Presents shall come, we the under signed Delegates of the States affixed to our Names send greeting. Whereas the Delegates of the United States of America in Congress assembled did on the fifteenth day of November in the Year of our Lord One Thousand Seven Hundred and Seventy seven, and in the Second Year of the Independence of America agree to certain articles of Confederation and perpetual Union between the States of Newhampshire, Massachusetts-bay, Rhodeisland and Providence Plantations, Connecticut, New York, New Jersey, Pennsylvania, Delaware, Maryland, Virginia, North-Carolina, South-Carolina and Georgia in the Words following, viz, "Articles of Confederation and perpetual Union between the States of Newhampshire, Massachusetts-bay, Rhodeisland and Providence Plantations, Connecticut, New-York, New-Jersey, Pennsylvania, Delaware, Maryland, Virginia, North-Carolina, South-Carolina and Georgia."

Article I. The Stile of this confederacy shall be "The United States of America."

Article II. Each state retains its sovereignty, freedom and independence, and every Power, Jurisdiction and right, which is not by this confederation expressly delegated to the United States, in Congress assembled.

Article III. The said states hereby severally enter into a firm league of friendship with each other, for their common defence, the security of their Liberties, and their mutual and general welfare, binding themselves to assist each other, against all force offered to, or attacks made upon them, or any of them, on account of religion, sovereignty, trade, or any other pretence whatever.

Article IV. The better to secure and perpetuate mutual friendship and intercourse among the people of the different states in this union, the free inhabitants of each of these states, paupers, vagabonds and fugitives from Justice excepted, shall be entitled to all privileges and immunities of free citizens in the several states; and the people of each state shall have free ingress and regress to and from any other state, and shall enjoy therein all the privileges of trade and commerce, subject to the same duties, impositions and restrictions as the inhabitants thereof respectively, provided that such restriction shall not extend so far as to prevent the removal of property imported into any state, to any other state of which the Owner is an inhabitant; provided also that no imposition, duties or restriction shall be laid by any state, on the property of the united states, or either of them.

If any Person guilty of, or charged with treason, felony, or other high misdemeanor in any state, shall flee from Justice, and be found in any of the united states, he shall upon demand of the Governor or executive power, of the state from which he fled, be delivered up and removed to the state having jurisdiction of his offence.

Full faith and credit shall be given in each of these states to the records, acts and judicial proceedings of the courts and magistrates of every other state.

Article V. For the more convenient management of the general interests of the united states, delegates shall be annually appointed in such manner as the legislature of each state shall direct, to meet in Congress on the first Monday in November, in every year, with a power reserved to each state, to recal its delegates, or any of them, at any time within the year, and to send others in their stead, for the remainder of the Year.

No state shall be represented in Congress by less than two, nor by more than seven Members; and no person shall be capable of being a delegate for more than three years in any term of six years; nor shall any person, being a delegate, be capable of holding any office under the united states, for which he, or another for his benefit receives any salary, fees or emolument of any kind.

Each state shall maintain its own delegates in a meeting of the states, and while they act as members of the committee of the states.

In determining questions in the united states, in Congress assembled, each state shall have one vote.

Freedom of speech and debate in Congress shall not be impeached or questioned in any Court, or place out of Congress, and the members of congress shall be protected in their persons from arrests and imprisonments, during the time of their going to and from, and attendance on congress, except for treason, felony, or breach of the peace.

Article VI. No state without the Consent of the united states in congress assembled, shall send any embassy to, or receive any embassy from, or enter into any conference, agreement, alliance or treaty with any King prince or state; nor shall any person holding any office of profit or trust under the united states, or any of them, accept of any present, emolument, office or title of any kind whatever from any king, prince or foreign state; nor shall the united states in congress assembled, or any of them, grant any title of nobility.

No two or more states shall enter into any treaty, confederation or alliance whatever between them, without the consent of the united states in congress assembled, specifying accurately the purposes for which the same is to be entered into, and how long it shall continue.

No state shall lay any imposts or duties, which may interfere with any stipulations in treaties, entered into by the united states in congress assembled, with any king, prince or state, in pursuance of any treaties already proposed by congress, to the courts of France and Spain.

No vessels of war shall be kept up in time of peace by any state, except such number only, as shall be deemed necessary by the united states in congress assembled, for the defence of such state, or its trade; nor shall any body of forces be kept up by any state, in time of peace, except such number only, as in the judgment of the united states, in congress assembled, shall be deemed requisite to garrison the forts necessary for the defence of such state; but every state shall always keep up a well regulated and disciplined militia, sufficiently armed and accoutred, and shall provide and constantly have ready for use, in public stores, a due number of field pieces and tents, and a proper quantity of arms, ammunition and camp equipage.

No state shall engage in any war without the consent of the united states in congress assembled, unless such state be actually invaded by enemies, or shall have received certain advice of a resolution being formed by some nation of Indians to invade such state, and the danger is so imminent as not to admit of a delay, till the united states in congress assembled can be consulted: nor shall any state grant commissions to any ships or vessels of war, nor letters of marque or reprisal, except it be after a declaration of war by the united states in congress assembled, and then only against the kingdom or state and the subjects thereof, against which war has been so declared, and under such regulations as shall be established by the united states in congress assembled, unless such state be infested by pirates, in which case vessels of war may be fitted out for that occasion, and kept so long as the danger shall continue, or until the united states in congress assembled shall determine otherwise.

Article VII. When land-forces are raised by any state for the common defence, all officers of or under the rank of colonel, shall be appointed by the legislature of each state respectively by whom such forces shall be raised, or in such manner as such state shall direct, and all vacancies shall be filled up by the state which first made the appointment.

Article VIII. All charges of war, and all other expences that shall be incurred for the common defence or general welfare, and allowed by the united states in congress assembled, shall be defrayed out of a common treasury, which shall be supplied by the several states, in proportion to the value of all land within each state, granted to or surveyed for any Person, as such land and the buildings and improvements thereon shall be estimated according to such mode as the united states in congress assembled, shall from time to time direct and appoint. The taxes for paying that proportion shall be laid and levied by the authority and direction of the legislatures of the several states within the time agreed upon by the united states in congress assembled.

Article IX. The united states in congress assembled, shall have the sole and exclusive right and power of determining on peace and war, except in the cases mentioned in the sixth article—of sending and receiving ambassadors—entering into treaties and alliances, provided that no treaty of commerce shall be made whereby the legislative power of the respective states shall be restrained from imposing such imposts and duties on foreigners, as their own people are subjected to, or from prohibiting the exportation or importation of any species of goods or commodities whatsoever—of establishing rules for deciding in all cases, what captures on land or water shall be legal, and in what manner prizes taken by land or naval forces in the service of the united states shall be divided or appropriated—of granting letters of marque and reprisal in times of peace—appointing courts for the trial of piracies and felonies committed on the high seas and establishing courts for receiving and determining finally appeals in all cases of captures, provided that no member of congress shall be appointed a judge of any of the said courts.

The united states in congress assembled shall also be the last resort on appeal in all disputes and differences now subsisting or that hereafter may arise between two or more states concerning boundary, jurisdiction or any other cause whatever; which authority shall always be exercised in the manner following. Whenever the legislative or executive authority or lawful agent of any state in controversy with another shall present a petition to congress stating the matter in question and praying for a hearing, notice thereof shall be given by order of congress to the legislative or executive authority of the other state in controversy, and a day assigned for the appearance of the parties by their lawful agents, who shall then be directed to appoint by joint consent, commissioners or judges to constitute a court for hearing and determining the matter in question: but if they cannot agree, congress shall name three persons out of each of the united states, and from the list of such persons each party shall alternately strike out one, the petitioners beginning, until the number shall be reduced to thirteen; and from that number not less than seven, nor more than nine names as congress shall direct, shall in the presence of congress be drawn out by lot, and the persons whose names shall be so drawn or any five of them, shall be commissioners or judges, to hear and finally determine the controversy, so always as a major part of the judges who shall hear the cause shall agree in the determination: and if either party shall neglect to attend at the day appointed, without shewing reasons, which congress shall judge sufficient, or being present shall refuse to strike, the congress shall proceed to nominate three persons out of each state, and the secretary of congress shall strike in behalf of such party absent or refusing; and the judgment and sentence of the court to be appointed, in the manner before prescribed, shall be final and conclusive; and if any of the parties shall refuse to submit to the authority of such court, or to appear or defend their claim or cause, the court shall nevertheless proceed to pronounce sentence, or judgment, which shall in like manner be final and decisive, the judgment or sentence and other proceedings being in either case transmitted to congress, and lodged among the acts of congress for the security of the parties concerned: provided that every commissioner, before he sits in judgment, shall take an oath to be administered by one of the judges of the supreme or superior court of the state, where the cause shall be tried, "well and truly to hear and determine the matter in question, according to the best of his judgment, without favour, affection or hope of reward:" provided also that no state shall be deprived of territory for the benefit of the united states.

All controversies concerning the private right of soil claimed under different grants of two or more states, whose jurisdictions as they may respect such lands, and the states which passed such grants are adjusted, the said grants or either of them being at the same time claimed to have originated antecedent to such settlement of jurisdiction, shall on the petition of either party to the congress of the united states, be finally determined as near as maybe in the same manner as is before prescribed for deciding disputes respecting territorial jurisdiction between different states.

The united states in congress assembled shall also have the sole and exclusive right and power of regulating the alloy and value of coin struck by their own authority, or by that of the respective states—fixing the standard of weights and measures throughout the united states—regulating the trade and managing all affairs with the Indians, not members of any of the states, provided that the legislative right of any state within its own limits be not infringed or violated—establishing and regulating post-offices from one state to another, throughout all the united states, and exacting such postage on the papers passing thro' the same as may be requisite to defray the expences of the said office—appointing all officers of the land forces, in the service of the united states, excepting regimental officers—appointing all the officers of the naval forces, and commissioning all officers whatever in the service of the united states—making rules for the government and regulation of the said land and naval forces, and directing their operations.

The united states in congress assembled shall have authority to appoint a committee, to sit in the recess of congress, to be denominated "A Committee of the States," and to consist of one delegate from each state; and to appoint such other committees and civil officers as may be necessary for managing the general affairs of the united states under their direction—to appoint one of their number to preside, provided that no person be allowed to serve in the office of president more than one year in any term of three years; to ascertain the necessary sums of Money to be raised for the service of the united states, and to appropriate and apply the same for defraying the public expenses—to borrow money, or emit bills on the credit of the united states, transmitting every half year to the respective states an account of the sums of money so borrowed or emitted,—to build and equip a navy—to agree upon the number of land forces, and to make requisitions from each state for its quota, in proportion to the number of white inhabitants in such state; which requisition shall be binding, and thereupon the legislature of each state shall appoint the regimental officers, raise the men and cloath, arm and equip them in a soldier like manner, at the expence of the united states; and the officers and men so cloathed, armed and equipped shall march to the place appointed, and within the time agreed on by the united states in congress assembled: But if the united states in congress assembled shall, on consideration of circumstances judge proper that any state should not raise men, or should raise a smaller number than its quota thereof, and that any other state should raise a greater number of men than the quota thereof, such extra number shall be raised, officered, cloathed, armed and equipped in the same manner as the quota of such state, unless the legislature of such state shall judge that such extra number cannot be safely spared out of the same, in which case they shall raise, officer, cloath, arm and equip as many of such extra number as they judge can be safely spared. And the officers and men so cloathed, armed and equipped, shall march to the place appointed, and within the time agreed on by the united states in congress assembled.

The united states in congress assembled shall never engage in a war, nor grant letters of marque and reprisal in time of peace, nor enter into any treaties or alliances, nor coin money, nor regulate the value thereof, nor ascertain the sums and expences necessary for the defence and welfare of the united states, or any of them, nor emit bills, nor borrow money on the credit of the united states, nor appropriate money, nor agree upon the number of vessels of war, to be built or purchased, or the number of land or sea forces to be raised, nor appoint a commander in chief of the army or navy, unless nine states assent to the same: nor shall a question on any other point, except for adjourning from day to day be determined, unless by the votes of a majority of the united states in congress assembled.

The congress of the united states shall have power to adjourn to any time within the year, and to any place within the united states, so that no period of adjournment be for a longer duration than the space of six Months, and shall publish the Journal of their proceedings monthly, except such parts thereof relating to treaties, alliances or military operations as in their judgment require secresy; and the yeas and nays of the delegates of each state on any question shall be entered on the Journal, when it is desired by any delegate; and the delegates of a state, or any of them, at his or their request shall be furnished with a transcript of the said Journal, except such parts as are above excepted, to lay before the legislatures of the several states.

Article X. The committee of the states, or any nine of them, shall be authorized to execute, in the recess of congress, such of the powers of congress as the united states in congress assembled, by the consent of nine states, shall from time to time think expedient to vest them with; provided that no power be delegated to the said committee, for the exercise of which, by the articles of confederation, the voice of nine states in the congress of the united states assembled is requisite.

Article XI. Canada acceding to this confederation, and joining in the measures of the united states, shall be admitted into, and entitled to all the advantages of this union: but no other colony shall be admitted into the same, unless such admission be agreed to by nine states.

Article XII. All bills of credit emitted, monies borrowed and debts contracted by, or under the authority of congress, before the assembling of the united states, in pursuance of the present confederation, shall be deemed and considered as a charge against the united states, for payment and satisfaction whereof the said united states, and the public faith are hereby solemnly pledged.

Article XIII. Every state shall abide by the determinations of the united states in congress assembled, on all questions which by this confederation are submitted to them. And the Articles of this confederation shall be inviolably observed by every state, and the union shall be perpetual; nor shall any alteration at any time hereafter be made in any of them; unless such alteration be agreed to in a congress of the united states, and be afterwards confirmed by the legislatures of every state.

And Whereas it hath pleased the Great Governor of the World to incline the hearts of the legislatures we respectively represent in congress, to approve of, and to authorize us to ratify the said articles of confederation and perpetual union. Know Ye that we the undersigned delegates, by virtue of the power and authority to us given for that purpose, do by these presents, in the name and in behalf of our respective constituents, fully and entirely ratify and confirm each and every of the said articles of confederation and perpetual union, and all and singular the matters and things therein contained: And we do further solemnly plight and engage the faith of our respective constituents, that they shall abide by the determinations of the united states in congress assembled, on all questions, which by the said confederation are submitted to them. And that the articles thereof shall be inviolably observed by the states we respectively represent, and that the union shall be perpetual. In Witness whereof we have hereunto set our hands in Congress. Done at Philadelphia in the state of Pennsylvania the ninth Day of July in the Year of our Lord one Thousand seven Hundred and Seventy-eight, and in the third year of the independence of America.

The 1787 Constitution

Editor's note: The Constitution as formulated by the 1787 Constitutional Convention is reprinted here. Passages that have been superseded by subsequent amendments or are otherwise dated or no longer in effect are printed in italic type.

We the People of the United States, in Order to form a more perfect Union, establish Justice, insure domestic Tranquillity, provide for the common defence, promote the general Welfare, and secure the Blessings of Liberty to ourselves and our Posterity, do ordain and establish this Constitution for the United States of America.

Article I

SECTION 1. All legislative Powers herein granted shall be vested in a Congress of the United States, which shall consist of a Senate and House of Representatives.

SECTION 2. The House of Representatives shall be composed of Members chosen every second Year by the People of the several States, and the Electors in each State shall have the Qualifications requisite for Electors of the most numerous Branch of the State Legislature.

No Person shall be a Representative who shall not have attained to the age of twenty five Years, and been seven Years a Citizen of the United States, and who shall not, when elected, be an Inhabitant of that State in which he shall be chosen.

Representatives and direct Taxes shall be apportioned among the several States which may be included within this Union, according to their respective Numbers, *which shall be determined by adding to the whole Number of free Persons, including those bound to Service for a Term of Years, and excluding Indians not taxed, three fifths of all other Persons.* The actual Enumeration shall be made within three Years after the first Meeting of the Congress of the United States, and within every subsequent Term of ten Years, in such Manner as they shall by Law direct. The Number of Representatives shall not exceed one for every thirty Thousand, but each State shall have at Least one Representative; and until such enumeration shall be made, the State of New Hampshire shall be entitled to chuse three, Massachusetts eight, Rhode-Island and Providence Plantations one, Connecticut five, New-York six, New Jersey four, Pennsylvania eight, Delaware one, Maryland six, Virginia ten, North Carolina five, South Carolina five, and Georgia three.

When vacancies happen in the Representation from any State, the Executive Authority thereof shall issue Writs of Election to fill such Vacancies.

The House of Representatives shall chuse their Speaker and other Officers; and shall have the sole Power of Impeachment.

SECTION 3. The Senate of the United States shall be composed of two Senators from each State, *chosen by the Legislature thereof,* for six Years; and each Senator shall have one Vote.

Immediately after they shall be assembled in Consequence of the first Election, they shall be divided as equally as may be into three Classes. The Seats of the Senators of the first Class shall be vacated at the Expiration of the second Year, of the second Class at the Expiration of the fourth Year, and of the third Class at the Expiration of the sixth Year, so that one third may be chosen every second Year; and if Vacancies happen by Resignation, or otherwise, during the Recess of the Legislature of any State, the Executive thereof may make temporary Appointments until the next Meeting of the Legislature, which shall then fill such Vacancies.

No Person shall be a Senator who shall not have attained to the Age of thirty Years, and been nine Years a Citizen of the United States, and who shall not, when elected, be an Inhabitant of that State for which he shall be chosen.

The Vice President of the United States shall be President of the Senate, but shall have no Vote, unless they be equally divided.

The Senate shall chuse their other Officers, and also a President pro tempore, in the Absence of the Vice President, or when he shall exercise the Office of President of the United States.

The Senate shall have the sole Power to try all Impeachments. When sitting for that Purpose, they shall be on Oath or Affirmation. When the President of the United States is tried the Chief Justice shall preside: And no Person shall be convicted without the Concurrence of two thirds of the Members present.

Judgment in Cases of Impeachment shall not extend further than to removal from Office, and disqualification to hold and enjoy any Office of honor, Trust or Profit under the United States: but the Party convicted shall nevertheless be liable and subject to Indictment, Trial, Judgment and Punishment, according to Law.

SECTION 4. The Times, Places and Manner of holding Elections for Senators and Representatives, shall be prescribed in each State by the Legislature thereof; but the Congress may at any time by Law make or alter such Regulations, except as to the Places of chusing Senators.

The Congress shall assemble at least once in every Year, and such Meeting *shall be on the first Monday in December, unless they shall by Law appoint a different Day.*

SECTION 5. Each House shall be the Judge of the Elections, Returns and Qualifications of its own Members, and a Majority of each shall constitute a Quorum to do Business; but a smaller Number may adjourn from day to day, and may be authorized to compel the Attendance of absent Members, in such Manner, and under such Penalties as each House may provide.

Each House may determine the Rules of its Proceedings, punish its Members for disorderly Behaviour, and, with the Concurrence of two thirds, expel a Member.

Each House shall keep a Journal of its Proceedings, and from time to time publish the same, excepting such Parts as may in their Judgment require Secrecy; and the Yeas and Nays of the Members of either House on any question shall, at the Desire of one fifth of those Present, be entered on the Journal.

Neither House, during the Session of Congress, shall, without the Consent of the other, adjourn for more than three days, nor to any other Place than that in which the two Houses shall be sitting.

SECTION 6. The Senators and Representatives shall receive a Compensation for their Services, to be ascertained by Law, and paid out of the Treasury of the United States. They shall in all Cases, except Treason, Felony and Breach of the Peace, be privileged from Arrest during their Attendance at the Session of their respective Houses, and in going to and returning from the same; and for any Speech or Debate in either House, they shall not be questioned in any other Place.

No Senator or Representative shall, during the Time for which he was elected, be appointed to any civil Office under the Authority of the United States, which shall have been created, or the Emoluments whereof shall have been encreased during such time; and no Person holding any Office under the United States, shall be a Member of either House during his Continuance in Office.

SECTION 7. All Bills for raising Revenue shall originate in the House of Representatives; but the Senate may propose or concur with Amendments as on other Bills.

Every Bill which shall have passed the House of Representatives and the Senate, shall, before it become a Law, be presented to the President of the United States; If he approve he shall sign it, but if not he shall return it, with his Objections to that House in which it shall have originated, who shall enter the Objections at large on their Journal, and proceed to reconsider it. If after such Reconsideration two thirds of that House shall agree to pass the Bill, it shall be sent, together with the Objections, to the other House, by which it shall likewise be reconsidered, and if approved by two thirds of that House, it shall become a Law. But in all such Cases the Votes of both Houses shall be determined by yeas and Nays, and the Names of the Persons voting for and against the Bill shall be entered on the Journal of each House respectively. If any Bill shall not be returned by the President within ten Days (Sundays excepted) after it shall have been presented to him, the Same shall be a Law, in like Manner as if he had signed it, unless the Congress by their Adjournment prevent its Return, in which Case it shall not be a Law.

Every Order, Resolution, or Vote to which the Concurrence of the Senate and House of Representatives may be necessary (except on a question of Adjournment) shall be presented to the President of the United States; and before the Same shall take Effect, shall be approved by him, or being disapproved by him, shall be repassed by two thirds of the Senate and House of Representatives, according to the Rules and Limitations prescribed in the Case of a Bill.

SECTION 8. The Congress shall have Power To lay and collect Taxes, Duties, Imposts and Excises, to pay the Debts and provide for the common Defence and general Welfare of the United States; but all Duties, Imposts and Excises shall be uniform throughout the United States;

To borrow Money on the credit of the United States;

To regulate Commerce with foreign Nations, and among the several States, and with the Indian Tribes;

To establish an uniform Rule of Naturalization, and uniform Laws on the subject of Bankruptcies throughout the United States;

To coin Money, regulate the Value thereof, and of foreign Coin, and fix the Standard of Weights and Measures;

To provide for the Punishment of counterfeiting the Securities and current Coin of the United States;

To establish Post Offices and post Roads;

To promote the Progress of Science and useful Arts, by securing for limited Times to Authors and Inventors the exclusive Right to their respective Writings and Discoveries;

To constitute Tribunals inferior to the supreme Court;

To define and punish Piracies and Felonies committed on the high Seas, and Offences against the Law of Nations;

To declare War, grant Letters of Marque and Reprisal, and make Rules concerning Captures on Land and Water;

To raise and support Armies, but no Appropriation of Money to that Use shall be for a longer Term than two Years;

To provide and maintain a Navy;

To make Rules for the Government and Regulation of the land and naval Forces;

To provide for calling forth the Militia to execute the Laws of the Union, suppress Insurrections and repel Invasions;

To provide for organizing, arming, and disciplining, the Militia, and for governing such Part of them as may be employed in the Service of the United States, reserving to the States respectively, the Appointment of the Officers, and the Authority of training the Militia according to the discipline prescribed by Congress;

To exercise exclusive Legislation in all Cases whatsoever, over such District (not exceeding ten Miles square) as may, by Cession of Particular States, and the Acceptance of Congress, become the Seat of the Government of the United States, and to exercise like Authority over all Places purchased by the Consent of the Legislature of the State in which the Same shall be, for the Erection of Forts, Magazines, Arsenals, dock-Yards, and other needful Buildings;—And

To make all Laws which shall be necessary and proper for carrying into Execution the foregoing Powers, and all other Powers vested by this Constitution in the Government of the United States, or in any Department or Officer thereof.

SECTION 9. *The Migration or Importation of such Persons as any of the States now existing shall think proper to admit, shall not be prohibited by the Congress prior to the Year one thousand eight hundred and eight, but a Tax or duty may be imposed on such Importation, not exceeding ten dollars for each Person.*

The Privilege of the Writ of Habeas Corpus shall not be suspended, unless when in Cases of Rebellion or Invasion the public Safety may require it.

No Bill of Attainder or ex post facto Law shall be passed.

No Capitation, or other direct, Tax shall be laid, unless in Proportion to the Census or Enumeration herein before directed to be taken.

No Tax or Duty shall be laid on Articles exported from any State.

No Preference shall be given by any Regulation of Commerce or Revenue to the Ports of one State over those of another: nor shall Vessels bound to, or from, one

State, be obliged to enter, clear or pay Duties in another.

No Money shall be drawn from the Treasury, but in Consequence of Appropriations made by Law; and a regular Statement and Account of the Receipts and Expenditures of all public Money shall be published from time to time.

No Title of Nobility shall be granted by the United States: And no Person holding any Office of Profit or Trust under them, shall, without the Consent of the Congress, accept of any present, Emolument, Office, or Title, of any kind whatever, from any King, Prince, or foreign State.

SECTION 10. No State shall enter into any Treaty, Alliance, or Confederation; grant Letters of Marque and Reprisal; coin Money; emit Bills of Credit; make any Thing but gold and silver Coin a Tender in Payment of Debts; pass any Bill of Attainder, ex post facto Law, or Law impairing the Obligation of Contracts, or grant any Title of Nobility.

No State shall, without the Consent of the Congress, lay any Imposts or Duties on Imports or Exports, except what may be absolutely necessary for executing its inspection Laws: and the net Produce of all Duties and Imposts, laid by any State on Imports or Exports, shall be for the Use of the Treasury of the United States; and all such Laws shall be subject to the Revision and Controul of the Congress.

No State shall, without the Consent of Congress, lay any Duty of Tonnage, keep Troops, or Ships of War in time of Peace, enter into any Agreement or Compact with another State, or with a foreign Power, or engage in War, unless actually invaded, or in such imminent Danger as will not admit of delay.

Article II

SECTION 1. The executive Power shall be vested in a President of the United States of America. He shall hold his Office during the Term of four Years, and, together with the Vice President, chosen for the same Term, be elected, as follows

Each State shall appoint, in such Manner as the Legislature thereof may direct, a Number of Electors, equal to the whole Number of Senators and Representatives to which the State may be entitled in the Congress: but no Senator or Representative, or Person holding an Office of Trust or Profit under the United States, shall be appointed an Elector.

The Electors shall meet in their respective States, and vote by Ballot for two Persons, of whom one at least shall not be an Inhabitant of the same State with themselves. And they shall make a List of all the Persons voted for, and of the Number of Votes for each; which List they shall sign and certify, and transmit sealed to the Seat of the Government of the United States, directed to the President of the Senate. The President of the Senate shall, in the Presence of the Senate and House of Representatives, open all the Certificates, and the Votes shall then be counted. The Person having the greatest Number of Votes shall be the President, if such Number be a Majority of the whole Number of Electors appointed; and if there be more than one who have such Majority, and have an equal Number of Votes, then the House of Representatives shall immediately chuse by Ballot one of them for President; and if no Person have a Majority, then from the five highest on the List the said House shall in like Manner chuse the President. But in chusing the President, the Votes shall be taken by States, the Representation from each State having one Vote; a quorum for this Purpose shall consist of a Member or Members from two thirds of the States, and a Majority of all the States shall be necessary to a Choice. In every Case, after the Choice of the President, the Person having the greatest Number of Votes of the Electors shall be the Vice President. But if there should remain two or more who have equal Votes, the Senate shall chuse from them by Ballot the Vice President.

The Congress may determine the Time of chusing the Electors, and the Day on which they shall give their Votes; which Day shall be the same throughout the United States.

No Person except a natural born Citizen, *or a Citizen of the United States, at the time of the Adoption of this Constitution,* shall be eligible to the Office of President; neither shall any Person be eligible to that Office who shall not have attained to the Age of thirty five Years, and been fourteen Years a Resident within the United States.

In Case of the Removal of the President from Office, or of his Death, Resignation, or Inability to discharge the Powers and Duties of the said Office, the Same shall devolve on the Vice President, and the Congress may by Law provide for the Case of Removal, Death, Resignation or Inability, both of the President and Vice President, declaring what Officer shall then act as President, and such Officer shall act accordingly, until the Disability be removed, or a President shall be elected.

The President shall, at stated Times, receive for his Services, a Compensation, which shall neither be encreased nor diminished during the Period for which he shall have been elected, and he shall not receive within that Period any other Emolument from the United States, or any of them.

Before he enter on the Execution of his Office, he shall take the following Oath or Affirmation:—"I do solemnly swear (or affirm) that I will faithfully execute the Office of President of the United States, and will to the best of my Ability, preserve, protect and defend the Constitution of the United States."

SECTION 2. The President shall be Commander in Chief of the Army and Navy of the United States, and of the Militia of the several States, when called into the actual Service of the United States; he may require the Opinion, in writing, of the principal Officer in each of the executive Departments, upon any Subject relating to the Duties of their respective Offices, and he shall have Power to grant Reprieves and Pardons for Offences against the United States, except in Cases of Impeachment.

He shall have Power, by and with the Advice and Consent of the Senate, to make Treaties, provided two thirds of the Senators present concur; and he shall nominate, and by and with the Advice and Consent of the Senate, shall appoint Ambassadors, other public Ministers and Consuls, Judges of the supreme Court, and all other Officers of the United States, whose Appointments are not herein otherwise provided for, and which shall be established by Law: but the Congress may by Law vest the Appointment of such inferior Officers, as they think proper, in the President alone, in the Courts of Law, or in the Heads of Departments.

The President shall have Power to fill up all Vacancies that may happen during the Recess of the Senate, by granting Commissions which shall expire at the End of their next Session.

SECTION 3. He shall from time to time give to the Congress Information of the State of the Union, and recommend to their Consideration such Measures as he shall judge necessary and expedient; he may, on extraordinary Occasions, convene both Houses, or either of them, and in Case of Disagreement between them, with Respect to the Time of Adjournment, he may adjourn them to such Time as he shall think proper; he shall receive Ambassadors and other public Ministers; he shall take Care that the Laws be faithfully executed, and shall Commission all the Officers of the United States.

SECTION 4. The President, Vice President and all civil Officers of the United States, shall be removed from Office on Impeachment for, and Conviction of, Treason, Bribery, or other high Crimes and Misdemeanors.

Article III

SECTION 1. The judicial Power of the United States, shall be vested in one supreme Court, and in such inferior Courts as the Congress may from time to time ordain and establish. The Judges, both of the supreme and inferior Courts, shall hold their Offices during good Behaviour, and shall, at stated Times, receive for their Services, a Compensation, which shall not be diminished during their Continuance in Office.

SECTION 2. The judicial Power shall extend to all Cases, in Law and Equity, arising under this Constitution, the Laws of the United States, and Treaties made, or which shall be made, under their Authority;—to all Cases affecting Ambassadors, other public Ministers and Consuls;—to all Cases of admiralty and maritime Jurisdiction;—to Controversies to which the United States shall be a Party;—to Controversies between two or more States;—*between a State and Citizens of another State;*—between Citizens of different States;—between Citizens of the same State claiming Lands under Grants of different States, and between a State, or the Citizens thereof, and foreign States, Citizens or Subjects.

In all Cases affecting Ambassadors, other public Ministers and Consuls, and those in which a State shall be Party, the supreme Court shall have original Jurisdiction. In all the other Cases before mentioned, the supreme Court shall have appellate Jurisdiction, both as to Law and Fact, with such Exceptions, and under such Regulations as the Congress shall make.

The Trial of all Crimes, except in Cases of Impeachment, shall be by Jury; and such Trial shall be held in the State where the said Crimes shall have been committed; but when not committed within any State, the Trial shall be at such Place or Places as the Congress may by Law have directed.

SECTION 3. Treason against the United States, shall consist only in levying War against them, or in adhering to their Enemies, giving them Aid and Comfort. No Person shall be convicted of Treason unless on the Testimony of two Witnesses to the same overt Act, or on Confession in open Court.

The Congress shall have Power to declare the Punishment of Treason, but no Attainder of Treason shall work Corruption of Blood, or Forfeiture except during the Life of the Person attainted.

Article IV

SECTION 1. Full Faith and Credit shall be given in each State to the public Acts, Records, and judicial Proceedings of every other State. And the Congress may by general Laws prescribe the Manner in which such Acts, Records and Proceedings shall be proved, and the Effect thereof.

SECTION 2. The Citizens of each State shall be entitled to all Privileges and Immunities of Citizens in the several States.

A Person charged in any State with Treason, Felony, or other Crime, who shall flee from Justice, and be found in another State, shall on Demand of the executive Authority of the State from which he fled, be delivered up, to be removed to the State having Jurisdiction of the Crime.

No Person held to Service or Labour in one State, under the Laws thereof, escaping into another, shall, in Consequence of any Law or Regulation therein, be discharged from such Service or Labour, but shall be delivered up on Claim of the Party to whom such Service or Labour may be due.

SECTION 3. New States may be admitted by the Congress into this Union; but no new State shall be formed or erected within the Jurisdiction of any other State; nor any State be formed by the Junction of two or more States, or Parts of States, without the Consent of the Legislatures of the States concerned as well as of the Congress.

The Congress shall have Power to dispose of and make all needful Rules and Regulations respecting the Territory or other Property belonging to the United States; and nothing in this Constitution shall be so construed as to Prejudice any Claims of the United States, or of any particular State.

SECTION 4. The United States shall guarantee to every State in this Union a Republican Form of Government, and shall protect each of them against Invasion; and on Application of the Legislature, or of the Executive (when the Legislature cannot be convened) against domestic Violence.

Article V

The Congress, whenever two thirds of both Houses shall deem it necessary, shall propose Amendments to this Constitution, or, on the Application of the Legislatures of two thirds of the several States, shall call a Convention for proposing Amendments, which, in either Case, shall be valid to all Intents and Purposes, as Part of this Constitution, when ratified by the Legislatures of three fourths of the several States, or by Conventions in three fourths thereof, as the one or the other Mode of Ratification may be proposed by the Congress; Provided *that no Amendment which may be made prior to the Year One thousand eight hundred and eight shall in any Manner affect the first and fourth Clauses in the Ninth Section of the first Article;* and that no State, without its Consent, shall be deprived of its equal Suffrage in the Senate.

Article VI

All Debts contracted and Engagements entered into, before the Adoption of this Constitution, shall be as valid against the United States under this Constitution, as under the Confederation.

This Constitution, and the Laws of the United States which shall be made in Pursuance thereof; and all Treaties made, or which shall be made, under the Authority of the United States, shall be the supreme Law of the Land; and the Judges in every State shall be bound thereby, any Thing in the Constitution or Laws of any State to the Contrary notwithstanding.

The Senators and Representatives before mentioned, and the Members of the several State Legislatures, and all executive and judicial Officers, both of the United States and of the several States, shall be bound by Oath or Affirmation, to support this Constitution; but no religious Test shall ever be required as a Qualification to any Office or public Trust under the United States.

Article VII

The Ratification of the Conventions of nine States, shall be sufficient for the Establishment of this Constitution between the States so ratifying the Same.

Done in Convention by the Unanimous Consent of the States present the Seventeenth Day of September in the Year of our Lord one thousand seven hundred and Eighty seven and of the Independence of the United States of America the Twelfth In witness whereof We have hereunto subscribed our Names,

George Washington
President and deputy from Virginia

New Hampshire
John Langdon
Nicholas Gilman

Massachusetts
Nathaniel Gorham
Rufus King

Connecticut
William Samuel Johnson
Roger Sherman

New York
Alexander Hamilton

New Jersey
William Livingston
David Brearley
William Paterson
Jonathan Dayton

Pennsylvania
Benjamin Franklin
Thomas Mifflin
Robert Morris
George Clymer
Thomas FitzSimons
Jared Ingersoll
James Wilson
Gouverneur Morris

Delaware
George Read
Gunning Bedford, Jr.
John Dickinson
Richard Bassett
Jacob Broom

Maryland
James McHenry
Daniel of St. Thomas
Jenifer
Daniel Carroll

Virginia
John Blair
James Madison, Jr.

North Carolina
William Blount
Richard Dobbs Spaight
Hugh Williamson

South Carolina
John Rutledge
Charles Cotesworth
Pinckney
Charles Pinckney
Pierce Butler

Georgia
William Few
Abraham Baldwin

The First Ten Amendments (The Bill of Rights)

AMENDMENT I

Congress shall make no law respecting an establishment of religion, or prohibiting the free exercise thereof; or abridging the freedom of speech, or of the press; or the right of the people peaceably to assemble, and to petition the Government for a redress of grievances.

AMENDMENT II

A well regulated Militia, being necessary to the security of a free State, the right of the people to keep and bear Arms, shall not be infringed.

AMENDMENT III

No Soldier shall, in time of peace be quartered in any house, without the consent of the Owner, nor in time of war, but in a manner to be prescribed by law.

AMENDMENT IV

The right of the people to be secure in their persons, houses, papers, and effects, against unreasonable searches and seizures, shall not be violated, and no Warrants shall issue, but upon probable cause, supported by Oath or affirmation, and particularly describing the place to be searched, and the persons or things to be seized.

AMENDMENT V

No person shall be held to answer for a capital, or otherwise infamous crime, unless on a presentment or indictment of a Grand Jury, except in cases arising in the land or naval forces, or in the Militia, when in actual service in time of War or public danger; nor shall any person be subject for the same offence to be twice put in jeopardy of life or limb; nor shall be compelled in any criminal case to be a witness against himself, nor be deprived of life, liberty, or property, without due process of law; nor shall private property be taken for public use, without just compensation.

AMENDMENT VI

In all criminal prosecutions, the accused shall enjoy the right to a speedy and public trial, by an impartial jury of the State and district wherein the crime shall have been committed, which district shall have been previously ascertained by law, and to be informed of the nature and cause of the accusation; to be confronted with the witnesses against him; to have compulsory process for obtaining witnesses in his favor, and to have the Assistance of Counsel for his defence.

AMENDMENT VII

In Suits at common law, where the value in controversy shall exceed twenty dollars, the right of trial by jury shall be preserved, and no fact tried by a jury, shall be otherwise re-examined in any Court of the United States, than according to the rules of the common law.

AMENDMENT VIII

Excessive bail shall not be required, nor excessive fines imposed, nor cruel and unusual punishments inflicted.

AMENDMENT IX

The enumeration in the Constitution, of certain rights, shall not be construed to deny or disparage others retained by the people.

AMENDMENT X

The powers not delegated to the United States by the Constitution, nor prohibited by it to the States, are reserved to the States respectively, or to the people.

For Discussion

Chapter One

1. How are James Madison's and Benjamin Rush's arguments about what is wrong in America similar? How are they different? Would you characterize the two as being in general agreement? Why or why not?

2. To what extent does "Z" concede the case of James Madison and Benjamin Rush? What parts of the Constitution (see appendix) might "Z" object to? Explain your answer.

3. What reasoning does Thomas Jefferson use to argue that rebellions in general, and Shays's Rebellion in particular, are not necessarily bad? Might his arguments have convinced George Washington? Why or why not?

Chapter Two

1. How much of the Virginia Plan presented by Edmund Randolph made it into the Constitution (see appendix)? Which elements were dropped or changed? Which deleted elements, if any, do you think should have been retained?

2. Judging from their letter, would any compromise at the Constitutional Convention have been acceptable for Robert Yates and John Lansing? Were they correct, at least technically, in arguing that the Convention had exceeded its authority? Explain.

3. Was the New Jersey Plan presented by William Paterson significantly different from, or a mere repetition of, the Articles of Confederation (see appendix)? Explain your answer.

4. What were the two main objectives of the Constitutional Convention, according to James Madison? Why does he argue that the New Jersey Plan fails to achieve those objectives?

5. List the main differences between the Virginia Plan and the New Jersey Plan. Do you agree or disagree with Alexander Hamilton's contention that they are similar (and similarly flawed)? Why?

6. What aspects of the British system of government does Alexander Hamilton admire most? Do you agree or disagree with his opinions on democracy? Why?

7. What differences between the United States and Great Britain does Charles Pinckney emphasize? What aspects of the British constitution praised by Alexander Hamilton does he find objectionable?

Chapter Three

1. What reasons does "Brutus" give for contending that a republic cannot survive in a country as large as the United States? Have some of his predictions come to pass? Explain.

2. What does James Madison mean by "faction"? How does the Constitution solve the problems posed by factions, according to Madison?

3. What are the great differences between a democracy and a republic, according to Madison? How do his views on democracy differ from those of Samuel Bryan?

4. What views does James Madison express about human nature in his two essays in this chapter? Are humans fundamentally good or evil in his eyes? Do you agree with his views? Why or why not?

5. James Madison and Alexander Hamilton have featured in this book both their speeches at the Constitutional Convention and their writings after the Convention, when they were united in their support for ratification. Find an instance in which one of them expresses arguments and opinions that are different for these two different circumstances (during and after the Convention). Do such differences weaken the arguments? Why or why not?

6. Today the House of Representatives consists of 435 people, each representing a congressional district with a population of more than a half million people. After reading the arguments of Melancton Smith and Alexander Hamilton, do you think the House of Representatives should be expanded? Do Smith's and Hamilton's arguments relate to today's conditions? Why or why not?

7. Should the Constitutional Convention have taken steps to abolish slavery, or was James Wilson correct in believing compromise was necessary? Is it fair to judge the decisions of the Convention by today's standards? Why or why not?

Chapter Four

1. What does Alexander Hamilton view as the chief stumbling block for the creation of a successful executive branch? What does George Mason see as the main problem? Do their answers to this question account for their differences over whether the executive should be singular or plural? Explain.

2. What similarities between the president under the Constitution and the king of Great Britain does "Cato" see? What predictions of "Cato" have come to pass?

3. What differences between the president and the king of Great

Britain does Tenche Coxe list? What constitutional safeguards does he emphasize?

Chapter Five

1. In his attack on Benjamin Franklin's speech before the Convention, "Z" quotes heavily from the speech itself. Are his quotations accurate? Is his use of them fair, or does he distort Franklin's meaning? Explain.

2. Which five of the objections listed by "An Officer" do you find most compelling? Are they adequately answered by "Plain Truth"? Why or why not?

3. What differing attitudes toward the wealthy are displayed in the exchange between Amos Singletary and Jonathan Smith? Who do you think was the more realistic?

4. Compare the amendments offered by the Massachusetts ratifying convention with the Bill of Rights as finally adopted in 1791 (see appendix). How many of the demands of Massachusetts were met? Which were not?

5. "An Officer," Mercy Otis Warren, and Patrick Henry all attack the Constitution for its lack of a bill of rights. Are their reasons for wanting a bill of rights similar? Do you believe their arguments are adequately answered by "Plain Truth" and Edmund Randolph? Why or why not?

Chapter Six

1. Judging from their viewpoints, what do you think Clinton Rossiter and Alfred F. Young would say about Charles Beard's thesis (described in the chapter preface) that the framers of the Constitution were acting primarily to advance their economic interests? Explain your answer.

2. Do you agree or disagree with Clinton Rossiter's assessments of the participants of the Constitutional Convention? Why or why not?

3. What is meant by the "people" in Alfred F. Young's viewpoint? What role did they play in the creation of the Constitution? Do they include women or minorities?

General

1. Both sides of the ratification debate claimed that they were fulfilling the ideals of the American Revolution and the Declaration of Independence. Which do you think had the better claim? Why?

2. Do the accounts in this book of the Constitutional Convention and ratification debates increase or lessen your regard for the creators of the Constitution? Explain your answer.

Chronology

November 15, 1777	The Continental Congress, after months of debate, votes to adopt the Articles of Confederation. The articles must be ratified by all thirteen states to become effective.
March 1, 1781	Maryland is the final state to ratify and sign the Articles of Confederation.
August 1786	Shays's Rebellion begins to erupt in Massachusetts as debt-ridden farmers violently resist efforts at tax and debt collection.
September 11–14, 1786	The Annapolis Convention meets to discuss trade matters; it issues a call for states to elect delegates to a convention to be held in Philadelphia in May 1787.
November 23, 1786	Virginia becomes the first state to authorize sending delegates to Philadelphia, electing delegates December 4. Other states except Rhode Island take similar steps over the next several months.
February 4, 1787	Shays's Rebellion is crushed when Massachusetts militia routs forces led by farmer/rebel Daniel Shays. The Massachusetts legislature enacts legislation providing some relief for debtors.
February 21, 1787	The Continental Congress authorizes a convention in Philadelphia for revising the Articles of Confederation.
May 14, 1787	Convention scheduled to begin in Philadelphia; quorum not present.
May 25, 1787	With the arrival in Philadelphia of three delegates from New Jersey, a quorum of seven states is achieved. The delegates elect George Washington as president of the Convention and settle on rules of procedure, including a rule of secrecy. Matters are to be decided by majority vote, with each state having a single vote.
May 29, 1787	Edmund Randolph presents the Virginia

Plan to the Convention. The plan is debated over the next two weeks.

June 15, 1787	William Paterson presents the New Jersey Plan as an alternative to the Virginia Plan.
June 18, 1787	Alexander Hamilton delivers a prolonged speech presenting his own plan for a national government.
June 19, 1787	After debate, including a lengthy James Madison speech criticizing the New Jersey Plan, the Convention votes to reject it and proceed using the Virginia Plan. Debate then focuses on the question of equal vs. proportional representation of the states in the national legislature.
June 28, 1787	Noting the lack of progress and frayed tempers of the delegates, Benjamin Franklin proposes that future sessions start with a morning prayer. The suggestion is not adopted.
July 13, 1787	While the Constitutional Convention meets in Philadelphia, the Continental Congress in New York votes to adopt the Northwest Ordinance instituting government for the territory north of the Ohio River. It provides for the future creation of three to five states "on an equal footing with the original states in all respects whatsoever." The ordinance, unlike the Constitution later to emerge from Philadelphia, guarantees freedom of worship, trial by jury, and public education, and also prohibits slavery.
July 16, 1787	After weeks of tumultuous proceedings in which the Constitutional Convention nearly breaks up over the question of state representation, the Connecticut Compromise is reached. Based on a proposal by Connecticut delegate Roger Sherman, the proposal divides the national legislature into two houses. Representation in the lower house is proportional to a state's population—the total of free residents (excluding Indians) and three-fifths of "all other persons" (i.e., slaves). States would be equally represented in the upper house. Adoption of the compromise is recognized by many as the turn-

ing point in the Convention.

July 27–
August 6, 1787
The Convention adjourns while a Committee of Detail works out unfinished business.

August 6–
September 10, 1787
Convention delegates reconvene and debate the draft constitution presented by the Committee of Detail. Key decisions include granting Congress the right to regulate foreign trade and interstate commerce, permitting the slave trade to continue for another twenty years, and mandating elections every four years for president, every six years for senators, and every two years for representatives.

September 8, 1787
A Committee of Style is appointed to prepare a finished text of the Constitution. Gouverneur Morris of New York is credited with doing most of the writing and polishing of the draft, including its preamble beginning with "We the People of the United States." The committee arranges all the proposed elements of the Constitution into seven articles.

September 12, 1787
The Committee of Style submits its draft of the Constitution to the Convention. George Mason of Virginia proposes adding a bill of rights to the Constitution. The motion, seconded by Elbridge Gerry of Massachusetts, is defeated with all states voting against it.

September 15, 1787
Edmund Randolph proposes that a second constitutional convention be held if state ratifying conventions wish to propose amendments to the document. Mason and Gerry also support a second convention, but the proposal is unanimously defeated. The Convention votes to approve the Constitution and orders a final official copy to be made.

September 17, 1787
Thirty-nine of the forty-two delegates present sign the official copy of the Constitution (the three exceptions being George Mason, Elbridge Gerry, and Edmund Randolph). The Convention adjourns.

September 20–28,
1787
The Continental Congress receives the proposed Constitution. After some debate, the Congress resolves to submit the Constitution to special state ratifying conventions. At least nine states must ratify for the Constitu-

tion to go into effect.

September 26, 1787	The first newspaper article critical of the Constitution appears in Philadelphia.
October 27, 1787	The first of eighty-five *Federalist* essays defending the Constitution is published in New York City. The articles are written by Alexander Hamilton, James Madison, and John Jay.
December 7, 1787	Delaware, by a unanimous vote, becomes the first state to ratify the Constitution.
December 12, 1787	After vociferous debate, the Pennsylvania convention votes 46–23 to ratify the Constitution. Opponents publish "Address and Reasons of Dissent," which is widely circulated throughout the states.
December 18, 1787	New Jersey ratifies the Constitution.
December 31, 1787	Georgia ratifies.
January 9, 1788	Connecticut ratifies.
February 6, 1788	The Massachusetts convention votes 187–168 to ratify the Constitution and to propose amendments.
March 1788	Rhode Island calls for a statewide referendum on the Constitution. Federalists boycott the election and the Constitution is rejected 2,708–237.
April 26, 1788	Maryland ratifies the Constitution.
June 21, 1788	New Hampshire becomes the ninth state to ratify the Constitution, thus putting it into effect.
June 25, 1788	Despite significant opposition by Patrick Henry, the Virginia convention votes 89–79 to ratify the Constitution. The convention proposes adding a bill of rights and other amendments.
July 2, 1788	Cyrus Griffin, president of the Continental Congress, receives the news of New Hampshire's ratification and announces that the Constitution has been ratified by the required nine states. A committee is formed to plan the transition to a new national government.
July 26, 1788	New York ratifies the Constitution, leaving North Carolina and Rhode Island holding out until after the new government is established.

Annotated Bibliography

Historical Studies

Douglass Adair, *Fame and the Founding Fathers.* New York: Norton, 1974. Essays on the thought of James Madison, Alexander Hamilton, and other key figures in the creation of the Constitution.

Willi P. Adams, *The First American Constitutions: Republican Ideology and the Making of State Constitutions in the Revolutionary Era.* Chapel Hill: University of North Carolina Press, 1980. Examines the contributions of state constitution makers to the country's political thought and eventual creation of the national Constitution.

John K. Alexander, *The Selling of the Constitutional Convention.* Madison, WI: Madison House, 1990. Analysis of newspaper coverage of the Constitutional Convention while it was meeting in secret; concludes that coverage was slanted in favor of replacing the Articles of Confederation and accepting whatever the Convention would produce.

Thornton Anderson, *Creating the Constitution.* University Park: Pennsylvania State University Press, 1993. A historical study that views the writers of the Constitution as experienced and astute politicians who created a new political structure with a dangerous concentration of power on the national level.

Bernard Bailyn, *Ideological Origins of the American Revolution.* Cambridge, MA: Harvard University Press, 1967. An intellectual history of the animating ideology of republicanism, which was crucial to the making of the Constitution.

Charles A. Beard, *An Economic Interpretation of the Constitution.* New York: Macmillan, 1913. A seminal book on the Constitution written by the famous progressive historian to make the case that the document was drafted by and for the wealthy.

Walter Berns, *Taking the Constitution Seriously.* New York: Simon & Schuster, 1987. An interpretive explanation of the Constitution that argues that its drafters sought to devise a government able to secure the rights established in the Declaration of Independence.

Richard B. Bernstein with Kym S. Rice, *Are We to Be a Nation? The Making of the Constitution.* Cambridge, MA: Harvard University Press, 1987. Richly illustrated history of the making of the Constitution.

Catherine Drinker Bowers, *Miracle at Philadelphia*. Boston: Little, Brown, 1966. A very readable popular history of the Constitutional Convention in Philadelphia.

Stephen Boyd, *The Politics of Opposition: Antifederalists and the Acceptance of the Constitution*. Millwood, NY: KTO Press, 1979. Analysis and study of the ratification debates, focusing on the anti-federalist opposition.

Robert Brown, *Charles Beard and the Constitution*. Princeton, NJ: Princeton University Press, 1956. A rebuttal of Beard's famous thesis of the economic origins of the Constitution.

George Carey, *The Federalist: Design for a Constitutional Republic*. Urbana: University of Illinois Press, 1989. An examination of the *Federalist Papers* of James Madison, Alexander Hamilton, and John Jay, focusing on the issues of representation, separation of powers, and the limits of federal power.

Christopher Collier and James Lincoln Collier, *Decision in Philadelphia*. New York: Random House, 1986. A scholarly yet popular history of the Constitutional Convention written to commemorate the bicentennial of the Constitution.

Patrick T. Conley and John P. Kaminski, eds., *The Constitution and the States*. Madison, WI: Madison House, 1988. A collection of thirteen essays—one for each of the original thirteen states—that examines the role of the states in the creation of the Constitution.

William W. Crosskey, *Politics and the Constitution*. Chicago: University of Chicago Press, 1953. A highly theoretical and legalistic work that accuses the Founders of seeking to create an all-too-powerful central government.

Paul Eidelberg, *The Philosophy of the American Constitution*. New York: Free Press, 1968. A work that argues that the Constitution's creators set out to create a "mixed regime" of democracy and aristocracy.

Paul Goodman, ed., *The American Constitution*. New York: John Wiley & Sons, 1970. Collection of primary and secondary sources that examine problems in government building faced by the makers of the Constitution.

Jack P. Greene, *Peripheries and Center: Constitutional Development in the Extended Politics of the British Empire and the United States, 1607-1788*. Athens: University of Georgia Press, 1986. Extended historical study that views the framers of the Constitution as inheritors of the problem faced by the British Empire and American colonies—how to reconcile local government and custom with central control.

Thurston Greene, *The Language of the Constitution*. New York: Greenwood Press, 1991. A sourcebook and guide to the political vocabulary employed by the writers of the Constitution. Includes a foreword by Warren Burger, former chief justice of the U.S. Supreme Court.

Peter Hoffer, *Revolution and Regeneration: Life Cycles and the Historical Vision of the Generation of 1776*. Athens: University of Georgia Press, 1983.

An exploration in psycho-history that follows the lives of twenty-one men, many of whom played important roles in the creation of the Constitution, from the American Revolution through the War of 1812.

Merrill Jensen, *The New Nation: A History of the United States During the Confederation*. New York: Knopf, 1950. A history of the 1780s that defends the Articles of Confederation against past and present critics and argues against the necessity of a more centralized government under a new constitution.

Michael Kammen, *A Machine That Would Go of Itself*. New York: Knopf, 1986. A study of how the Constitution has been interpreted and used by Americans over the course of its history.

Alfred H. Kelly, Winifred A. Harbison, and Herman Belz, *The American Constitution, Its Origins and Development*. 7th ed. New York: Norton, 1991. A general history of constitution making in the American colonies on the state level and at Philadelphia, as well as a history of constitutional interpretation.

Ralph Ketcham, *James Madison*. New York: Macmillan, 1971. A compact one-volume biography of Madison portraying him as being committed to both the union and republicanism.

Russell Kirk, *The Conservative Constitution*. Washington, DC: Regnery Gateway, 1990. A history that emphasizes what the author regards as the conservative ends of the Constitution and the influence of British political philosopher Edmund Burke on its creators.

Adrienne Koch, *Jefferson and Madison*. New York: Knopf, 1950. A history of the intellectual friendship of these two men who played such critical roles in the politics of the 1780s.

Leonard Levy, ed., *Essays on the Making of the Constitution*. New York: Oxford University Press, 1969. A collection of essays by historians discussing the background and process of the Constitutional Convention and the ratification debates.

Staughton Lynd, *Class Conflict, Slavery, and the U.S. Constitution: Ten Essays*. Indianapolis: Bobbs-Merrill, 1967. A collection of essays critical of the Constitution and written from the perspective of the 1960s American Left.

Jackson Main, *The Antifederalists*. Chapel Hill: University of North Carolina Press, 1961. A general social and political history of those who took the lead in seeking to block ratification of the Constitution.

Frederick Marks, *Independence on Trial: Foreign Affairs and the Making of the Constitution*. Baton Rouge: Louisiana State University Press, 1973. A history of the role of foreign policy in the drafting of the Constitution.

Henry Mayer, *Son of Thunder: Patrick Henry and the American Republic*. New York: Franklin Watts, 1986. A biography of an early American populist and opponent of the Constitution.

Forrest McDonald, *E Pluribus Unum: The Formation of the American Republic*.

Boston: Houghton Mifflin, 1965. A political and intellectual history of the years between 1776 and 1790 that sees the Constitution as a triumph of interests over ideals.

Charles L. Mee Jr., *The Genius of the People*. New York: Harper & Row, 1987. A popular history of the making of the Constitution written to coincide with its bicentennial.

Marvin Meyers, *The Mind of the Founder: Sources of the Political Thought of James Madison*. Hanover, NH: University Press of New England, 1981. An intellectual biography of Madison, republican and nationalist.

Max Mintz, *Gouverneur Morris and the American Revolution*. Norman: University of Oklahoma Press, 1970. A political biography of the Constitutional Convention delegate from New York that contrasts his support for civil liberties with his opposition to political democracy.

Broadus Mitchell, *Alexander Hamilton*. New York: Macmillan, 1957-1962. A two-volume biography of one of the most important and nationally oriented federalists.

Edmund Morgan, *The Birth of the Republic, 1763-1789*. Chicago: University of Chicago Press, 1956. A brief general history of the United States from the road to the Revolution through the creation of a new nation that culminates with the ratification of the Constitution.

Richard B. Morris, *The Forging of the Union, 1781-1789*. New York: Harper & Row, 1987. A general history of the United States in the 1780s that is less sanguine about the Articles of Confederation than are Merrill Jensen and other historians.

Richard B. Morris, *Witnesses at the Creation: Hamilton, Madison, Jay, and the Constitution*. New York: Holt, Rinehart and Winston, 1985. A biographical look at the three people who wrote *The Federalist*, examining how their political careers shaped their opinions on creating a new national government.

Peter Onuf, *The Origins of the Federal Republic: Jurisdictional Controversies in the United States, 1775-1787*. Philadelphia: University of Pennsylvania Press, 1983. Examines the history of conflicts between the thirteen states and their roles in the creation of the Constitution.

John Reardon, *Edmund Randolph: A Biography*. New York: Macmillan, 1974. A biography of the Virginian political leader who became one of the leading critics of the Constitution yet eventually supported it.

Donald Robinson, *Slavery in the Structure of American Politics, 1765-1820*. New York: Harcourt Brace Jovanovich, 1971. A history of the role that slavery played in the early national period, including its role in the creation of the Constitution.

Clinton Rossiter, *Alexander Hamilton and the Constitution*. New York: Harcourt Brace, 1964. A biography that argues that Hamilton was both a nationalist and the premier constitutionalist of his era.

Clinton Rossiter, *1787: The Grand Convention*. New York: Macmillan, 1966.

A narrative history of the Constitutional Convention that pays special attention to the various personalities gathered at Philadelphia.

Robert Rutland, *James Madison and the Search for Nationhood.* Washington, DC: Library of Congress, 1981. A succinct biography of the main architect of the Constitution.

Robert Rutland, *The Ordeal of the Constitution: The Antifederalists and the Ratification Struggle of 1787-1788.* Norman: University of Oklahoma Press, 1966. A study of the ratification process from the point of view of those opposed to the Constitution.

Stephen L. Schechter, ed., *The Reluctant Pillar: New York and the Adoption of the Federal Constitution.* Troy, NY: Russell Sage College, 1985. Essays on the ratification debate in the pivotal state of New York, placing it in historical context.

Geoffrey Seed, *James Wilson.* Millwood, NY: KTO Press, 1978. A judicious, well-written analysis of the political ideas of one of the more prominent, yet almost forgotten, delegates to the Constitutional Convention.

Page Smith, *The Constitution: A Documentary and Narrative History.* 2nd ed. New York: Morrow, 1980. A useful single-volume history that provides both primary sources and a narrative account of the making of the Constitution.

Jeffrey St. John, *Constitutional Journal.* Ottawa, IL: Jameson Books, 1987. A popular history of the Constitutional Convention told in simulated "correspondent's reports" that re-create the debates and tension of the time.

Jeffrey St. John, *A Child of Fortune.* Ottawa, IL: Jameson Books, 1990. A continuation of the "correspondent's reports" focusing on the battle for the ratification of the Constitution.

Herbert Storing, *What the Antifederalists Were For.* Chicago: University of Chicago Press, 1981. A sympathetic treatment of those who took the lead in opposing the Constitution.

Gerald Stourzh, *Alexander Hamilton and the Idea of Republican Government.* Stanford, CA: Stanford University Press, 1970. A study of Hamilton's thinking, with special emphasis on the interplay of republican government and foreign policy.

David Szatmary, *Shays' Rebellion.* Amherst: University of Massachusetts Press, 1980. A history of one of the critical events that helped trigger the gathering at Philadelphia to create a stronger central government.

Carl Van Doren, *The Great Rehearsal.* New York: Viking, 1948. A study of the Constitution that views that document as a forerunner of the United Nations and the creation of an international commonwealth.

Morton White, *Philosophy, the Federalist and the Constitution.* New York: Oxford University Press, 1987. An extended essay analyzing the intellectual underpinnings of the Constitution provided by John Locke and David Hume.

Garry Wills, *Explaining America: The Federalist.* New York: Doubleday,

1982. An intellectual history of the background of the *Federalist Papers*.

Gordon Wood, *The Creation of the American Republic 1776-1787*. Chapel Hill: University of North Carolina Press, 1969. A history of republican ideology from the Declaration of Independence to the Constitution.

Gordon Wood, *The Radicalism of the American Revolution*. New York: Knopf, 1992. An original, compelling history of the impact of republican ideology on American politics and American society from the Constitution to the presidency of Andrew Jackson.

Esmond Wright, *Franklin of Philadelphia*. Cambridge, MA: Harvard University Press, 1986. A biography of the oldest delegate to the Constitutional Convention.

Primary Source Collections

Bernard Bailyn, ed., *The Debate on the Constitution*. New York: Library of America, 1993. A thorough collection of newspaper articles and state convention speeches covering the debate over the Constitution's ratification.

Jonathan Elliot, ed., *The Debates in the Several State Conventions on the Adoption of the Federal Constitution, etc. etc.* 2nd ed. New York: 1888. Useful if somewhat dated collection of documents pertaining to the state ratification conventions.

Max Farrand, ed., *The Records of the Federal Convention of 1787*. New Haven, CT: Yale University Press, 1937. For many years since its original publication in 1911 this was the definitive source for primary documents relating to the Constitutional Convention, including the notes of James Madison, Robert Yates, and others.

John C. Fitzpatrick, ed., *The Diaries of George Washington*. Boston: Houghton Mifflin, 1925. A firsthand source that offers clues to Washington's support for a new constitution.

Paul L. Ford, ed., *Essays on the Constitution of the United States, Published During Its Discussion by the People, 1787-1788*. Brooklyn: Historical Printing Club, 1892. *Pamphlets on the Constitution of the United States, Published During Its Discussion by the People, 1787-1788*. Brooklyn: Historical Printing Club, 1888. Two collections of primary sources, originally printed for the Constitution's centennial. Partially replaced by newer anthologies, but still useful.

James H. Hutson, ed., *Supplement to Max Farrand's Records of the Federal Convention of 1787*. New Haven, CT: Yale University Press, 1987. A source volume containing important documents discovered since 1937, including selected diary entries and private letters of important participants of the Constitutional Convention. An introductory essay defends the reliability of James Madison's notes on the Convention.

Merrill Jensen, John P. Kaminski, Gaspare J. Saladino, and Richard Leffler, eds., *The Documentary History of the Ratification of the Constitution*. Madison, WI: State Historical Society, 1976- . A massive and comprehensive multivolume collection of documents tracing the history of the creation and ratification of the Constitution.

Michael Kammen, ed., *The Origins of the American Constitution*. New York: Penguin, 1986. A paperback sourcebook of primary documents relating to the background of, debates during, and ratification of the Constitution.

Cecilia Kenyon, ed., *The Antifederalists*. Indianapolis: Bobbs-Merrill, 1966. A collection of primary sources concerning the ideas and strategies of those opposed to the new Constitution.

Ralph Ketcham, ed., *The Anti-Federalist Papers and the Constitutional Convention Debates*. New York: Mentor Books, 1986. Conveniently compact collection of speeches and writings debating the Constitution.

Adrienne Koch, ed., *Notes of Debates in the Federal Convention of 1787 by James Madison*. Athens: Ohio University Press, 1966. A collection of primary sources relating to Madison's thinking and strategy during the Constitutional Convention.

James Madison, Alexander Hamilton, and John Jay, *The Federalist Papers*. New York: New American Library, 1961. A collection of eighty-seven essays written to promote the cause of ratification, but which also constitute an important statement of American republican political theory. One of many available editions.

John F. Manley and Kenneth M. Dolbeare, *The Case Against the Constitution*. Armonk, NY: M.E. Sharpe, 1987. Anthology of writings critical of the Constitution, dating from anti-federalist writings to modern assessments.

Herbert Storing, ed., *The Complete Anti-Federalist*. Chicago: University of Chicago Press, 1981. Definitive multivolume primary source collection of the writings and speeches of the people who opposed the Constitution during the debates for its ratification.

Charles C. Tansill, ed., *Documents Illustrative of the Formation of the Union of the American States*. Washington, DC: Government Printing Office, 1927. Large collection of documents, including James Madison's notes on the Constitutional Convention.

Index